# Justice, Institutions, and Luck

Kok-Chor Tan addresses three key questions in egalitarian distributive justice: *Where* does distributive equality matter?; *Why* does it matter?; And among *whom* does it matter? He argues for an institutional site for egalitarian justice, and suggests that the mitigation of arbitrariness or luck is the basis for distributive commitments. He also argues that distributive obligations are global in scope, applying between individuals across borders. Tan's objectives are tripartite: to clarify the basis of an institutional approach to justice; to establish luck egalitarianism as an account of the ground of equality; and to realize the global nature of egalitarian justice. The outcome is 'institutional luck egalitarianism'—a new cosmopolitan position on distributive justice.

**Kok-Chor Tan** is Professor of Philosophy at the University of Pennsylvania

# Justice, Institutions, and Luck

*The Site, Ground, and Scope of Equality*

Kok-Chor Tan

OXFORD
UNIVERSITY PRESS

# OXFORD
## UNIVERSITY PRESS

Great Clarendon Street, Oxford, OX2 6DP,
United Kingdom

Oxford University Press is a department of the University of Oxford.
It furthers the University's objective of excellence in research, scholarship,
and education by publishing worldwide. Oxford is a registered trade mark of
Oxford University Press in the UK and in certain other countries

First Edition published in 2012
First published in paperback 2014

Published in the United States of America by Oxford University Press,
198 Madison Avenue, New York, NY 10016, United States of America

British Library Cataloguing in Publication Data
Data available

Library of Congress Cataloguing in Publication Data
Data available

ISBN 978-0-19-958885-5 (Hbk)
ISBN 978-0-19-870154-5 (Pbk)

*For Amalia*

# Preface and Acknowledgments

This book surveys and evaluates three central philosophical debates within distributive justice: Where is the site of distributive equality, that is, to what entity do distributive principles primarily apply? What is the ground of distributive equality, that is, why does distributive equality matter? And is the reach or scope of the ideal of distributive equality limited to the confines of the state or is it global?

My objective is to provide an overview of some of the main arguments and positions in the contemporary discussions surrounding these questions. I cannot attempt to engage all the different positions at play in the vast and still growing literature on these matters. Instead, I wish to identify what I take to be the general forms of the most important positions and arguments for the purpose of organizing and tidying an increasingly crowded field. As a result some details may be sacrificed, but the hope is that a tidying-up of the philosophical terrain and the identification of the key issues at stake in these debates will compensate for this shortcoming.

This critical survey will suggest that *institutional egalitarianism* provides the most reasonable understanding of the site of equality; that *luck egalitarianism* provides a plausible understanding of the grounds of equality; and that the scope of equality is realizably *global*. To do this, the book will attempt to clarify the basis of the institutional approach to equality, the proper contours of luck egalitarianism, and the case for the global reach of egalitarian concerns in spite of equality's institutional site. It will also propose a way of understanding how the institutional site, the luck egalitarian ground, and global scope of equality—even though engaged with different aspects of equality—can come together to support a particular ideal of distributive justice that I will call *institutional luck egalitarianism*. In this regard, although the main goal of this book is to provide a critical introduction to some of the main questions on equality, I hope some of the arguments it advances can contribute to the contemporary philosophical literature on distributive justice and be of interest to readers already engaged in this discourse.

I enjoyed the benefit of discussing several parts of this book in various stages of its development with students in different advanced undergraduate and graduate seminars since Fall 2005 at the University of Pennsylvania. I am grateful for their criticisms and for their own views on the subject. I owe special thanks to the following (some of whom are now only former students): Collin Anthony, Chris Melenovsky, Mark Navin, and Doug Paletta.

Colleagues and friends at the University of Pennsylvania have been supportive and kind enough to discuss different aspects of this book with me. I am especially grateful to Samuel Freeman in many ways, including for the frequent discussions on the topic of this book, and whose own writings have provided one of the sparks for this work. I also thank Karen Detlefsen for entertaining my thoughts on this subject on more occasions than she would care to recall, and whose comments and feedback provided valuable guidance at crucial points. Colleagues and friends in the field at large have also offered comments and criticisms on different sub-parts of this work at various occasions. In particular I thank: Richard Arneson, Simon Caney, Deen Chatterjee, the late Jerry Cohen, Bruce Landesman, Carol Gould, Aaron James, Alistair Macleod, Darrel Moellendorf, Margaret Moore, Christine Sypnowich, Cindy Stark, and Bob Talisse.

Peter Momtchiloff of Oxford University Press generously supported and encouraged this work from the beginning, and adroitly arranged for invaluable feedback on both the proposal and manuscript. I benefited from different readers' comments on the proposal, among them Thomas Pogge and Andrea Sangiovanni. Two readers took the additional trouble of offering careful criticisms and comments on the manuscript, and I hope they will find the revisions prompted by their remarks on track. I am certainly grateful for their attention. One of these readers, now revealed to me to be Peter Vallentyne, deserves special thanks for his detailed and incisive suggestions and criticisms that he turned around with astonishing rapidity. I have not addressed all of Peter's and the other reader's concerns to my full satisfaction (and no doubt neither to theirs); but I hope I have done enough to temper at least some of their more powerful challenges. Many thanks also to Brenda Stones for her excellent copy-editing of the script.

Finally, and most of all, thanks to Karen again for her good patience and encouragement, and to Amalia for providing the necessary life distractions that put things in their rightful place.

Chapter 6 includes passages from "Luck, Institutions, and Global Distributive Justice," *The European Journal of Political Theory* (July 2011). I am grateful for permission to reproduce parts of this paper here, and to the editors and readers of the journal for helpful criticisms on the draft of this paper.

Part I and Part II expand (with revisions in most cases) on some arguments first presented in the following papers:

"Justice and Personal Pursuits," *The Journal of Philosophy* 101/7 (2004).

"A Defense of Luck Egalitarianism," *The Journal of Philosophy* 105/11 (2008).

I thank the editors and readers of *The Journal of Philosophy* for helpful feedback on these papers.

# Contents

# 1

# Introduction

## 1.1 The questions

This work surveys and evaluates the following three questions of egalitarian
distributive justice: *Where* does distributive equality matter? *Why* does it
matter? And among *whom* does it matter? These questions may be referred
to, respectively, as the questions of the site, ground, and scope of distributive
equality.

The question of the site of distributive equality asks what the primary
subject of justice is, that is, to which agents or entities do principles of
distributive justice apply. Do distributive principles apply directly to individual agents in their day-to-day decisions and choices, or do they apply
primarily to the background institutions of society within which rules
individuals may do as they wish so long as background justice is preserved?

The question of the ground of distributive equality asks why distributive
equality matters, or, more precisely, why economic inequalities in a social
order ought to be regulated. Does the commitment to distributive equality
derive from a more fundamental commitment to democratic ideals, or is
the commitment to equality an independently valuable one? For instance,
is the aim of a distributive principle one of ensuring that democratic
relations among persons are not strained due to excessive inequalities
among them, or is the aim of a distributive principle more basically one
of ensuring that no persons qua moral agents are disadvantaged due to
circumstances not of their doing?

Finally, the question of boundary or scope concerns the proper set of
agents among whom principles of distributive justice apply. Does the
commitment to distributive justice apply only among participating members of a democratic political order, or does it apply among persons more
generally and independently of their political membership? For instance,

does distributive equality matter only domestically (i.e. within a state), or does it matter globally as well?

As partially indicated by its title, this book will defend, to borrow standard labels, an *institutional* focus in egalitarian justice, a *luck egalitarian* ideal of why equality matters, and the idea that the scope of distributive justice is *global*. Consequently, the book will propose an account of equality that I will label "institutional luck egalitarianism" that is global in scope.

These individual questions of equality are very much in the forefront of the contemporary debate on distributive justice, and the main objective of this work is to offer a critical overview and evaluation of the discussions surrounding these questions, and to provide some conceptual organization to the various positions and arguments at play. But this survey also aims to clarify what I take to be the motivation for the institutional approach, the contours of luck egalitarianism, and a basis of global egalitarianism, and programmatically to advance an account of equality unified by the way it understands these aspects of equality.

## 1.2 Institutional, luck and global egalitarianism: The challenges

The subject of this book is egalitarian distributive justice, that is, the ideal that economic inequality between persons ought to be regulated by some distributive principle. The term equality in this work is understood in this specific sense. I will say more to stake out the subject of egalitarian distributive justice in the next section. Here, let me elaborate more on the questions and challenges of equality so understood that propel this study.

On the question of the site of equality, a common view is that principles of justice are meant to apply primarily to the institutions of society, or what John Rawls calls its "basic structure," that is, its main political, social and economic institutions that determine persons' fundamental rights and entitlements (Rawls 1971: 7, 54; 2001: 10). While individual agents have the duty of justice to bring about an institutional order that satisfies the principles of justice, in their day-to-day life they may do as they wish within the rules of this just institutional order (Rawls 2001: 50; also Nagel 1991). We may refer to this generally as the "institutional approach" to justice or more specifically "institutional egalitarianism."

Regarding the ground of egalitarian justice, or why distributive equality should matter, one view is that distributive equality matters because of the need to counteract the effects of luck on persons' life prospects. On this  view, any departure from the benchmark of equal distribution is acceptable when this is due to persons' efforts and choices, but not when it is due to contingencies over which they have no control, such as good or bad luck. A just distributive arrangement should thus reflect the efforts and choices of persons and not their good or bad luck and unchosen circumstances. The point of a distributive commitment is to direct a social order towards this ideal (G. A. Cohen 1989, 2000; Dworkin 2000, 2003; Arneson 1989, 2000). This position is commonly known in the literature as "luck egalitarianism." Since the ground of equality also specifies its point—that is, if the reason why equality matters is that society cannot allow the vagaries of luck to affect persons' life prospects, then the point of an egalitarian principle on this ideal is to mitigate the effects of luck on persons' life prospects—I will for stylistic reasons sometimes refer to the ground of equality as the point of equality.

On the question of scope, one position, which I will call "global egalitarianism," takes the reach of distributive equality to be global and not restricted by state borders. On this view, equality is a commitment that holds not only among persons within the confines of the state but between persons across state borders as well, and that global justice properly understood includes such a distributive egalitarian ideal (Beitz 1979; Pogge 1989; Caney 2005; Moellendorf 2002). For convenience, I will sometimes refer to this egalitarian ideal as the cosmopolitan ideal.

But each of these positions I have just described—the institutional approach, luck egalitarianism, and global egalitarianism—has been subject to extensive criticisms in the recent literature. On the first, some critics argue that restricting the principles of justice to the institutions of a social order amounts to an "evasion" of the burdens of justice because it does not demand enough of individuals in their day-to-day choices and actions (e.g. G. A. Cohen 2000, 2008). On their view, the demands of distributive justice transcend institutions so to speak, and should also regulate personal choices and decisions within the rules of justly regulated institutions. As G. A. Cohen puts it, a just society must have more than merely just or justly regulated institutions within which rules persons may do as they wish; it must also exhibit an egalitarian "ethos" that is expressed in the way its members make decisions in the "thick of daily life" within the rules of institutions (id. 2000: 3–4).

Others have rejected the luck egalitarian position on why equality matters, holding that the aim of distributive equality is to secure the social relationship among persons that is constitutive and requisite of membership in a democratic political order, rather than that of mitigating the effects of luck on individuals' life prospects (Anderson 1999; Scheffler 2003a, 2005; Freeman 2006a). For these critics, distributive equality matters not because equality in distribution is the moral default and that acceptable departures from this have to be due to choice and not luck (as in the luck egalitarian view). Instead, they argue, equality in distribution matters because of the more fundamental values associated with the ideal of democracy. To put it generally, the democratic ideal of reciprocity is undermined if the gap between rich and poor in society cannot be reasonably accepted by those disadvantaged under the arrangement. This alternative view of why distributive equality matters can be broadly labeled "democratic equality." One implication of this account of why equality matters is that equality is a *political* ideal in the sense that it matters only amongst persons who are first of all members of a common democratic political association.

*[margin note:] This could bring about a strong criticism of democratic equality. Are those outside the confines of the state or a particular form of governance not entitled to equality?*

Finally, the cosmopolitan ideal is rejected by egalitarians who believe that the scope of equality is given, and thus limited, by the boundaries of political societies. For them, distributive egalitarian commitments apply only within the state because of the special conditions of the state that give rise to these commitments, and these conditions don't obtain (at least presently) at the global level (Nagel 2005; Blake 2001; Sangiovanni 2007; Freeman 2006a; Rawls 1999a). Indeed, in the current debate, many democratic egalitarians are skeptical of cosmopolitanism precisely because of their view that the value of equality derives from the more basic ideals of democracy. Since there is no global democratic political order in their view, global egalitarian commitments simply do not arise.[1]

As mentioned above, I will defend, respectively, the institutional approach, the luck egalitarian position, and the global egalitarian view

---

[1] The anti-cosmopolitan egalitarian view I am concerned with in this book is that of egalitarians who deny that egalitarian commitments apply globally. That is, the concern regards the scope of equality, not whether equality matters at all. Of course there are those who reject cosmopolitan egalitarianism because they reject egalitarianism *tout court*. But this opposition falls outside the inquiry of this work, which is about how distributive equality should be conceived (its site, its ground, and its scope), not whether it should be conceived at all.

against these recent criticisms. But this project is not merely defensive in the limited way of recapitulating established views and showing how these evade the stated objections. The defense will involve some reformulation and reconstruction of different aspects of each of these positions. So although the book is motivated in the first instance by the need to defend existing positions under siege, it does so by proposing distinctive and, I hope, more plausible accounts of each of these positions on equality.

More significantly, while each of these questions on the site, ground, and scope of justice is interesting and important enough by themselves (as reflected by the growing body of literature on these different questions), I hope to offer more than just a piecemeal inquiry of each of these questions. There is a central thesis that connects my discussion of each of these questions. My overarching goal is to defend an institutional approach to luck egalitarianism that is also consequently global in scope. Indeed, to anticipate some of the connections between the different questions, my justification of the institutional approach will lend support to my account of luck egalitarianism. And I will suggest that my institutional luck egalitarianism plausibly grounds global egalitarian justice. More positively, thus, this work can be seen as an attempt at substantiating cosmopolitan egalitarianism by defending the luck egalitarian ideal and the institutional approach.

One of the intended contributions of this work lies in the way I distinguish these three questions of equality and my claim that to evaluate properly the debates surrounding equality it is important first to get clear which of these (or other) questions of equality a particular commentator is attempting to address. There is no denying that these questions are related or interdependent, in that the response one gives to one could shape the response one could give to another. In fact, instead of denying that these are related questions, one of the aims of this work, as already mentioned, is to forward an account of equality that answers these questions in a coherent and unified way. But these are nonetheless distinct questions in that they address different aspects of equality and a response to one does not directly furnish a response to another. For example, as I will point out below, it will be too hasty to reject luck egalitarianism just because we disagree with a particular luck egalitarian's understanding of the site of equality; or to reject global egalitarianism because we disagree with how some global egalitarians understand the ground or site of equality.

## 1.3   The terrain of inquiry: Egalitarian distributive justice

The term "equality" in this work, unless otherwise qualified or fixed by the context, refers specifically to "egalitarian distributive justice." But this term needs further clarification and specification. Below are some preliminary comments for the purpose of defining more clearly the terrain of inquiry. Roughly, I take distributive justice to be an aspect of social justice, and *egalitarian* distributive justice to be a form of distributive justice that is comparative and that tends towards an equal distribution of the relevant economic goods. The aim of this section is not to provide an analytical account of egalitarian distributive justice, for no doubt other definitions of egalitarian distributive justice can be proposed. The purpose is simply to provide an understanding of egalitarian distributive justice that is commensurate with some of the dominant egalitarian theories on offer, and for which the questions of equality's site, ground, and scope have bearing.

### 1.3.1   Social justice, political justice, and distributive justice

One might say that distributive justice belongs to the larger category of social justice. Social justice concerns the background social conditions that assign persons their fundamental political and economic rights and responsibilities. As a concept, then, social justice is concerned with the appropriate allocation by society of persons' basic political and economic rights and entitlements, and what counts as an appropriate allocation of these rights, and what are to be considered among these rights, are specified by a given theory of justice. A claim of justice is thus a moral claim individuals have against each other for a social order that meets a specified standard.

Social justice, as described, consists of two dimensions or "two coordinate roles" (e.g. Rawls 2001: 48; 1971: 7, 61), corresponding to what may be called political justice and distributive justice.[2] Political justice is concerned with the basic civil and political liberties of persons, whereas distributive justice is concerned with their basic entitlements to economic

---

[2] As an aside, one might note that, in a very basic sense, political justice is distributive in that it is concerned with the distribution of basic rights and liberties, and hence social justice on the whole is distributive justice in this way as Rawls notes (Rawls 1971: 7, 84). But the term "distributive justice" is normally understood specifically in the economic sense, and I adopt this conventional usage. Rawls adopts this usage as well, at one point referring to this as distribution in the "narrow sense" (id. 2001: 42, 43).

goods, such as resources or opportunities. Strictly speaking, distributive justice is also political in that matters of economic justice, as it is with matters of justice generally, are subject to the regulation of the state (Rawls 2001: 48, 61). So the distinction does not mean that distributive justice is apolitical, but that its focus is on the distribution of economic goods or opportunities as opposed to political rights and liberties. Nor does the fact that they are distinct dimensions mean that they are separate. The justness of a social order depends on the package of political and economic justice it delivers, and it is possible that what counts as justice along the economic dimension is informed (or even limited) by what counts as justice in the political dimension. But they present distinct arenas of social justice that can be examined on their own terms. The term economic justice is sometimes used to refer to distributive justice, and I use these terms interchangeably (Dworkin 2000: 12).

### 1.3.2 Equality and justice

Equality as an ideal of distributive justice has to be distinguished from equality as a more general and fundamental moral ideal. Several philosophers have noted that all plausible theories of social justice begin with some notion of the moral equality of persons. Where each theory differs, they point out, is in how it specifies what this moral equality or equal respect entails from the standpoint of justice. In this rather general sense any plausible theory of justice is fundamentally egalitarian. As Dworkin puts it, each must begin from an "egalitarian plateau" (Dworkin 1983: 25–6; Kymlicka 1990: 4; Sen 1992). This is a non-trivial claim, for it reveals a common, however general, reference point against which competing theories of justice can be evaluated. The dispute between competing accounts is settled by deciding which gives the most reasonable understanding of what it means (and what is entailed) by the ideal of equal respect and concern for persons. A theory of justice that denies that individual subjects under its coverage are entitled to equal moral respect in some general sense is one which we will find hard to take seriously.

But there is another, more substantive and specific, sense of equality in discussions of justice that has to do with the distribution or assignment of economic goods (such as resources, opportunities or welfare) among agents. It is this particular notion of equality, equality as an ideal of *economic* or *distributive* justice, with which this book is concerned. On this narrower and more substantive definition of equality, *not* all theories of justice at play in contemporary political philosophy, even if they begin from an egalitarian plateau as specified above, endorse equality. That is, not all accept that equality in the distribution of economic opportunities, goods, or resources matters. John Rawls's theory of justice will qualify as egalitarian in this narrower sense as it does not only begin with the presumption that persons are free and equal citizens, but is also committed to the ideal that they are entitled to an economic order in which inequalities among them are regulated and constrained by a distributive principle (Rawls 1971). But neither will utilitarianism nor libertarianism count as egalitarian in this narrower sense. While utilitarianism may be egalitarian in the general way that everyone is to count for one and no one is to count for more than one, utilitarianism is not egalitarian with respect to distributive justice since it has no basic commitment to equal shares or distribution. Similarly, libertarianism does not endorse equality as an ideal of distributive justice, even if we take it to be affirming at the basic level the ideal of equal respect, which libertarians will specify in terms of equal individual liberties (Sen 1992: 12–13; cf. Nozick).[3] Equality as a distributive ideal concerning the allocation of economic goods is thus a more specific commitment that is not shared by all theories of justice.

### 1.3.3  Egalitarian distributive justice (i): Comparative

Not all distributive principles are egalitarian. One way of distinguishing an egalitarian distributive principle from distributive principles in general is to note two formal features that make a distributive principle egalitarian. One is that it is *comparative* in the inter-personal sense; the other is that the default comparative baseline is that of equal distribution or shares.

---

[3] This remark on libertarianism does not apply to so-called "left-libertarianism" (e.g. Otsuka 2003). Left-libertarianism endorses an egalitarian presumption denied by libertarians, namely that natural resources are owned equally and that any private appropriation of these has to be with the permission of all others. What left-libertarians share with libertarians, or right-libertarians (to distinguish the two views for the present purpose), is the idea of individual self-ownership. But, its label notwithstanding, its commitment to equal ownership of natural resources, and the condition of their acceptable appropriation, makes it substantively a different position from right-libertarianism. Left-libertarianism is in fact an egalitarian position; libertarianism only in name. As Freeman puts it, "Left-libertarianism thus rejects almost entirely the economic libertarianism endorsed by advocates on the right. It is understandable if right-libertarians might see this as libertarianism's surrender to, rather than its reconciliation with, egalitarianism" (Freeman 2008: 467). For a discussion of its possible coherence, see Risse (2004). For reply see Vallentyne, Otsuka, and Steiner (2005).

Let me remark first on the comparative feature. For a group of persons in the relevant distributive unit, an egalitarian distributive principle is comparative when it determines how much a person should get in relation to what others have (D. Miller 1998: 169; 1988).[4] This comparative feature of an egalitarian principle is most vividly highlighted when we contrast an egalitarian principle with what is normally called a principle of humanitarian assistance. A principle of humanitarian assistance has as its goal that of helping persons meet some defined level of basic subsistence rights or needs, and a humanitarian duty is discharged when the recipients of the duty are able to enjoy their basic rights or satisfy their basic needs. Unlike an egalitarian principle, a principle of humanitarian assistance has no comparative commitment: persons' entitlements are understood absolutely rather than comparatively in relation to what others have, that is, by reference to some defined threshold of minimum rights or basic needs. To say that humanitarian duty is defined absolutely does not mean, obviously, that the threshold of human basic needs is fixed and static. Naturally a society's understanding of the basic minimum its members are entitled to is dynamic and shifts with changing social conditions, wealth, and expectations. The point is that persons' humanitarian entitlements are determined by reference to some criteria of human needs (that is fixed at least at a given point in time) rather than in comparison to how others are faring.[5]

*[margin handwriting: Lower threshold for what is minimally necessary is concept w/ n'esslitarian distributive principle]*

This formal comparative feature of egalitarian distributive justice sets it apart not just from basic humanitarian duties, which as I will suggest later in this work belong to a different moral category from that of social justice, but also from any threshold conceptions of social justice, including what is commonly known as "sufficientist" conceptions of distributive justice. For instance, egalitarianism differs from Frankfurt's account of sufficiency, even if sufficiency here is defined more substantially than merely meeting humanitarian needs.[6] The difference, again, is that the latter is non-comparative and has a fixed target, whereas an egalitarian principle is

*[margin handwriting: ✱✱✱]*

---

[4] As David Miller puts it, a distributive principle is "comparative in form—it specifies how people are to be treated relative to one another" (D. Miller 1988: 660).

[5] Understood in this specific way, as more than just a social commitment to ensuring basic welfare for members of society, the ideal of distributive justice is thus a relatively modern ideal perhaps. Compare Fleischacker, who traces the ideal of distributive justice back to the ancients; but Fleischacker uses the term in a broader sense to cover the idea of basic social welfare. See Freeman (2009) on the history of the idea of distributive justice.

[6] See Frankfurt (1987) for an account of sufficientism; and Casal (2007) for why sufficientism is not egalitarianism.

comparative and remains operational as long as there are economic inequalities to regulate. Similarly, Rawls's duty of assistance in his theory of international justice can be read as a sufficientist principle because that duty is discharged when the goal of ensuring that societies are able to support decent institutions of their own is met, in contrast to a global egalitarian principle which is comparative and ongoing, so to speak (Rawls 1999a: Part III).[7] As Rawls himself contrasts his duty of assistance with a global egalitarian distributive principle, the duty of assistance has a target (to empower societies to support decent institutions of their own) and a cut-off (the duty is discharged when all societies are able to do so), whereas a global egalitarian principle continues to apply as long as inequalities remain between societies, even when each is able to support decent institutions of their own.

To be sure, sufficiency and equality are not independent of each other, and in fact in practice they are often closely related. It is possible that the meeting of some sufficiency criteria entails distribution towards greater equality in order to meet the needs of those falling short of the benchmark. In this way sufficiency can lead to a commitment to equality. But equality here enters only as a strategic consideration and does not factor as an intrinsic goal of the position. And if a sufficientist approach prioritizes the needs of the worst-off (taking the form of prioritarianism), this can have the result of narrowing the gap between the least advantaged and the rest of society. Still, the egalitarian outcome here is incidental and not an objective of the sufficientist commitment. The fundamental commitment of a sufficientist approach remains this: that all persons ought to be able to meet some standard of adequacy, which may entail equality under some circumstances, as opposed to egalitarianism, which holds that so long as inequalities exist among persons, some accounting is necessary even when all are able to meet a defined basic minimum.

[7] Rawls's duty of assistance is not merely humanitarian (as that term is commonly understood) as it requires more than ensuring the persons' basic needs are met. Rawls holds that assistance be given to societies that are unable to support decent functioning institutions. It is perhaps more accurate to refer to Rawls's duty of assistance as a sufficientist principle rather than a humanitarian principle. As an aside, to the extent that sufficientism is a distributive principle, it would have been more precise had Rawls distinguished his international duty of assistance from a global egalitarian principle not in terms of assistance versus distributive justice (as he does), but in terms of sufficiencientism versus egalitarianism in distribution.

## 1.3.4 Egalitarian distributive justice (ii): Egalitarian default

An egalitarian principle is thus a comparative principle. But not every comparative distributive principle is thereby egalitarian. We can imagine a comparative distributive principle in a hierarchical society that takes as its starting presumption that members of some castes ought to get more than members of others. So while this principle is still comparative, in that how much a person gets is determined by reference to what others have, the principle is not an egalitarian one because the baseline of comparison is caste-differentiated. For example, a distributive principle that says that members of caste B will get 20 percent of what members of caste A get is clearly comparative, but it is hardly an egalitarian distributive principle. An egalitarian distributive principle is therefore not only comparative but it also takes the default to be that of an equal distribution of the relevant objects of distribution, and specifies the conditions under which departures from this benchmark of equality are acceptable. In presuming an egalitarian default, this means that a distributive principle will tend towards an equal distribution unless a departure from equality meets its stated conditions.

This is how Rawls describes the egalitarian character of his difference principle: An "equal division is accepted as the benchmark because it reflects how people are situated when they are represented as free and equal persons" and departures from this egalitarian default are acceptable when they can be justified to those benefiting least (Rawls 1993: 282, 281–2; and 2001).[8] An egalitarian principle in effect, then, is a principle offering justifications for inequalities by specifying the conditions under which inequalities in distribution are justifiable. Put another way, it is egalitarian in that it sets the limits of acceptable inequalities.[9] Rawls's difference

---

[8] Rawls thus characterizes the difference principle as a "strongly egalitarian conception in the sense that unless there is a distribution that makes both persons better off...equal distribution is to be preferred" (Rawls 1971: 76, 538). Those benefiting least from the departure from the egalitarian default have a "veto," so to speak (Rawls 1993: 282, 284). One might say that the idea of maximizing the situation of the worst-off within the difference principle might not in itself be comparative. But the reason why we have the commitment to maximize the situation of the worst-off in the first place is because we have an interest in regulating the gap between the most advantaged and the worst-off (therein the comparative element).

[9] One might think that this definition of egalitarianism is too broad, for it also picks out principles of distribution that are ostensibly not egalitarian, such as utilitarianism. For instance, one might say that utilitarianism begins from the default of equal shares of individual well-

principle is a paradigm example of an egalitarian distributive principle in this respect. The difference principle presumes an equal distribution of income and wealth *and* provides an account of how much inequality is permissible. It holds that an unequal distribution is justifiable only on the condition that the given distributive arrangement is one in which the worst-off representative class of society benefits most. A feature of an egalitarian distributive principle then is that it justifies inequalities.[10]

Egalitarian distributive justice is thus an aspect of social justice, and is egalitarian in that it has the objective of limiting inequalities in the distribution of economic goods or resources among persons within the relevant social order. It is, for instance, concerned with more than just ensuring that persons are able to meet some criteria of sufficiency, but is concerned with how persons fare in relation to others. An egalitarian distributive principle remains in effect so long as inequalities between the relevant subjects persist. The subject in this work is egalitarian distributive justice thus defined, and the questions I am exploring are, to restate, to what entity or subject does an egalitarian distributive principle apply, what is the ground for this egalitarian commitment, and what is its scope or reach. For convenience and stylistic reasons I will often use the terms "equality," "distributive justice," or simply "justice" to refer to the idea of egalitarian distributive justice unless the context necessitates finer distinctions.

being and holds that deviations from this equality are acceptable when aggregate utility is maximized. But the problem with this reading is that utilitarianism does not begin with a presumption of equal shares. Its sole goal is to maximize utility. Any commitment to equality in distribution it might have is derivative, for example, on the grounds that equality in shares among persons contributes to overall greater social utility. That is, utilitarianism does not say: let the distribution of shares tend towards equality unless unequal distribution maximizes utility. It says: let utility be maximized, and equality in distribution matters when this contributes to utility. The offered definition also leaves out libertarianism. Even though Nozick holds that if manna were to fall from heaven, an equal distribution would be the most plausible starting point (Nozick 1975: 198), this initial equal distribution is only *a starting point* and not a *default* for Nozick. It is a starting point that is quickly transcended; but, more to the point, there is no distributive principle that tends towards equality in Nozick's account. A commitment to an egalitarian default is not just the presumption of an egalitarian starting point but a commitment to incline distribution towards equality.

[10]   This definition captures also "strict egalitarianism," as Rawls calls a conception that aims at equal outcomes as the goal (Rawls 1971: 538). Strict egalitarianism simply denies that any deviation from the benchmark of equality can be justified. This is not to suggest that strict egalitarianism is a plausible conception of distributive justice, but that the claim that an egalitarian principle is in the business of justifying inequalities captures this ideal of equality as well.

The above classifications are meant to clarify and limit the field of inquiry, and the terms and labels by which I denote the different aspects of social justice and forms of distributive justice are not meant to carry any theoretical or normative baggage. What matters is not what we call the different duties and domains of justice as described above, but that we recognize that these different categories do pick out substantively different kinds of duties and expectations. However we label it, it is I hope relatively uncontroversial that what I refer to as egalitarian distributive justice is a specific ideal within economic justice (as distinct from the more general idea of equal respect), and is egalitarian (as opposed to sufficientist) in that it presumes an egalitarian default in the distribution of the relevant economic goods from which departures have to be justified.

## 1.4  The approach: Outline of chapters

The book is divided into three parts corresponding to the three central questions as follows: Part I: Institutions (Chapters 2 and 3); Part II: Luck and Equality (Chapters 4 and 5); and Part III: Global Justice (Chapters 6 and 7).

*Part I: Institutions.* Part I aims to justify the institutional approach and defend it against some common objections. To begin, Chapter 2 recounts the justifications for the institutional approach, arguing in particular that an institutional focus allows for a way of balancing the demands of justice and the legitimate demands of personal life. The argument is not simply that institutions affect persons' life prospects profoundly and pervasively from the start. More importantly, and less often appreciated, is the idea that an exclusive focus on institutions preserves space for individuals to be engaged in meaningful and valuable personal pursuits. On the reasonable presumption of value pluralism, so I argue, the institutional approach provides the most plausible demarcation of the site of equality.

Chapter 3 develops and clarifies the institutional account proposed in the previous chapter by posing it against some of the important criticisms leveled against the institutional approach. Special attention will be given to objections of the form advanced by G. A. Cohen, as well as to Cohen's recent replies to his own critics (G. A. Cohen 1989, 2000, 2008). In so doing, this chapter invokes and reinforces the idea advanced in Chapter 2, that in light of value pluralism the institutional focus provides a plausible

*Tan's criticism on Cohen's Site* ⮡  understanding of the site of egalitarian justice, whereas a more encom-
passing trans-institutional approach does not provide proper space for
valued and valuable personal pursuits. The latter thus contradicts the end
of liberal justice, namely that of providing the appropriate framework
within which persons may freely and equally, but permissibly and fervently, pursue their ends. It stresses that the institutional approach is not a
compromise of justice against personal pursuits; in fact, the primacy of
justice is preserved in this approach for the rules of just institutions set the
range of personal ends that persons may permissibly pursue and the means
by which they can pursue them.

   *Part II: Luck and Equality.* Part II turns to the question of why equality
matters and defends luck egalitarianism against "democratic equality."
Chapter 4 begins by recalling the familiar core ideas of luck egalitarianism
and affirms its initial plausibility. More originally, it will go on to clarify the
basic contours of luck egalitarianism. Specifically, it will argue that the
conceptual space of luck egalitarianism should be limited to the *special
domain of distributive justice,* that its site is the basic *institutions* of a social
order, and its limited *justificatory purpose* is that of explaining why equality
matters. While the outline of the luck egalitarian view I sketch out may
appear in the eyes of some luck egalitarians to be too modest with regards
to its domain, site, and justificatory purpose, I contend that my account
remains staunchly and significantly a luck egalitarian one. In addition, as
will be argued for in the succeeding chapter, my luck egalitarian account is
able to evade criticisms of the luck egalitarian position to which existing
accounts are vulnerable.

   Thus Chapter 5 examines some influential objections raised by proponents of democratic equality (e.g. Anderson 1999; Scheffler 2003, 2005;
Freeman 2006a) against luck egalitarianism, objections that fundamentally
aim to call into question its initial plausibility. I argue that these objections
are deflected when the domain, site, and purpose of luck egalitarianism are
understood in the way I have proposed. While various aspects of luck
egalitarianism are no doubt in need of further refinement and development (as is the case with other competing conceptions of equality), the
main conclusion of this chapter is that the standard worries that luck
egalitarianism is so implausible as not even to get off the ground as a
justification of equality are unfounded. Luck egalitarianism as an account
of the grounds of equality is both attractive and plausible, so I will argue,
and therefore deserving of further attention and defense.

An outcome of the discussion is that luck egalitarianism can, and should, be understood to have an institutional focus, a position already independently defended in Part I. I refer to this version of luck egalitarianism as "institutional luck egalitarianism." The key idea of this luck egalitarianism is that it is not mere facts such as good and bad luck in themselves that generate a problem of justice, but how entrenched social arrangements and practices handle luck that raises considerations of justice.

*Part III: Global Justice.* Part III will show that institutional luck egalitarianism supports the cosmopolitan idea that equality is global in scope. Chapter 6 builds on the luck egalitarian ideal defended in Part II, arguing that since equality matters independently of the ideal of democracy, it potentially applies outside the confines of the (democratic) state. On my institutional luck egalitarian account, what is significant is whether there are global practices and institutions that systemically translate natural and arbitrary facts about persons into significant advantages for some and disadvantages for others. The chapter thus elaborates on the ways global institutions and practices turn facts that are "arbitrary from a moral point of view" and contingencies into actual social advantages and disadvantages for persons. It points out that the institutional focus prevents global luck egalitarianism from sliding into the absurdity often attributed to it, namely, that global luck egalitarianism has to take on distributive (not just humanitarian) commitments to anyone who so happens to be worse off, even if these are (to follow fantastical examples favored by some philosophers) imaginary aliens on different planets with whom we have no prior contact. Chapter 7 examines objections against extending luck egalitarian considerations to the global domain. These are objections that even if nationality is arbitrary, and that the aim of egalitarian justice is to mitigate arbitrary influences on persons' life options, it is not obvious that global egalitarianism will be the result.

A concluding chapter (Chapter 8) highlights the main points of the book, recapitulates the plausibility of the account of equality I have sketched, and responds to some possible objections.

## 1.5 The currency and pattern of equality

The questions of the site, ground, and scope of equality are not the only significant questions of egalitarian distributive justice. There is also the important, and well-discussed, question of the currency of equality, the

"Equality of What?" question as labeled by Sen (Sen 1980; G. A. Cohen 1989; Daniels 1990). That is, what is it that an egalitarian principle should seek to distribute more equally: is it resources, welfare, or capability? I believe my arguments will be neutral with respect to this matter of the currency of equality, and so I will largely leave this question to one side. But to ground some of my discussion, I will often presume resource egalitarianism for illustrative purpose when it does not prejudice the arguments.

Similarly, the book does not directly discuss what the pattern of *egalitarian* distribution ought to be. By a "pattern of egalitarian distribution" I mean here the operational form of the egalitarian principle, how the distributive scheme is to be specified.[11] This specification will be done by what I will call a *substantive* distributive principle. An example of a substantive distributive principle is Rawls's difference principle, to recap, the principle which limits inequality by stating that social and economic inequalities in society are acceptable only when they obtain under a social arrangement that most benefits the worst-off class. Or, as another example of a substantive egalitarian principle, Cohen's principle of "equal access to advantage" (G. A. Cohen 1989: 916–17). Even though I will suggest later how luck egalitarianism could perhaps support something like the difference principle (in order to show that it is not an account of equality that is under-specified necessarily), the question of substantive distributive principle is largely unaddressed in this work. As with the currency question, my discussion of the site, ground, and scope of equality does not presume a prior commitment to a substantive distributive principle.

The above remarks are meant to distinguish two further questions of equality from the ones I will be discussing in this book, and to note that my argument for institutional, luck, and global egalitarianism will not presuppose settlement on the currency and pattern questions. These two questions are important but their resolution does not affect, as I will argue, the site, ground, and scope questions. And although I will not substantiate this point in the work, my conjecture is that clarifying the site, grounds, and scope of equality can help clarify the important questions about its currency and pattern.

---

[11] Since this work is concerned with *egalitarian* distributive justice, it is not neutral about the pattern of distribution in a more general sense: that is, it is not neutral as to whether a pattern of distribution should be sufficientist, utilitarian, or egalitarian. What it is neutral about is the pattern of *egalitarian* distribution.

# PART I

# Institutions

# 2

# Institutions and Justice

## 2.1 The institutional approach

In the opening pages of *A Theory of Justice*, John Rawls writes that "the primary subject of justice is the basic structure of society, or more exactly, the way in which the major social institutions distribute fundamental rights and duties and determine the division of advantages from social cooperation" (Rawls 1971: 7, 54; 1993: 257; 1999c: 6–7; 2001: 10). On this understanding of the locus of justice, *the site* of distributive equality is principally the background institutions of society. Principles of justice are directed primarily at the basic social, economic, and political institutions of society, rather than at the choices and decisions of individuals within the rules of institutions. This means that the commitment to distributive equality is in effect a commitment on the part of members of society to order and regulate the basic institutions of their society against certain distributive principles. For Rawls, society's basic institutions are to be structured such that any resulting inequalities in persons' fundamental economic entitlements are acceptable only where there is fair equality of opportunity (equal opportunity principle) and where there are no alternative feasible institutional arrangements in which the worst-off will benefit more (the difference principle).

But this institutional focus also means that persons are not expected to exercise direct regulation of their day-to-day decisions and actions against these egalitarian principles. In a similar remark later on in *Theory* on the institutional focus of justice, Rawls goes on to add that "[t]he principles of justice for institutions must not be confused with principles which apply to individuals and their actions in particular circumstances. These two kinds of principles apply to different subject and must be discussed separately" (Rawls 1971: 54). On the contrary, persons may be left free to pursue ends that are neither egalitarian in motivation nor in outcome so long as they do so within the rules of institutions that are properly regulated by egalitarian principles. As Rawls puts it in a later work, "within the framework of background justice set up by the basic structure, individuals and associations may do as they wish insofar as the rules of institutions permit" (id. 2001: 50; 1971: 213).[1] For convenience, I will call this the institutional approach, or institutional egalitarianism.

The claim is not that interpersonal conduct within the rules of institutions need not be regulated by certain principles; quite the contrary, and we may even call these principles regulating personal conduct principles of justice (id. 1971: 7). The point is that the principles of justice for the purpose of regulating the social background order *are distinct* from principles of personal conduct, regardless of whether we choose to label the latter principles of justice or not. It is this substantive matter that is affirmed in adopting the institutional approach, namely that the principles of justice applicable specifically to the basic institutions of society are distinct from those regulating personal conduct and choices. For more precision, we could describe this concern with the background social order as that of *social* justice to allow conceptual room for the fact that personal choices, attitudes, and so on can be aptly described as just or unjust (in other senses of justice). But for brevity I will use the term "justice" to mean social justice as described.

Nor does the institutional approach hold that personal decisions and conduct are not constrained at all by the demands of institutional justice. Given that individuals are free to pursue their ends only within the terms of just institutions, it is obvious that personal choices and decisions are limited in this way by the requirements of institutional justice. They may not form personal ends that violate the requirements of justice; and even if these ends are in conformity with justice, the means of their pursuit and realization are subject to the requirements of justice. Moreover, individuals are expected to establish and support institutions that meet standards of institutional justice. Thus their choices as to what kinds of institutions to put in place and support are subject to the constraints of justice. The

---

[1] For one historical type of this approach, see Kant's remarks in his discussion of the principles for a civil constitution in "On the Common Saying: 'This may be true in theory but it does not apply in practice'": "for each may seek his happiness in whatever way he sees fit, so long as he does not infringe upon the freedom of others to pursue a similar end which can be reconciled with the freedom of everyone else *within a workable general law*" (Reiss: 74, my stress).

crucial point of the institutional approach is that principles for institutions do not directly bear on personal conduct and decisions within the rules of just institutions. There is a dualism of perspective presumed here: that individuals support and maintain institutions against certain principles of justice without expecting that the same principles also serve to regulate their day-to-day choices within the rules of justly regulated institutions.

The institutional approach is widely endorsed in the contemporary literature. Besides Rawls, Thomas Nagel writes that the ideal of justice is "a set of institutions" that meets the requirements of social justice while allowing persons to lead their personal lives within the rules of these institutions (Nagel 1991: 18). It is an approach also affirmed in a different way by Brian Barry, who holds that the notion of justice as impartiality applies to the institutions of society but not to personal conduct and choices within the rules of institutions, or, as he puts it, not to "behavior in everyday life" (B. Barry 1995: 194). Similarly Ronald Dworkin takes it that distributive justice is basically concerned with the background institutions of a society that assigns benefits and burdens, and that the aim of egalitarian justice is to identify the requisite institutional arrangement within which differences in persons' life prospects reflect the outcome of their choices and not circumstances (Dworkin 2000: Ch. 2).

But what justifies this special and exclusive focus on the basic structure or the background political, social, and economic institutions of society? Why shouldn't the principles of distributive justice regulate not only the background institutions of society but also the personal conduct and choices of individuals within the rules of these institutions? This question is particularly bothersome for conceptions of justice such as Rawls's: after all, if individuals *are expected to endorse and willingly to support* egalitarian basic institutions for the right reasons on Rawls's own ideal of a well-ordered society, why should they not also be expected to govern their personal conduct within the rules of just institutions by egalitarian principles? Put generally, why should professed egalitarians concern themselves only with the basic institutions of their society and not with personal conduct within the framework given by egalitarian institutions? If egalitarian personal choices in addition to egalitarian institutions can bring about more distributive equality, shouldn't egalitarian justice require egalitarian personal conduct? While the institutional approach is very much in the mainstream, it has thus come under some very powerful criticisms in recent debate: that it represents an evasion of the burdens of justice by not demanding more of

It's not about more distribution equality. The principle, if correct, should satisfy that. It is about sustainability and legitimacy

individuals in their day-to-day choices and decisions (G. A. Cohen 2000, 2008; Murphy 1999).

In the next chapter, I will turn to some of these criticisms. In the present chapter, I recount and clarify the special motivation behind the institutional approach. Gaining a clearer understanding of its motivation, and the background presumptions that compel this approach to equality, will allow us to make a better assessment of the objections that have been leveled against it. As I will explicate below, the institutional approach presumes a form of value pluralism, and it is motivated by the need, in light of this presumption, to provide a plausible means of identifying and demarcating the demands of justice from the demands of personal life. A key point is that the institutional approach does not offer a compromise of justice in favor of personal pursuits; rather, it proposes an understanding of the proper domain and demands of justice in relation to personal pursuits.

## 2.2  The significance of institutions

Rawls's passage quoted in the opening of this chapter is one exemplary statement of the institutional approach. So a good place to start might be to ask what Rawls's stated reasons are for taking "institutions" to be the primary subject of justice.

One reason Rawls gives for taking institutions to be the primary site of distributive justice is that the effects of the basic structure on persons' life chances are "profound and pervasive" from the start (Rawls 1971: 7–8; 1999c: 7; 2001: 55 ff.). The basic structure determines fundamentally persons' basic entitlements and rights and hence the life prospects of persons living under it. From the perspective of economic justice, the basic structure provides the set of background rules, including the basic terms of ownership—"who is to own what," that structure economic activity and the allocation of its costs and rewards in society. In other words, the basic structure of society sets the terms of property rights and ownership and of transaction, laws of contracts, laws regulating capital ownership and wages, and so on.[2] Given this very basic and widespread

---

[2]  As Rawls puts it, the basic structure consists of "the major social institutions" of society that "distribute fundamental rights and duties and determine the division of advantages from social cooperation" (Rawls 1971: 7, 54–5; 2001: 10).

effect of the basic structure on persons' entitlements and hence their life prospects, it is essential that the basic structure of society be regulated by some principles of justice. For instance, a just society would want to regulate its economic background condition as given by the basic structure to ensure that persons' fundamental entitlements are not improperly influenced by contingencies like their social class, native endowment, "good or ill fortune," and the like (id. 2001: 55).

But the fact that the basic structure affects the lives of persons profoundly and pervasively explains why the basic structure is a *necessary* subject of social justice; it does not show that it is also *sufficient* to focus on it, that it is the sole subject of justice. That is, it does not *justify a limited and exclusive* focus on the basic structure. For, after all, one can easily point to other aspects of society that have profound and pervasive impact on persons' life options that are not institutionally based, such as personal attitudes, choices, and actions. If individuals in a society are selfishly driven in their personal decisions—if, for example, skilled individuals are disinclined to do work that has beneficial social consequences unless they are given extra compensation—that can have profound and pervasive impact on the lives of members of that society. G. A. Cohen thus notes that what he calls the "ethos" of society can have profound and pervasive impact on individual lives, and argues that if the purpose of justice is to respond to features of society that impact on persons profoundly and pervasively, there is no good reason to limit justice to institutions (G. A. Cohen 2000: 3). Institutional design will still be important for justice on this view, but so are other social elements, such as personal attitudes and conduct. A society's ethos or culture of selfish acquisitiveness should be as much a concern of justice as its basic institutional structures if the reason for caring about basic institutions is because of their profound and pervasive impact on persons' lives.

So we need to know why we may focus *exclusively* on institutions, not just why we should attend to institutions. Now Rawls also says that focusing on the basic structure allows us "to regard distributive justice as a case of background procedural justice," which consequently frees society from having to regulate each and every personal transaction within the rules of institutions (Rawls 2001: 54). That is, in treating distributive justice as procedural justice, our concern would be with the process by which distributional outcomes are reached, rather than with the outcomes themselves. There are several related reasons for why distributive justice ought to be regarded as procedural. If the background conditions of ownership aren't reasonably fixed and regulated by principles of justice, persons living under this structure will not be able to form legitimate expectations. Without secure and publicly accepted institutions, they will not be confident that what they currently hold (e.g. the resources that they have) are legitimately theirs since the terms of ownership aren't regulated; hence they will not be able to make plans. That is, failure to limit the focus of justice to institutions risks excessive and unpredictable political interference with individual lives.

*[margin handwritten: Cohen's idea is not to make rules for elimate behviur, rather it is to create an ethos that alons w/ the institutions]*

In addition, besides securing personal interests by providing a procedure in which individuals can make decisions without worry of unpredictability, the institutional focus also secures persons' interest in justice itself, that is, their commitment to living in a just society. In the absence of just background institutions, individuals will not be able to make plans confident that social justice is being preserved. With just institutions firmly in place, individuals can freely pursue their ends within the rules of these institutions, "secure in the knowledge that elsewhere in the social system the regulations necessary to preserve background justice are in force" (Rawls 2001: 54). The institutional approach, by establishing and clarifying the terms of ownership and entitlements, establishes the ground rules against which individuals may pursue their life goals confident that these pursuits will not be arbitrarily stymied and that they can pursue their goals without necessarily upsetting justice. Consequently, individuals can live their day-to-day life relieved of the burden of asking at every instance whether a given personal transaction or decision is consistent with the requirements of social justice. The complexities of making such considerations about background justice with regard to each personal decision and action are thus avoided by adopting the institutional focus (id. 1993: 267; 2001: 54–5). So long as that transaction or decision is admissible within the rules of an institutional arrangement taken to be just, they may proceed with confidence that justice is not compromised.

*[margin handwritten: Main point on why inst. approach is better]*

Thus we get closer to why institutions are exclusive: focusing exclusively on institutions preserves space for individual day-to-day activities, decisions, and the setting of expectations free from continuous state intervention, and relieves individuals of the complex (if not practically impossible) task of evaluating their daily decisions in light of egalitarian considerations. The institutional approach addresses two potential conflicting interests that we presume individuals to have: an interest in pursuing lives of their own without excessive interference, and an interest in pursuing these consistent with the requirements of justice.

Still, this fact that the institutional approach makes space for just personal pursuits does not *fully* justify an exclusive institutional focus. For the question remains as to why it should be the case that an ideally just society need not subject personal transactions to the demands of justice instead of seeking to provide space for non-egalitarian pursuits within just institutional rules. Why should we think that individuals ought to be relieved of the responsibility of regulating, to the best of their ability, their personal pursuits by egalitarian principles, complex as this might be? Rawls's second set of reasons presumes that when institutions are just and its justness actually preserved, individuals can proceed with their personal lives secure in the knowledge that they are doing so justly. Even if we accept that it is indeed a tall and unreasonable order that individuals take into account egalitarian justice considerations each time they make an economic decision, a basic presumption needs substantiation if the institutional approach is to be given full justification: why should egalitarian justice be exclusively concerned with the background institutional conditions?[3]

Thus, while the two arguments discussed go some way toward justifying the institutional approach by explaining why an institutional focus is essential, they don't justify the special and exclusive focus on institutions. The first reason, having to do with the pervasiveness and profundity of the effects of background institutions on persons' life chances, shows why it is necessary to focus on institutions, but it does not justify the limited focus on institutions. That is, it does not show that it is sufficient to address only institutions. Likewise, the second set of reasons, that focusing on institutions frees up space for personal pursuits within the parameters set by justly regulated institutions, explains the significance of focusing only on institutions, but this presumes that which is at issue: why should justice free up space for personal pursuits in this way? Why presume that justice ought to provide space for non-egalitarian personal pursuits instead of regulating personal choices and conduct within the rules of just institutions?

---

[3] Without further argument, the difficulty of personal computation can be a difficulty of implementing ideal justice, not a difficulty with regard to our ideal of justice. In which case, as suggested by Peter Vallentyne, act consequentialist responses against parallel objections can be attempted here. Thus, it is important to show why the institutional approach is a specification of what justice is and demands, and is not simply a strategy compelled by the difficulties of implementation.

A defense of the institutional approach needs to show why it is *both* necessary and sufficient for justice to focus on institutions. To have a full appreciation of the basis for an exclusive focus on institutions, we need to explicate the starting assumptions behind the institutional approach concerning the role of justice and the fact of *value pluralism*.

## 2.3  Justice and personal pursuits

Justice is an important social virtue, in part because it defines the appropriate social background conditions against which persons can freely and equally pursue their ends in life or their conceptions of the good human life (Rawls 2001: 2–3, 40–1). Indeed the problem of justice arises precisely because of the fact that individuals have different legitimate personal interests that may come into conflict (id. 1971: 189). Individual personal pursuits, as we may call them, are not limited to asocial private goals but include a range of socially shared ends and associational commitments and can be other-regarding as well, such as those ends and commitments having to do with familial relations, friendship, and so on. It is because of the importance of such pursuits of persons' ends that society should care to ensure that each and every one is able to pursue his or her conception of the good as a free and equal person and not be arbitrarily disadvantaged against in this regard. One might say that there would be no occasion for the concept of justice were it not to matter to us whether individuals are able to pursue their valued ends freely and equally with respect to others. As Rawls puts it in a pithy but suggestive remark, "while justice draws the limit and the good shows the point, justice cannot draw the limit too narrowly" (id. 1993: 174). Justice is an important value because it defines the boundaries within which individuals may pursue their own conceptions of the good life, and it is these pursuits that give value and point to their individual lives.[4]

---

[4] Consider Bernard Williams's related remarks that "the public order, if it is to carry conviction, and also *not flatten human experience*, has to find ways in which it can be adequately related to private sentiment, which remains more intuitive and open to conflict than public rules can be" (B. Williams 1981: 82, my stress). None of this implies that justice cannot be constitutive of the good or that the truly good life has to be one that is justly realized. And indeed for some individuals the pursuits of justice itself could be their dominant conception of the good life. The point is that in general, while justice of course matters for individuals, there are other things that matter that are distinct from justice.

A background assumption of the institutional approach is that even *[margin note: Wholeheartedly agree. But, this is not incompatible w/ Cohen's view of site of J]* though egalitarian justice defines the parameters within which persons may pursue the ends of life, these ends themselves need not be egalitarian in their motivation or consequence. Put another way, personal pursuits can be valuable independently of egalitarian principles. They need not be *derived from* egalitarian principles, nor need their worth be *justified by* their tendency to realize these principles. The only standard for evaluating one's personal projects, once they satisfy the external constraints set by justice, is that they meet the requirements of rationality; that is, these pursuits are consistent with and further rather than thwart the individual's own under- standing of the good. There is no basis by which to compare "the worth of the different conceptions of persons once it is supposed they are compati- ble with the principles of justice. Everyone is assured of an equal liberty to pursue whatever plan of life he pleases as long as it does not violate what justice demands" (Rawls 1971: 94, 447).[5] For example, a person's show of special concern for his family within the bounds set by institutional justice need not, and is usually not, justified because this special concern derives from an egalitarian principle; nor is it defended on the grounds that this is how, through a division of social labor, economic equality is best en- hanced. Familial special concern, within the bounds of societal justice, is valuable independently of social equality. It is a value independent of egalitarian justice.[6]

The independence of personal justice of justice in the way spelled out above reflects a kind of value pluralism, or what Nagel would call "the fragmentation of value," namely that there are diverse moral values not all of which are reducible to or subsumable under a single dominant principle (Nagel 1979; also B. Williams 1981). Egalitarians are committed to living in a society regulated by some egalitarian distributive principle; but they also have personal projects that are valuable independently of their egalitarian commitments. It is this presumption of moral pluralism that compels the institutional approach. As Samuel Freeman writes, "The fact of reasonable pluralism says that people will have many different

---

[5] Another example, Rawls writes: "within the limits allowed by the principles of right, there need be no standard of correctness beyond that of deliberative rationality" (Rawls 1971: 564). For more on Rawls's view on the principles of rational choice, and how they provide constraints relative to a system of ends rather than external constraints on the system of ends itself, see 1971: 408–9, 424–6.

[6] For one discussion on parental partiality and background justice, see C. Macleod (2011).

worthwhile aims and pursuits in a well-ordered democratic society, in addition to concern for the economic status of the least advantaged" (Freeman 2007: 124; also 2006a: Ch. 6; and Scheffler 2006).[7]

Because of this independence of justice and personal pursuits, a question arises: how is it possible to reconcile the demands of egalitarian justice on the one side and the various demands of personal life on the other? This is a particularly taxing challenge for the committed egalitarian, for she is committed both to promoting equality and to pursuing her ends. How does an egalitarian live up to her egalitarian commitments on the one side while also pursuing her non-egalitarian but legitimate ends? Justice, as Rawls notes, "supposes that individuals and groups put forward competing claims, and while they are willing to act justly, they are not prepared to abandon their interests" (Rawls 1971: 281). It is as a response to this challenge that the institutional approach is best appreciated. Taking the principles of justice to be primarily concerned with the basic institutions of society allows for a division of moral labor between the demands of justice on the one side, and the demands of personal commitments and ends on the other. The institutional focus thus attempts a reconciliation of these two potentially competing demands in the following way: in the name of justice, persons have the duty to establish and support just institutions, but within the rules of these institutions persons may freely pursue their ends. They may "do as they wish" insofar as the rules of institutions permit, secure in the knowledge that so long as they pursue their ends within just rules, justice for society is preserved. The institutional focus thus provides a way of balancing the pursuit of egalitarian justice on the one hand and personal pursuits on the other. The institutional approach, by training the principles of justice primarily at the basic structure of society, provides a means by which to "approximate the boundaries" (id. 1971: 566) within which individuals and their associations may pursue their conceptions of the good while meeting the requirements of justice.

The problem the institutional approach is meant to address can be framed in terms of the two moral powers Rawls attributes to individuals: (i) their capacity for a sense of justice and (ii) their capacity for forming, pursuing, and revising their conceptions of the good (e.g. id. 2001: 19). On the presumption of value pluralism, while justice limits the good, it need

[7] For remarks suggestive of value pluralism as I have defined it in Rawls's *Theory of Justice*, see Rawls 1971: 485, 447–8, 512, 528.

not justify or ground the good. Thus it is not available to Rawlsian individuals to try to reconcile justice and the good by limiting the good to only those that promote justice or those that derive from shared principles of justice. They must therefore have an alternative way of aligning their pursuit of justice and their pursuit of the good. The institutional approach offers a way of demarcating the demands of justice from that of personal pursuits.

The sense of value pluralism presumed under the institutional approach does not claim that there is an irresolvable conflict between justice and personal life. And certainly it does not deny that there can be an agreed upon reasonable standard of justice for society. So the idea of value pluralism invoked here is relatively modest compared to other usages of that term, in that it is not presumed to support the thesis that there are irresolvable moral dilemmas. To the contrary, the institutional view holds that at least conflicts between justice and personal life can be resolved institutionally. What this pluralism invokes is that persons have diverse and not necessarily compatible ideas of the good life, and one person's conception need not be necessarily rationally justifiable to others. It affirms the regulative primacy of justice: that justice constrains the range of personal goals and the means by which they may be realized. Thus although personal ends are not necessarily justified by reference to justice, conflicts between justice and personal ends are resolved in favor of justice. What counts as an admissible conception of the good life, and what qualifies as acceptable means of pursuing that conception, is constrained by what social justice demands of persons. The institutional approach reconciles justice and personal pursuits by securing the antecedent background conditions of justice against which only individuals may pursue their personal ends; it "frames" the range of admissible personal pursuits (Rawls 1971: 548, 563, 31). A workable approach to justice must therefore also present a means of granting justice this regulative primacy over the good. That is, it has to be able to provide a method of parameter-setting such that the limits of how one may live one's life can be practically located. Focusing on institutions—the identifiable background social, political, and economic institutions of society—provides just the way to make locatable the bounds of personal pursuits (e.g. Nagel 1991: 18).

Accordingly, the institutional focus offers a reconciliation of these two superficially competing demands in the following way: in the name of justice, persons have the duty to establish and support just institutions, but within the rules of these institutions, persons may freely pursue their ends. To recall, persons may "do as they wish" so long as the rules of institutional justice permit, and they can do so confident that justice is being upheld if they play by the rules. A procedure is provided for balancing the demands of equality on the one hand and personal life on the other. It tells the committed egalitarian who is also an individual with her own life to live that her obligation to egalitarian justice extends to her supporting and sustaining a just egalitarian basic structure in her society, but that she is free to pursue her personal ends within the rules of the basic structure. To use a simplified example for the purpose of illustration, imagine that to sustain an egalitarian basic structure would require that persons comply with a particular taxation scheme. On the institutional approach, once a person has paid her share of taxes under this arrangement, and this can be very substantial in principle, she is free to use her post-tax wealth to do as she wishes so long as background institutional justice is preserved. Justice thus defines the parameters for personal pursuits, but within the parameters set, personal life falls outside the reach of justice directly. The institutional approach provides a focus for the demands of justice, a means by which the parameters of justice may be set, and within which persons are left free to pursue their personal ends.

In short, in light of value pluralism—the idea that the various diverse ends that persons have need not necessarily be derived from principles of egalitarian justice or promote egalitarianism—a feasible approach to egalitarian justice (i) has to be able to provide a means of approximating the bounds of justice and personal pursuits, and do that in a way that (ii) accords justice primacy over personal pursuits. The institutional approach meets these two conditions. The crucial point is that the institutional approach is not proposed as a method by which individuals can be relieved of the burdens of justice. That is, it does not propose a compromise of justice's demands. Instead, it is, as Scheffler puts it, a "response to a form of pluralism about moral values and principles," an implication of the idea that "the principles for the basic structure do not supersede the complex and varied principles and values that apply to individuals" (Scheffler 2006: 107). To put the contrast simply, it is one thing to say: "Achieving equality across the board is what justice demands, but since this would be too burdensome, we limit this demand to institutions," and another to say: "Since justice cannot demand that persons attempt to achieve equality across the board (on account of value pluralism), we should limit the demands of justice to institutions." The latter is an implication of value pluralism that is the rationale behind the institutional approach.

I have not defended value pluralism here. My central point is that it is the presumption of pluralism that crucially explains the motivation for the institutional approach: in light of the fragmented character of values, an institutional focus allows for a way of approximating the boundary of justice and its rightful demands on persons. To the extent that many critics of the institutional approach do not explicitly disavow value pluralism, my conditional claim is not trivial.[8]

One might ask if we could not adopt a form of "act egalitarianism" that is subject to personal prerogatives (in the spirit of a prerogative sensitive act consequentialism) as an alternative to the institutional approach outlined above.[9] But this proposal merely restates the very problem that the institutional approach is meant to solve: how to balance the demands of egalitarianism with the demands of personal prerogative. To say that we can allow egalitarian commitments to regulate all of life if we admit that there are personal prerogatives that will allow for legitimate departures from egalitarian demands does not answer the basic question: how do we determine in a principled manner legitimate personal prerogatives? The "act luck egalitarian" faces the problem with which we began the discussion, namely, how is she to act given her dual commitments to equality and to living a worthwhile personal life? The institutional approach as argued above is an attempt to locate in a feasible and plausible way the boundary between egalitarianism justice and admissible personal pursuits. That is, it defines the space for personal prerogatives (to depart from egalitarian demands) to be just that space provided for by the rules of egalitarian institutions.[10]

---

[8] For instance, see Cohen's reluctance to deny pluralism (G. A. Cohen 2008: 397–8).

[9] Scheffler labels as "agent-centered prerogatives" those morally justified permissions that agents can have for not promoting a moral goal (Scheffler 1982: Ch. 1). Cohen for instance holds that taking justice's demands to cover more than institutional rules does not mean that justice cannot allow for personal "prerogatives" (G. A. Cohen 2008: 61 f., 387 ff.; and 2000: n. 212–13). The idea of prerogatives within "act egalitarianism" is suggested by Peter Vallentyne, in his advice as reader to this script.

[10] Thus when Cohen says, in responding to Estlund's argument that prerogatives can sanction Rawlsian inequalities, that Rawls allows for departures from egalitarian demands within the rules of institutions *even when there is no prerogative-based justification* for these departures (G. A. Cohen 2008: 394), he fails to note that Rawls's institutional approach

## 2.4  Division of labor: Two senses

The institutional approach is often characterized as a form of "division of labor" in that it distinguishes the moral demands on institutions from the demands on personal life. But it is important that the sense of labor "division" here not be misunderstood. The term "division of labor" as understood normally in classical economics assumes that there is a common social goal whose most efficient attainment is facilitated by some social division of labor, with the different divided tasks shaped by reference to that shared end.  Here the justification for the diverse efforts is that the different assignments and jobs in totality promote the common end. For example, Adam Smith's famous example of the division and specialization of tasks in pin manufacturing is meant to show how the singular objective of increasing productivity in pin production is facilitated "as a consequence of a proper division and combination of their different operations" (Smith 1776:13).

But the institutional approach to justice invokes the idea of a division of labor in a fundamentally different sense. The institutional egalitarian approach does not hold the premise that there is an overriding common substantive moral objective of, say, achieving maximum equality across the whole of society, and that the division of tasks between institutions and personal choices is what best promotes this grand social objective. Rather, as  mentioned, its division of labor is instigated by the acknowledgment of the pluralism of value, the recognition that there are distinct moral ends and that within different moral domains different values and principles apply. The division of labor in this case reflects the fragmented nature of morality itself and is not a social strategy for the purpose of servicing a shared dominant end.

In other words, the division of labor invoked by the institutional approach does not occur against the background assumption that individuals in society share a common (substantive moral) goal that the division of tasks is meant to achieve in the best and greatest way (as opposed to pin-making). It begins from an opposite presumption, to wit, that there is a plurality of moral values, including those of egalitarian justice and personal  life, and an account of justice has to reflect this structural fragmentation of morality by acknowledging and specifying the limited and special domain

identifies the space for prerogatives (with regard to egalitarian justice) with that space allowed for by the rules of institutions. Now Cohen might say Rawls's institutionally given space is too generous, but then an argument has to be made as to why the boundaries between justice and personal life have to be drawn differently. See discussion in next chapter.

within which principles of egalitarian justice apply.[11] The division of labor offered by the institutional approach is not a means of maximizing a certain overriding common moral objective, but is a way of regulating and ordering the different compartments of a moral agent's life.

Thus the division of labor is an expression of or a response to the moral pluralism underlying the institutional approach, rather than the ideal that a common and dominant moral goal (i.e. social equality) is most efficiency  strived for by dividing up and assigning different tasks to different entities (Scheffler 2006:107–9; Rawls 1993: 268–9). To highlight this point, consider a possible utilitarian institutional approach. The institutional utilitarian will presume a monistic moral world in which utilitarianism is the dominant moral ideal, in that all other moral values are justified only by reference to the utility principle. The institutional utilitarian might hold, however, that as a matter of efficiency it would be better to divide up moral commitments between institutions and personal life (thus allowing persons to engage in pursuits that in themselves don't seem to promote social utility) in the belief that assigning the task of achieving social justice to institutions and allowing space for persons to pursue their ends within the rules of institutions best serves the objective of maximizing utility for all. On this account, it has to be argued that such a division *in fact* achieves this goal, for if an alternative division of labor or arrangement can be shown to be better at maximizing utility, there will be no reason for maintaining the institutional division of labor. Thus utilitarianism can arrive at an institutional approach based on a very different understanding of a division of labor on account of its value monism. Institutional egalitarians such as Rawls, as mentioned, begin from an opposition moral assumption, that of value pluralism, and the division of labor  between principles for institutions and principles for daily life under this approach is not a division of labor in the classical economics sense that it is efficient to divide up labor in this way, but because of the acknowledgment that morality is itself divided.[12] In other words, on the utilitarian view, there is a common objective that a division of labor is meant to serve

---

[11] For Rawls, utilitarianism's denial that "the plurality of distinct persons with separate system of ends is an essential feature of human societies" is one of his reasons for rejecting the utilitarian doctrine (Rawls 1971: 29).

[12] Rawls explicitly distinguished this utilitarian view of division of labor from his own account of the "institutional division of labor" (Rawls 1993: 260–1).

best; whereas on the institutional view, the division of labor is a reflection of the diversity of objectives.

This clarification is important because it shows that it is no objection to the institutional approach that the end of social egalitarianism could in fact be more efficiently served by extending the site of egalitarian justice beyond institutions. This objection would be guilty of reading the institutional approach as a division of labor in the instrumental (classical economics) sense. That the goal of social equality can be maximized by not differentiating principles for institutions and principles for personal conduct does not raise any difficulty for the institutional approach, because it is not its goal to maximize social equality across the board. Clarifying the sense of the division of labor offered by the institutional approach also shows that it is not its purpose to divide up moral labor in order to ease the burdens of justice on persons. The division marks the boundary of justice and its proper demands, rather than a compromise of justice for the sake of individual ends. The special and limited focus on institutions is not meant to further the goal of maximum social equality in some way, nor to make the move toward equality less demanding on individual agents. Its purpose is to make it possible for persons to live meaningful and worthwhile separate lives consistent with the demands of social justice given the assumption of value pluralism.

## 2.5  The basic structure as a public system of rules

The basic structure for Rawls, as mentioned, is the major social institutions of society that determine persons' fundamental rights and duties and the division of benefits and burdens (Rawls 1971: 7, 54–5; 1993: 258; 2001: 10). What is clear from the above discussion is that the basic structure is not co-terminous with the set of all features of society that have profound and pervasive influence on persons' life prospects. In addition to not being able to account for why it would be sufficient to focus just on the basic structure, as explained above, understanding the basic structure to be identical to any features of society that have profound and pervasive impact on persons would also make the definition of the basic structure too expansive and ill-defined to serve as the site of justice. The basic structure indeed has profound and pervasive effect on persons, but it is not the only thing in society that can have this impact on persons. Private associations and relationships (like churches and families) can have this effect on persons, indeed even more so as in the case of religious commitments for some individuals; yet these are not (in some respects to be elaborated on below) part of the basic structure. The ethos of society too, that is, the sum of the moral sentiments and attitudes of its members, has this impact, says Cohen.

What it is about the basic structure that makes it a determinant subject of justice is not that that it picks out those aspects of society that have profound and pervasive impact on persons living under it, though it of course has that impact, but that it is the set of society's political, social, and economic institutions that are *subject to public–political regulation*. Principles of justice are public principles of right, and can be directed only at entities that society can appropriately regulate via its system of laws.[13] Features of society like personal attitudes no doubt can have profound and pervasive effects on persons, but in general attitudes are not the kinds of things that the public sphere can or may directly regulate. In contrast, a person's political and civil rights, and their economic rights and entitlements—as these are determined by wage laws, property rights, contract laws, tax policies, access to basic social opportunities (such as education, etc.), and so on—are things that may be regulated by the state through its laws, public policy, taxation schemes, and the like. The basic structure shapes persons' fundamental *civil, political, and economic rights and responsibilities* precisely because they are subject to the regulatory power of the state. This is what gives the status of "rights" to these entitlements. In the case of the domestic political society, the basic structure consists in the political, social, and economic institutions of a society that the state can directly shape and regulate. In a sense, the basic structure is important in a distinctive way in that it is through the basic structure that *the state* directly profoundly and pervasively shapes and delimits the life prospects of persons. Thus it is not inappropriate to refer to the basic structure as the coercive institutions of society, given that state regulation is in a broad sense coercive regulation since the state is centrally a coercive institution. But "coercive" here has to be properly understood. It does not limit the basic structure to just those institutions of society that fall under criminal law where the coercive

---

[13] In *The Metaphysics of Morals*, Kant writes: "The sum total of those laws which can be incorporated in external legislation is termed the theory of right (jus)" (Reiss: 134). Rawls calls the basic structure "a public system of rules" (Rawls 1971: 55).

authority of the state is most tangible. Rather, anything that falls under the direct regulatory powers of the state falls under its coercive powers to the extent that the state has the right to use force to enforce its policies and decisions. Whether we refer to the basic structure as the coercive institutional features of society or the institutional features of society subject to state regulation, we are identifying the same set of social institutions. The crucial point is that the fact that the basic structure is directly subject to publicly recognized political regulation (and this is what makes it also a coercive structure) makes it, and only it, the proper subject of a system of public right.

While the basic institutions typical of the political society or state most vividly reveal how the basic structure presents a public system of rules subject to societal regulation, it does not follow that only state institutions have this relevant characteristic. As I will argue later, the set of global institutions present too a public system of rules subject to collective regulation, thus rendering it into a basic structure for the purpose of justice. For instance, the global economic order, with its trade rules, laws on property rights and so on, constitutes a public system of rules that can be regulated and enforced (even if the regulating and enforcing are not performed by a centralized global political authority).

G. A. Cohen has argued that the notion of a basic structure under Rawls's own explication suffers from a "fatal" ambiguity, leading him to conclude that since there is no clear subject that is the basic structure, the institutional approach fails from the very outset (G. A. Cohen 2000: 129 ff.). Indeed, this claim of Cohen's regarding the ambiguity of the basic structure is the lynchpin of his internal critique of Rawls's institutional focus. Cohen's opening move in his internal critique is that Rawls's exclusive institutional focus is at odds with his own ideal of a well-ordered society in which individuals, moved by fraternity, are to internalize the principles of justice. This argument, as Cohen himself anticipates, will elicit the obvious response that the principles Rawls expects persons to internalize are *principles for the basic structure*, and so it is not incoherent to say that individuals can genuinely endorse and accept (in the name of fraternity) as binding those principles that are meant not to apply to their day-to-day conduct as such but to the choice of institutions that they ought to support. To counter this obvious response, which he dubs "the basic structure objection," Cohen is compelled to show that the very notion of a basic structure is fraught. The success of Cohen's internal critique, therefore, rides wholly on the success of his reply to the basic structure objection. Since the idea of the basic structure, or the set of the basic social and political institutions of society, as an identifiable and tolerably determinate identity is crucial to the institutional approach, it is important to consider Cohen's arguments in this regard.

Why does Cohen think that Rawls's specification of the basic structure suffers from a fatal ambiguity? Cohen's central evidence for this alleged ambiguity in Rawls, it seems to me, is that Rawls sometimes refers to the family as part of the basic structure, sometimes not (Rawls 1993: 258). If the family is part of the basic structure of society, then the basic structure cannot be just those coercive (or regulated) institutions of society since the family is not, says Cohen, a coercive or state-regulated institution. On the other hand, if the family is not part of the basic structure, this is in tension with some of Rawls's own statements that the family is part of the basic structure of society (G. A. Cohen 2000: 136; cf. Rawls 1971: 463; 2001: 11). So, that Rawls apparently "wobbles" on this matter put paid to the idea that there is a clear enough notion of the basic structure that justice can regulate.

Yet these apparently conflicting statements about the family and its relation to the basic structure are not a case of "wobbling" on the part of Rawls, and do not sufficiently support Cohen's skepticism with regard to the basic structure. The seemingly conflicting statements about the family and the basic structure in Rawls are due to the complex character of the social institution of the family and the complicated ways in which the family relates to the background set of institutions of state, subject to state regulation. The family is both a part of the basic structure and not a part of, in the sense that some aspects of familial relations belong to the basic structure while other aspects and practices do not. On the one hand, the family is a social organization that partly falls outside state regulation because it is a private association between members of society. The state, for instance, does not regulate division of labor within the household by mandating some manner of egalitarian relationships between spouses, how children are to be raised and educated (beyond political liberal requirements of civic education), and so on. So with respect to these matters, the family is not part of the basic structure of society. On the other hand, there are practices and aspects of the family that fall directly under state regulation and hence are aspects of the basic structure of society. For instance, the state regulates the union of persons in marriage, and regulates terms of separation should this be sought. The state even directly constrains child-raising practices, though in tightly circumscribed ways, like educational and basic health requirements etc. On these matters, then, the family belongs to the basis structure of society, as these are kinds of practices and relationship that the state can and does regulate directly. Thus Rawls's apparent ambivalence about the family and the basic structure is only apparent and does not show that the basic structure is ill-defined. His different comments about the family and the basic structure reflect the complex nature of the family in relation to the basic structure of society (e.g. Scheffler 2006).

The question of what the basic structure is, for Rawls, is perhaps a more complex matter, and more can be said about how that is understood by Rawls.[14] I intended only to suggest a plausible reading of the basic structure that also addresses Cohen's charge that it is an insufficiently determinate entity because of its alleged ambiguity with respect to the family. Rawls scholarship aside, the general issue before us is whether institutional egalitarians have a clear target on which to locate the site of justice. The basic structure, I am suggesting, does present this clear and definable site if it is understood as those social, political, and economic institutions in society that fall under the regulatory power and authority of the state. It is also uncontroversial that such institutions also happen to be institutions that have profound and pervasive impact on persons' lives. If this is a reasonable way of understanding what the basic structure is, then we can, contra Cohen, take these institutions to be the site of justice because they are the sort of things that states can regulate and these institutions do present a clear and definitive enough target; and these institutions ought to be assessed against principles of justice because of the profound and pervasive impact they have on individuals.

## 2.6 The demands of institutional justice

The limitation of principles of justice to the institutions of a social order might give the impression that the institutional approach is not sufficiently demanding of persons, and to the extent that we might think that

---

[14] See Scheffler (2006) and also A. Williams (1998) for additional discussion on the basic structure.

justice has to impose certain demands on persons, this perceived undemandingness of the institutional approach might appear suspicious. And, relatedly, it might be argued that its undemandingness will result in excessive inequalities in society. Hence, I will try here to suggest that the institutional approach in fact imposes various demands on persons, including that of setting limits on what counts as legitimate personal pursuits and the requirement that they have a duty of vigilance with respect to the justness of their institutions. Moreover, these demands, including the fact that the institutional approach understands egalitarian justice to be part of a larger conception of social justice, need not necessarily allow for excessive inequalities. This last is important, as we will see in the next chapter, because the misperception that the institutional approach admits excessive inequalities is what sparks some of the main criticisms against it.

### 2.6.1 Not all individual decisions are strictly personal

As we have seen, the reconciliation of personal pursuits to justice offered by the institutional approach is not achieved by limiting the demands of justice against personal pursuits. On the contrary, the reconciliation affirms the primacy of justice over personal pursuits. Justice and personal pursuits come together when persons pursue their ends in a social order whose basic institutions are regulated by principles of justice. Individuals may pursue their own ends, secure in the knowledge that egalitarian justice is being preserved, only if they can presume that the basic institutions of their society conform to the demands of egalitarian justice.

Indeed, rather than compromising the demands of justice in relation to the concerns of personal life, a successful reconciliation of justice and personal pursuits through the institutional approach can require substantial revisions in persons' existing conceptions of the good. It could require individuals to temper their own wants and interests in light of the requirements of background justice; it will require that persons take responsibilities for assuming the costs of their preferences and wants, and that they pursue these only with resources that are rightly theirs.[15]

---

[15] Rawls 1993: 34, 280; 1971: 13, 31. As Nagel notes, a complete reconciliation of justice with personal life will involve significant transformation in individual moral outlook in light of what justice demands (Nagel 1991: 17).

Indeed individuals truly concerned about the success of their personal life will affirm the primacy of justice. In the context of grave social injustice, persons cannot be confident that their pursuit of personal ends is not tainted by injustice. They do not know whether they are using more than their fair share of resources, for example; they do not know whether privileging their own children's education is justifiable when their neighbors are not able to meet their children's basic needs. For individuals committed to the ideals of equal respect for others as well as their own ideas of the good life, a "just society is a prerequisite for a life that respects both of two ideals neither of which should be abandoned. So our private lives, our success or failure in leading the lives people like us should have, are in that limited but powerful way parasitic on our success together in politics. Political community has that ethical primacy over our individual lives" (Dworkin 1992: 223). The institutional approach recognizes this antecedence of justice and provides a workable means of securing justice while marking out space for personal pursuits.

Given the primacy of justice, what counts as properly personal pursuits against which we want to reconcile the demands of justice has to be carefully defined. The institutions of a society, clearly, are the result of the choices that individuals make. Thus, in as far as some choices individuals make do determine the kinds of institutions that can be established and supported, institutional egalitarians would be directly concerned about these choices of individuals and their evaluative postures toward these institutions (Rawls 1971: 13). That is, such politically salient choices of individuals, as we may call them, are not strictly *personal*, and institutional egalitarians can be critical of individuals who opt against institutional arrangements that are required by egalitarian principles, or whose preferences and pursuits make the establishment and maintenance of such institutions difficult. Thus if members of a society opt to vote into power a less egalitarian government because they find the egalitarian ideals of the incumbent government too taxing on their own interests, they are not really exercising a personal choice but a political one and hence a choice subject to the evaluation of justice. They are in effect making a choice about the sorts of institutions to be put in place, and so their decision is subject to judgment under the institutional approach. Certainly an adequate reconciliation of justice and personal life will involve transformation in individual moral outlook given how they currently are with regard to institutional choices.[16]

Genuinely *personal* choices, then, pertain only to those actions and decisions of individuals that are *not directed at* institutions, such as decisions to bring about or support a particular kind of social institutional arrangement over another. Only choices of individuals understood in this way, that is, choices that are not aimed at the basic structure of society *and* that are permitted by the rules of the basic structure, count as personal and outside the direct regulation of principles of egalitarian justice. But individual conduct or choices concerning the kinds of institutions to be established or supported are not personal choices, and fall directly within the purview of justice on the institutional approach. A distinction has to be observed between *individual* choices in general and *personal* choices in particular.

So while institutional egalitarians would reject the slogan "the personal is political" (if by this slogan it is meant literally that there are no personal choices as such, but that all individual choices are politically salient), they do not deny that *some* individual choices have direct institutional implications, and hence are political; and that these choices are subject to the critical evaluation of justice (G. A. Cohen 2000: 122–3). The institutional approach accepts the division between justice and personal pursuits; it is one important feature of this approach that not all individual choices qualify as *personal* choices properly understood. What counts as personal pursuits on the institutional view is more restricted than some of its critics might think. Personal pursuits are defined by reference to the requirements of justice impartially defined, not the other way around. Justice "is not at the mercy, so to speak, of existing wants and interests" (Rawls 1971: 261).

In his *Rescuing Justice and Equality*, Cohen argues that *economic* decisions in general cannot really be personal (in the sense described above) because they can impinge on and impair the background conditions of justice. He points out that a welfare state would not be able to maintain its egalitarian

---

[16] As Rawls notes, a successful reconciliation of justice and personal pursuits will require that persons be prepared to reform or revise their personal pursuits in light of what justice demands (Rawls 1993: 34, 280; 1971: 13, 31). Indeed, the institutional approach reconciles justice and personal life fully only when there is some transformation of personal life (Nagel 1991: 17).

redistributive programs should its talented and well-off, put off by the taxation structure necessary for supporting its welfare institutions, opt to work less hard. The lack of egalitarian ethos on the part of the talented, as is reflected by their unwillingness to contribute more under an incentive structure they deem unfavorable to them, can thus in fact compromise the egalitarian aspirations and objectives of the state. Thus he concludes that the economic choices of persons "do have strong implications for what sorts of institutions are possible" (G. A. Cohen 2008: 376).

As is clear, the problem Cohen is pressing here is not the banal one of citizens opting to vote into power another, less egalitarian, government because they resent the high taxes the present authority enforces. In such a case, institutional egalitarianism can straightforwardly condemn this collective decision if it is indeed the case that the preferred political institutions are indeed at odds with egalitarian justice. Choices about what kinds of institutions society should put in place, even though they are choices that persons make, are not personal in the relevant sense, as indicated above. Cohen's point is a more subtle one, namely, that that which is seemingly a personal economic choice, such as choosing to work less hard under a given incentive structure, can in fact undermine background egalitarian institutions, by diminishing the economic base (from taxation, for example) that is necessary for supporting social welfare programs. Such economic choices rarely if ever qualify as genuinely personal choices in his view.

In reply, it is not clear how a reduced tax base (because of the choice to work less hard by the talented) really presents a case of economic choices that undermine egalitarian *institutional* arrangements. It seems that what this choice compromises is not the egalitarian structure of institutions but the resources that these institutions would have with which to promote egalitarian ends. This does not mean that the egalitarian character of the background institutions is now compromised; they remain structurally egalitarian. To illustrate this point, imagine, for simplicity, a society with social institutions that are regulated as a whole by the difference principle. What these institutions can affect and achieve for the worst-off will depend on how big the economic pie is, and this will depend on the productivity of all participants including the most talented. If the talented opt to produce less because they are unmoved to work harder under the present incentive structure, it means that the pool of resources available to be allocated under the difference principle is smaller than it otherwise would be. But the difference principle remains the principle in effect, and these institutions are still organized on its terms. So personal economic choices have certainly determined the total amount of goods that egalitarian institutions have to pass around, but these choices remain *personal* in that they do not need to corrode the formal character of these institutions. They remain egalitarian, i.e. guided by the difference principle. Personal choices of the kind Cohen describes can indeed affect outcomes under a given set of rules, but do not change the rules themselves. It is in this sense that genuinely personal choices can be said to have no direct institutional impact. Unless we wish to say that egalitarianism means also acquiring the largest feasible bundle of resources in order to share it around, it is not obvious why just because personal decisions can affect the size of the bundle of resources to be distributed egalitarianly implies that these personal choices can be said to be undermining egalitarian institutions.[17]

Indeed, it is hard to know to what degree economic choices by persons of the sort that Cohen describes are responsible for the reduction in welfare commitments in some countries, like Sweden. One might conjecture that the waning of the welfare state in these countries is due more to the political (and institutional) decisions of persons—their decision no longer to keep in power governments who are committed to egalitarian goals. That is, the drift to the right politically speaking in these countries is not the result of these states being forced to abandon social welfare institutions on account of their reduced tax base, but because of the *non-personal* (and hence criticizable on the institutional account) decisions of individuals in voting into power a government more hostile to egalitarianism.[18]

---

[17] In other words, the criticism bites only if we presume a consequentialist approach to egalitarianism, whereby the objective is to mitigate inequality as far as is possible, and to maximize resource production as far as is possible, to the extent that with more resources we can have more equality.

[18] As a conjecture, that the social welfare state that Sweden long supported is on the retreat is due less to Swedes making certain economic decisions (like working less hard in reaction to high taxes) and more to their overtly political choice, as when in 2006 Swedes voted out of power the Social Democratic Party and replaced it by the Alliance for Sweden, a center-right coalition. This is an institutional decision.

### 2.6.2   The tendency toward injustice

The institutional approach is also sensitive to the effects of personal pursuits permitted by the rules of just institutions. Pursuits permissible under the current rules of an institutional scheme can have cumulative effects that may undermine the justness of that scheme. For example, an income taxation program that satisfies Rawls's difference principle at a given time (that is, a taxation program that supports a distributive arrangement that is to the greatest benefit of the worst-off compared with alternative programs) can, nonetheless, conceivably generate a distributive outcome over time, such that the same taxation program, unless revised or supplemented by, say, an estate tax, may no longer be to the best benefit of the worst-off. More generally, this cumulated disparity in wealth distribution that a just taxation program can permit over time may result in a social scenario in which worst-off individuals have little reason to accept the basic structure of their society as a just one. Given this tendency toward injustice, call it the *fragility of justice*, institutional egalitarians will recognize that the rules of institutions will have to be adjusted or revised from time to time to ensure that the cumulated effects of permissible pursuits do not undermine justice. Rules of institutions on the institutional approach, are not seen as fixed once and for all, but are subject to revisions and adjustments as conditions (such as distributive patterns over time) in society change due to the effects of (legitimate) personal pursuits. What this also means is that a given institutional rule may have to be supplemented by another rule, or other rules, in order to take account of the possible long-term (unjust) effects of personal pursuits that are permitted under that rule. As Rawls observes, "the tendency is . . . for background justice to be eroded even when individuals act fairly." Even when individuals act fairly, "the invisible hand guides things in the wrong direction and favors an oligopolistic configuration of accumulations that succeeds in maintaining unjustified inequalities and restrictions on fair opportunity" (Rawls 1993: 267, 266–7). Institutional egalitarians, therefore, are aware of the need regularly to adjust the basic structure in order to take care of excessive and potentially unjustified inequalities that can arise through the just conduct of individuals (ibid.: 266; 2001: 51, 52–3; 1993: 259, 266–7).

Thus the striving for justice does not cease when the right basic structure is in place such that individuals may go on to lead their lives without paying heed again to justice. The institutional approach, to the contrary, will demand continuing individual vigilance to ensure that background justice is preserved and maintained, and given the fact of the invisible hand's tendency to upset background justice, this is no small requirement. This duty of vigilance is no minor or light responsibility, and so it is a mistake to think that the institutional approach lets individuals off the hook of justice too easily. It just imposes different kinds of demands on persons. From the institutional approach, individuals may fervently pursue their own ends within the rules of just institutions, secure in the knowledge that background justice is preserved. But this knowledge is secure only when individuals remain attentive to the character and operations of their background institutions.

### 2.6.3  The mutual dependency of principles of justice

The fragility of justice points to another feature of the institutional approach, which we may call the *mutual dependency* of the principles of justice, or the holism of justice. Given "the tendency for background justice to be eroded even when individuals act fairly" (Rawls 1993: 267), the success of any given institutional rule in meeting the requirements of justice depends on there being in place, and adequately enforced, other appropriate institutional rules to block this tendency. For instance, to prevent wealth accumulation over time and across generations that can possibly undermine egalitarian justice, an income taxation scheme may have to be supplemented by an estate tax. Or the offering of incentives for skilled labor that is permitted under one institutional rule may have to be supplemented by rules supporting equal access in education and employment to prevent a concentration of wealth among a small privileged minority.

The mutual dependency condition about the rules of institutions can be generalized to the principles of justice: a given distributive principle may seem insufficiently egalitarian when regarded on its own because of the personal choices it permits; but this need not be so if that principle is only one part of a larger framework of justice in which other principles are enforced, including, for example, the principle of equal opportunity. As an example, Rawls's difference principle need not generate inequalities as excessive as some of his critics think, if the difference principle is understood to operate in conjunction with the principles of equal opportunity and basic liberties. I will elaborate on this point in the next chapter.

This mutual dependency of justice is one important feature of the institutional approach that some of its critics, as we will see, seem to overlook. A proper evaluation of any institutional approach to justice has to consider the principles it advances as a package and not in isolation from each other (Daniels 2003: 245). A single principle of justice examined in isolation may seem inadequate from an egalitarian perspective (say, because it appears to allow for excessive inequalities), though when evaluated in conjunction with other principles that ought to be operational in a just society it need not be so. Principles of justice within a single conception, in short, are mutually reinforcing and dependent, and the strength of any institutional approach to justice can be properly appreciated only by considering the principles that it proposes as a whole.[19]

To recap these relevant features and demands of the institutional approach: First, not all individual choices count as personal in the strict sense, and the institutional approach is more restrictive of individual choice (and hence less permissive of inequalities) than some of its critics might think. Second, the fragility of justice will compel institutional egalitarians to pay ongoing attention to the effects of personal choices that may be detrimental to justice, and to be prepared to revise, adjust, and supplement existing institutional rules in light of the demands of justice. In other words, institutional egalitarians can take care of any potentially unjust effects of personal conduct within the rules of institutions. Third, the mutual dependency of justice shows that any egalitarian principle is to be regarded in conjunction with other principles of justice as part of a complete theory of justice, and the plausibility of an institutional approach has to be assessed by considering the set of principles that the approach advances. Moreover, institutional egalitarians have to conform to the other demands of justice that their distributive principle presumes to be already enforced.

---

[19] What this means is that any non-egalitarian discretionary space permitted by a distributive principle on a given institutional account must be seen in the circumscribed context of other demands under that conception of justice. For example, on Rawls's Justice as Fairness, the difference principle may allow for the awarding of additional incentives to the talented, but this permissiveness is contingent on other requirements of Justice as Fairness being honored, including the respect for persons' basic liberties and fair equality of opportunity. And the requirements that basic liberties of persons be respected and that there be fair equality of opportunity for all (that provide the operative conditions for the difference principle) are not trivial burdens but entail that persons do make certain decisions about the kind of social order, with its obligations with respect to basic liberties and equal opportunities, that they are to support.

Thus the institutional approach does not easily let persons off from the standpoint of justice, as first impression might convey. The institutional approach stringently circumscribes the realm of the personal; next, it requires individual collective ongoing vigilance to ensure background justice is preserved; and finally, even if one of the principles of a given institutional conception considered in isolation appears overly lax, its principles work in tandem and can together impose significant demands on individuals.

## 2.7 Limits of the institutional approach

The institutional approach, as explained, is motivated by the presumption of value pluralism. But this does not mean that the institutional approach offers a reconciliation of all possible value conflicts. Its concern is that of the conflict between justice and personal life. Within the sphere of the personal, there can be other value conflicts, and about these conflicts the institutional approach offers no direct solution. Thus, the dilemma confronting Bernard Williams's Gauguin between his commitment to his art and his familial duties is not a matter for which the institutional approach offers a solution (B. Williams 1981: Ch. 2). Gauguin's problem is that of competing personal demands (the pursuit of his art on the one side, the call of his familial life on the other) and not those of social justice versus personal demands. To be sure, many kinds of conflicts of obligation in personal life can be traced to institutional failures that in turn generate this conflict for a person within the social arrangement. Conflicts that individuals may experience between the demands of career and family life may be traced to modes of organizing the workplace that presume a certain gendered division of labor. These kinds of conflicts between competing personal demands, because they have an institutional cause, can be mitigated by institutional reforms, in this case, by making the professions more family-friendly. Thus the institutional approach, to the extent that it seeks to eliminate institutional injustices, can have the effect of minimizing some of the more common forms of conflicting personal demands that individuals face in social life. Following Nussbaum, we might refer to this as the "Hegelian" solution to moral conflict, that is, the idea that many of the conflicts of obligations that persons regularly face in the course of life can be resolved by political institutional reforms (Nussbaum 2001: xxxi; 2000b).[20]

Still, one could accept, as does Nussbaum herself, that there will remain ineliminable duty conflicts in the personal domain for which there can be no systematic institutional solution. Gauguin's problem is an example of a duty conflict that is not amenable to a feasible institutional solution.[21] But this is a comment on intractable conflicts within the domain of the personal, and is compatible with the claim that the conflict between justice and personal pursuits can be systematically addressed via the institutional approach. The institutional approach need not, thus, take a stance on the question of commensurability in morality more generally.[22] Its claim of reconciliation is limited to that of justice and personal life, leaving open the possibility that there are demands within personal life that can present ineliminable moral conflicts.

There is a more important limitation. The reconciliation of the personal with justice, via the primacy of the latter, which the institutional approach aims to provide, is realizable only when institutions, within which rules personal conduct are to be confined, are in fact regulated by principles of justice. For instance, only when the social and economic institutions defining the bounds of proper ownership and economic activities are themselves regulated by acceptable principles of distributive justice can we safely conclude that persons are pursuing their ends and special commitments with resources that are rightly theirs and not with more or less than their just share. Thus individuals concerned with justice may be fervently engaged in economic activities with their own interests in mind within the rules of institutions only when they know that the institutions satisfy the requirements of justice. The reconciliation of justice and personal pursuits aspired

[20] Nussbaum drawing on this Hegelian idea writes: "many [moral] conflicts that at first seem intractable can themselves be surmounted with intelligent [public] planning" (Nussbaum 2001). She draws on Hegel's *The Philosophy of Fine Art* (1835), trans. Osmaston 1920. Rawls also writes: "social wisdom consists in framing institutions so that intractable difficulties do not often arise" (Rawls 1971: 90, 110). One might say that a moral dilemma arising because of failures of institutional justice belongs to the class of moral conflicts that Aquinas calls "perplexity secundum quid," that is, moral conflicts that obtain because of a prior violation of duty (Donagan 1987: 285). And institutionally derived moral dilemmas are in principle resolvable by institutional means.

[21] Assuming that Gauguin's dilemma is that *he* cannot *himself* look out for his family if he pursues his artistic ambition, his personal dilemma persists even if the state were, however unlikely that may be, to take on the responsibility of providing for the families of aspiring artists.

[22] See here B. Williams 1981: 82. For more discussion on moral conflict at the level of interpersonal morality, see Kelly 2000.

to by the institutional approach is attained only when institutions meet the requirements of justice, that they are satisfactorily regulated by the accepted principles of justice for society, The division of labor between principles for institutions and principles for personal conduct presumes that principles of justice for institutions are in fact realized by existing institutions. In short, the reconciliation of justice and the personal is achievable only under *ideal conditions*, that is, under conditions in which institutions are in compliance with the principles of justice.

That the institutional approach makes space for personal conduct under the presumption of ideal conditions is an important one, for in non-ideal situations, that is, situations in which the basic institutions of society fall far short of the requirements of justice, it is less certain that space for personal pursuits may still be rightly preserved within the rules of these (unjust) institutions. The institutional approach provides a reconciliation of justice with the personal when it is acknowledged that the rules of institutions do in fact justly determine persons' fundamental entitlements and resources with which to pursue their ends. But when institutions are unjust, one can no longer with confidence say that persons are pursuing their ends with their just entitlements and therefore should be left free to seek these ends within the confines of institutional rules. Rather, in severely unjust situations, some are likely to be pursuing their goals with more than their rightful share of resources while others are doing with much less. In this context, it is a violation of the primacy of justice to say that persons may be left uncontested to pursue their goals within the rules of institutions. One can imagine that, in cases of the grossest injustice, all personal pursuits ought to be halted for the foremost purpose of achieving just institutions. The space for personal pursuits may shrink or collapse significantly in the face of injustice. I will say more about personal expectation in the face of severe institutional failures in the following chapter. For now the main point is that on the institution approach, personal pursuits are admissible only within the rules of justly regulated institutions. It addresses an ideal situation. That there is something amiss from the perspective of justice in the case of individuals fervently pursuing personal ends in the context of *unjust* institutions is a conclusion the institutionalist shares. This is an important point, for it means that, in order to be on target, a criticism of the institutional approach has to fault it for allowing space for personal pursuits in the *context of just institutional rules*. As we shall see in the next chapter, this idealizing presumption blunts the force of some of the criticisms against the institutional approach.

# 3

# Evading the Demands of Justice?

The previous chapter tried to account for the basis of and motivation for the institutional approach or institutional egalitarianism. The central argument is that, given the presumption of value pluralism, that is, the presumption that persons committed to egalitarian justice are also individuals with independently valuable personal commitments and ends, indeed commitments and ends that add value and meaning to individuals' lives, the institutional approach allows for a way of reconciling the impersonal demands of egalitarian justice and the pursuit of personal ends and commitments. But it does this while preserving the primacy of egalitarian justice, in that the demands of justice define the bounds of admissible personal pursuits. By confining the site of egalitarian justice to the basic institutions of society, institutional egalitarianism allows for personal pursuits within the rules of justly regulated institutions while regulating and constraining these pursuits. In limiting the site of egalitarian justice to institutions, we can have it both ways, so to speak: honor the demands of justice but at the same time preserve space for our morally valuable personal commitments and ends. Institutional egalitarianism thus provides a moral division of labor that reflects the pluralistic character of morality itself.

Roughly, the institutional approach makes three essential points: (i) there is an identifiable background system of public rules within which persons interact and that determines the fair terms of this interaction (the idea of the basic structure); (ii) that this basic structure is to be regulated by  principles specific to it and not derived from some overarching general moral principle, and that the objective of a conception of distributive justice is to identify principles for the basic structure as distinct from principles regulating personal conduct within the rules of the basic structure (value pluralism); and (iii) that the principles regulating the basic structure enjoy a certain "regulative primacy" over other principles of personal conduct and choices (the primacy of justice). Distributive justice on this account has a limited but not insignificant purview.

But the institutional approach has been criticized in recent discussions for permitting an evasion of the burdens of egalitarian justice. According to critics, by focusing primarily on institutional design and not on personal conduct as such, it releases individuals too easily from the requirements of justice. And in so shielding personal conduct from the strictures of egalitarian principles, institutional egalitarianism permits inequalities that would not have arisen but for selfish personal choices and conduct. The thrust for this objection may be put as follows: if individuals claim to support egalitarian principles for their shared institutions, shouldn't they also accept that these principles, or at least their underlying justifications, ought to inform and constrain their personal conduct and choices within the rules of institutions? This line of criticism has been most powerfully and influentially advanced by G. A. Cohen. My aim in this chapter is to assess this criticism.[1]

## 3.1 Cohen's basic challenge

In several important writings, G. A. Cohen takes issue with the limited focus of institutional justice (G. A. Cohen 1992, 1997, 2000, 2008; also Murphy 1999). He argues that justice should be concerned not only with the background institutions of society but also with the choices and decisions of persons within the rules of institutions. After all, wouldn't real egalitarians want not only just institutional rules but also to be prepared to subject their personal choices and decisions against some egalitarian considerations? A truly egalitarian and just society for Cohen thus will not only have just institutions but will also exhibit what he calls an "ethos" of justice (and that will be reflected by the decisions of persons

---

[1] Cohen's most sustained and developed version of his institutional critique takes the form of an internal criticism, a criticism within the Rawlsian framework, to wit that the institutional approach (along with the incentive provision it permits via the difference principle) is inconsistent with other (more fundamental) aspects of Rawls's professed commitments (G. A. Cohen 2008: "Introduction"). But his general and external criticism of the institutional approach is powerful and significant in its own right, and my concern is with the general criticism rather than with the criticism internal to the Rawlsian project.

in "the thick of daily life" within the rules of just institutions). The institutional approach according to Cohen seems to be "an evasion" of the burdens of justice (Cohen 2000: 4).

Taking Rawls as his representative and target institutional egalitarian, Cohen draws attention to Rawls's difference principle to substantiate his claim that institutional egalitarianism evades the burdens of justice. The difference principle, to recall, permits inequalities so long as these inequalities are also to the advantage of the worst-off in society. There is thus an incentive provision built into the difference principle: the talented may be specially rewarded if this is what it takes to move them to benefit society. But is this not a case of catering to the acquisitiveness of the talented, wonders Cohen? In a society informed by an egalitarian ethos, the talented would not require the "extra-incentives" in order to be inclined to provide the service, and so the worst-off would stand to benefit even more (since additional resources could be passed onto them instead of being given to the talented as incentives). To be sure, Cohen accepts that the talented may need some incentives without which they could not "literally" do the job that is asked of them. This would include compensation for additional training and education that they may have to undergo, compensation if the work they are asked to do is indeed especially arduous, and so on; and these are incentives that Rawls also recognizes (Cohen 2000: 127; 1992, 2008). Indeed Cohen would say that incentives for especially hard work should be seen as a restoration of equality in distribution rather than a justification for a move away from inequality (id. 2008: 103; also A. Macleod 1985: 187–8). After all, in the larger scheme of things, the person doing the harder but socially more beneficial job, if not additionally compensated, will be treated less equally than others with easier jobs. Her life overall would be poorer than the average person's.[2]

Be that as it may, Cohen's main objection is that the difference principle allows also for what we may call *extra-incentives*, that is incentives that are asked for and paid out to the talented not because they literally

***

[2] We are not forced to accept a welfarist egalitarian position in order to accept Cohen's point. It can be extended to a resource egalitarian theory, such as Rawls's, if we include, as does Rawls, leisure as among the economic primary goods to equalize. In this case, extra compensation by way of extra income for one who has given up her leisure to do extra work is more accurately an *adjustment towards equality* than a *justified departure from equality*.

need the extra-rewards in order to be able to perform the needed task but simply because of their "acquisitiveness." And this is a failure of justice, a failing due to the institutional approach's indifference to personal choice  and decisions within the rules of institutions. For our current purpose, I do not need to ask if Cohen is hostile to the difference principle in itself. What we are interested in is his objection to the general approach to justice that the difference principle expresses, namely the institutional approach. Again, this approach holds that the site of justice is confined to institutions for the sake of allowing space for non-egalitarian personal decisions and conduct within the rules of institutions. The difference principle is one instantiation of this view of justice, for its incentive provision holds that as long as the basic institutions of society are arranged so as to be to the best advantage of the worst-off persons in society, then persons may do and decide as they wish within the rules of such institutions. This includes granting the talented, whose support is needed to benefit the worst-off, the option of demanding extra-incentives in order to be compelled to act accordingly. Cohen targets the difference principle because it vividly exposes what he takes to be a basic failure of the institutional approach—the failure of permitting individual discretion within the rules of justice institutions—thus, likewise our discussion will focus on the difference principle.

To get clear on Cohen's criticism, it is important to avoid the misunderstanding that Cohen is proposing *to replace* the institutional approach to justice with an interactional one, where by interactional we mean interpersonal interaction apart from institutions. Cohen does not deny that institutional design is important with respect to justice; his claim is that just institutions have to *be supplemented* (not replaced) by just interpersonal conduct as well within the rules of just institutions. It is not that, for Cohen, justice should not be concerned with institutions. His concern is that justice cannot just be concerned with institutions.[3] For this reason, I will occasionally describe Cohen's account of equality as transinstitutional (that is, as in addition to institutions) rather than misleadingly as interactional or non-institutional.

_Important Clarification about Cohen_

---

[3] This point is worth noting if only because some commentators take Cohen to be dismissing institutions as a site of justice altogether (G. A. Cohen 2008: 374–5).

## 3.2  Responding to Cohen's challenge

Cohen's challenge that the institutional approach represents an evasion of
the demands of justice has elicited a range of responses, and it will be
helpful here to canvas some of these responses.[4]

The first line of defense is to cushion Cohen's challenge by trying to
minimize the perceived flaw of the institutional approach, as illustrated via
the operations of the difference principle. That is, one might try to show
that the degree of inequality that the difference principle can admit via its
incentive provision is not really as large as Cohen's line of criticism may
imply to some readers. To be sure, minimizing a problem of course is not
the same as addressing the problem, but it at least helps if we can first locate
and confine the problem. As a first response, then, one might point out
that it is plausible, under Rawls's overall scheme, that the extra-incentives
that the talented can demand and actually receive are reduced drastically in
an ideal society in which the difference principle operates in tandem with a
principle of equal basic liberties and a principle of fair equality of opportunity. After discounting for discriminations of various sorts that involve
violations of persons' basic liberties, and inequality in opportunities, one
can plausibly believe that the special skills required of certain professions
need not be so scarce as to command the kind of market price that they
tend to do in our society with all its various forms of historic and
background injustices. So, if the difference principle, with its incentive
provision, is understood to be part of a package of principles of justice and
not as an isolated principle, the worry that it can allow acquisitive talented
individuals to receive extra-incentives over and above that which they
need to do the socially beneficial job is perhaps blunted (Rawls 1971: 79,
158; 2001: 61; also Daniels 2003; Tan 2004a).

Another mitigating factor is available to Rawls: it is basic to the institutional view that just institutions can have educative effects on persons, and
one can surmise that a society whose institutions live up to Rawlsian
principles will be a society characterized by strong mutuality and reciprocity
among its members. This, plausibly, would temper the acquisitiveness of
the talented: their inculcated sense of solidarity for their fellow citizens can

---

[4] Cohen's criticism of the institutional approach has generated a substantial debate in
contemporary political philosophy. See, for example, papers by A. Williams (1998); Scheffler
(2006); Estlund (1998); Daniels (2003); J. Cohen (2002); Pogge (2000); Freeman (2006a,
2007). The discussion here also draws on Tan (2004a, 2008).

overcome whatever selfish acquisitiveness they would otherwise be prone to have. Thus, the educative effects on individual character and attitudes of institutions ought not to be overlooked. The basic structure for Rawls shapes and fashions persons' wants and desires (Rawls 1971: 32, 259), and just institutions will have the effect of tempering the selfish acquisitiveness of the talented that moves Cohen. Consider Cohen's own illustration (G. A. Cohen 2000: 144–5), the fact that executives (just assuming for the sake of discussion that their service does somehow benefit the worst-off in society) in contemporary American society make outlandish demands for compensation. This situation that rightly troubles Cohen may be due to certain deformations of their character as a result of living in a society with serious unjust background institutions. Excessive expectations may be fueled by failures of justice somewhere in the system (Rawls 1971: 79). If there is this institutional causal explanation for personal selfishness, then in correcting for institutional failings institutional egalitarianism effectively tackles these problems of personal attitudes rather than being irresponsive to them (J. Cohen 2002: 381).

Thus, the presumption that a just Rawlsian society will ensure equal protection of persons' liberties and fair equality of opportunity, coupled with the presumption of the educative effects of just institutions on persons living under them, go some way towards tempering the inequalities that the incentive provision in the difference principle can allow. If this is right, then Rawlsian institutional justice need not result in incentives-based inequalities to the degree characteristic of contemporary American life that rightly exercises Cohen and other egalitarians. The inequalities between the talented and the worst-off that an ideal Rawlsian society permits need not be as great as Cohen's criticisms seem to be propelled by, Rawls's institutional focus notwithstanding.

So if the degree of inequality that the difference principle can allow under conditions of a well-ordered society is quite tightly confined, the force of Cohen's objection may be blunted a little. To be sure, Cohen himself notes that he is not objecting to excessive inequalities as such, but to the fact of any inequalities (however large or small) that need not be but for the acquisitiveness of the talented (that is, inequalities that would not exist if the talented did not demand extra-incentives). But to the extent that some critics might be moved to reject the institutional approach because of the perceived degree of inequalities permitted under the difference principle, it is worth clarifying that the difference principle allows for inequalities only under closely regulated circumstances, that is, under a social institutional order regulated not just by the difference principle but also by its companion principles of justice, and where personal selfishness is tempered as a consequence of living under such institutions. The inequalities admitted by the difference principle need not be so excessive as to be troublesome for some erstwhile critics of the difference principle.

Still, even though glaring inequalities motivate Cohen's critical project, the basic challenge it raises once his criticism gets moving is not deflected by pointing out that permitted inequalities under the institutional approach need not be as excessive as he had thought.[5] The response to Cohen canvassed so far at best assuages his challenge but does not ultimately address it. The problem remains that the Rawlsian institutional approach allows for certain inequalities that need not exist in a society that is also informed by an egalitarian "ethos." Even if these inequalities are not as excessive as one might think, they are nonetheless inequalities that need not exist but for the acquisitiveness of the talented.[6] For Cohen, individuals with an egalitarian ethos will not take advantage of the incentive provision of the difference principle to demand incentives beyond that without which they could not *literally* do the socially beneficial job. After all, if they are true egalitarians, the skilled or talented will see that their worst-off compatriots stand to benefit even more should they, the talented, not make demand for any rewards beyond those that they literally need in order to provide the required services. Thus the institutional approach, in excusing personal conduct from the strictures of egalitarianism, permits residual inequalities that would not exist in a society were personal choices also regulated by egalitarian considerations. Does this not show, then, that personal choices and attitude do matter from the point of view of egalitarian justice, and does this not expose a limitation to the view that social

[5] Thus while Cohen acknowledges that his belief that Rawls's approach allows for excessive inequalities "animates" his criticism, he stresses that Rawls's *justification of inequalities*, however large or not these might be, is his central concern (G. A. Cohen 2008: 382).

[6] Cohen, moreover, denies that substantial inequalities will be eliminated even when the difference principle is understood to apply in conjunction with the other principles of Rawlsian justice (G. A. Cohen 2008: 383–5). But I will leave this matter to one side for, either way, Cohen's central objection remains and must be confronted: there are inequalities present that need not be but for the incentives that the difference principle grants the talented. It is this conceptual and more challenging worry that I want to focus on.

justice is only concerned with the justice of institutions but not with personal conduct within the rules of institutions?

To get some grip on this objection, let us imagine a highly skilled surgeon (we will assume she contributes to societal good, given her special talents) who now wishes to abandon her career in medicine to pursue the arts. She has come to see the life of an artist, even a struggling and comparatively unsuccessful one, to be more valuable to her, given the overall conception of the good life she now has, and she holds this view even though she knows that her contribution to society as an artist will be quite limited. Thus to remain a surgeon she will incur a great personal opportunity cost, indeed a moral opportunity cost, namely that of not pursuing a life plan that she now finds more worthwhile and meaningful. Suppose, however, that society can offer her additional monetary compensation that, in her eyes, can offset this opportunity cost to her of continuing in medicine. Should the artist–surgeon, if she is a true egalitarian, not require such enticement but be prepared to compromise her pursuits simply out of concern for the worst-off? Should she, were she a true egalitarian, not be willing to forego her idea of the good without compensation for the sake of the worst-off in her society?

This example, I think, rather than calling the institutional approach into question, illustrates the importance of giving persons space within the rules of justice to pursue a meaningful personal life. It illustrates the significance of the incentive provision allowed under the difference principle: that it is out of recognition of the importance of the freedom of occupational choices and the diverse valuable ends and conceptions of the good life that persons have that Rawls provides room for incentives in his principle. A just society will need persons of special skills to perform socially beneficial tasks; but a just society also has to recognize that persons are free to pursue a diversity of ends, including occupational choices, that need not have any egalitarian consequence. Offering incentives for talented persons to take on certain socially useful professions is a legitimate way of re-weighting the opportunity sets available to such persons (Rawls 1971: 306, 271–2, 311; 2001: 78; also A. Williams 1998; Estlund 1998; and Tan 2004a). It provides a means to entice persons, like our artist–surgeon, freely to take on or stay in a socially beneficial profession in spite of other independently morally valuable and acceptable alternatives they might have.

Thus, it is the belief that persons ought to be free to pursue a variety of personal commitments and that there is a plurality of valuable ends, including considerations like career and occupational choices as well as other social commitments like familial ones, that motivates the institutional approach. The aim of justice, as said, is to secure the appropriate social conditions against which persons may pursue their various ends and conceptions of the good freely and fairly. As Freeman writes, "The primary reason Rawls builds incentives into the difference principle is not to encourage capitalist self-seeking but to accommodate the plurality of goods and citizens' freedom to determine and pursue their conception of the good" (Freeman 2006a: 12, 136–7; 2007: 124–5; Scheffler 2006). If we accept with Rawls (and many modern moral and political philosophers do) the idea of the reasonable plurality of ends—that is, that there are various morally worthy ends and goods that persons may pursue that need not be subsumed under one unified account of what the good is—it is not so clear that allowing individuals appropriate space within the rules of just institutions to pursue their ends and structuring a scheme of incentives to entice persons to take on socially needed roles represents an evasion of the burdens of justice. On the contrary, this meets the point of justice, namely, to ensure that persons are able freely and equally to pursue their different valuable ends. Even though Cohen does not deny pluralism, his view of egalitarian justice seems to "underestimate the significance of 'the fact of reasonable pluralism'," and consequently he grants "undue priority to the position of the least advantaged over all other claims" (Freeman 2007: 124).

The incentive provision of the difference principle is thus not a capitulation of the demands of justice but a *specification* of its demands. It is not designed for the purpose of allowing society a means of submitting to the exhortations of *selfish acquisitive*. Rather, it is compelled by the acknowledgment that persons can have genuinely *legitimate* reasons for pursuing ends that need not have egalitarian consequences. The focus on institutions provides a way of drawing a sensible boundary between the demands of justice and the concerns of personal life, and the end of the incentive provision in the difference principle on the institutional approach is to allow for a way of aligning personal pursuits with the needs of society. It marks the space for individuals to pursue their ends, including the exercise of their freedom of occupational choices, *while* aiming to satisfy the needs of society by presenting a means of restructuring persons' overall preferences that could motivate them to take on freely certain socially beneficial occupational tasks. As Rawls puts it, "The priority of liberty means that we

[Handwritten margin notes left side:]

✱✱✱✱✱
Important to note this idea is willing to accept inequalities if they are absolutely necessary

✱✱✱✱✱
Use this definition against them to illustrate Cohen's view is not only compatible w/ these ideals, but also a better formulation of a theory that expresses these ideals

[Handwritten note at bottom:]
Already concede that restructuring a person's preferences (ie influencing personal choices) is permissible

cannot be forced to engage in work that is highly productive in terms of material goods. What kind of work people do, and how hard they do it, is up to them to decide in light of the various incentives society offers" (Rawls 2001: 64).

It is true that the fact that the difference principle is designed for the purpose of reconciling personal pursuits with the demands of social justice does not mean that it could not be appropriated and misused by acquisitive individuals. Consider another surgeon who, unlike the surgeon–poet in the above, demands extra-incentives simply for what we standardly call "selfish" reasons, as opposed to merely self-regarding reasons. That is, to make the case as blunt and straightforward as possible, let us just say that the selfish surgeon simply yearns for the material rewards for their own sake. In contrast to the artist–surgeon, the selfish surgeon is not facing a conflict among opposing options concerning the life she wants to lead that the extra-incentive is meant to help resolve in a particular direction, since she would prefer the life of a doctor. It is her selfish material acquisitive-ness, plain and simple, that compels her to demand extra-rewards and she does so knowing that she has the threat advantage. She can withhold services (although it is not the case that she would rather be doing something else) and she will do so if she does not get her way (she is prepared to hold out and compromise her own doctoring preference in the hopes of getting it all her way eventually). So even though the difference principle is designed with people like the artist–surgeon in mind, its formal structure unfortunately also provides convenient cover for people like the selfish surgeon. But the point remains that it is not for the sake of such selfish exploiters that the difference principle allows for incentives. The incentive provision in the difference principle can be exploited (in the bad sense) by the selfish, but this does not mean that the difference principle was designed with them in mind. As Freeman says, the difference principle and its incentive provision "is not designed to encourage such choices even if it tolerates them" (Freeman 2006a: 140–1). Just as the fact that free speech principles can be taken advantage of by hate-mongers to insult a minority does not mean that free speech is designed for the purpose of promoting hate, so the fact that the incentive provision under the difference principle can be taken advantage of by selfish acquisitive individuals does not mean that the principle is designed for this purpose. And as the ideal of free speech is not a compromise of justice just because bigots can misappropriate the principle, so the

Solid
Assment

difference principle is not a compromise of justice just because selfish individuals can take advantage of it.

So if the above interpretation of the difference principle is acceptable, that it is designed to encourage people toward socially useful occupations in light of their legitimate diversity of ends, rather than to allow selfish acquisitors to take advantage of the need society has for their skills and talents, then the criticism of the incentive provision has to be made more precise. It is not that the difference principle allows the artist–surgeon to receive extra compensation to stay as a doctor that makes it objectionable; Why not try to eliminate the loophole? the problem is that the difference principle also inevitably lets in those it is not designed for, that is, it admits a loophole. The exception provides an easy shield for objectionable demands, like those of the selfish surgeon. So the recast objection is that the difference principle is too permissive a principle in that it offers protection to individuals that it is not meant to protect.

What can we make of this reformulated worry? A response to this challenge, I believe, will parallel how society normally deals with problems of individuals exploiting a principle or a policy for personal gains. By exploiting a principle, I mean untechnically the taking advantage of an accepted principle to justify one's conduct that is contrary to the spirit of that principle. That is, the letter of the principle permits actions at odds with the spirit of the principle. Typically, unless the exploitation of the principle is so pervasive as to undermine its purpose, society can assume the cost of such exploitations. The ideal of free speech, for example, can be co-opted by persons to promulgate racist or sexist prejudices, contrary to the ends of the ideal of free speech, which is to facilitate the free and equal exchange of ideas, social criticisms, and arguments. Hate speech lacks ideas or arguments and has no political value. The principle of free speech is not designed to provide room for hate speech, yet it can be misused for this end. However, we do not necessarily as a result reject the principle of free speech for being too permissive. As a possible response, society might be prepared to accept the exploitation of a free speech principle by hate-mongers as part of the cost of having such a principle, on the grounds that it is better to have a principle that errs on the side of permissiveness than one that is too restrictive. The independent justification for free speech is not defeated just because the practice that it justifies can be abused.

So too with the incentive provision in difference principle: that it is subject to exploitation by the selfish is a price society can possibly bear if there are compelling independent reasons for the difference principle and its incentive provision, and especially so if its exploitation can in fact be minimized and contained.[7] On the last point, recall the earlier argument that in an ideally just society selfish acquisitiveness is minimized. With regard to the compellingness of the difference principle, it is not clear if there is an alternative to the difference principle, given the necessity of both protecting individual freedom and promoting social ends. The difference principle may be permissive in that it can also rationalize selfish acquisition. But, on the other hand, to replace the difference principle with another distributive principle that gives no room for the kinds of genuine personal pursuits as illustrated in the artist–surgeon example is to implement an overly restrictive principle: it will remove protection for the selfish surgeon but it also penalizes the artist–surgeon.

One might ask here: why not forward an incentive principle (rather than the non-discriminating difference principle) that is able to distinguish cases like that of the artist–surgeon from those of the selfish surgeon? But such a discerning principle would have to be capable of examining and regulating persons' intentions. This principle would not simply accede to the artist–surgeon's or the selfish surgeon's demands, but it would have to be able to discern why each is requesting the extra-rewards to stay on the job. We can easily see why this principle can't possibly be successfully implemented (an applicant could simply lie), and even if it could be implemented it would be unaccepted in a liberal society where persons are not required to explain themselves so long as their conduct falls within the bounds of justice. More significantly, even if members of a liberal society would hold the selfish surgeon in lower moral esteem, it is hard to  see how there can be a principled way of judging her conception of the good to be less just from the social point of view than that of the artist–surgeon. Both, after all, are demanding, by hypothesis, the same level of material rewards; the only difference is that one does so because she sees no reason to forego the artistic life otherwise, and the other because she is

---

[7] The analogy with free speech is not meant to indicate an independent argument for the difference principle and its incentive provision, but just to show that because acquisitive individuals can free-ride or exploit the difference principle, that alone does not defeat the independent arguments in its favor. As an aside, it is worth noting that Shiffrin uses the principle of free speech as an analogy to support Cohen's position (with modifications), arguing that a principle applying to social institutions may have implications for individual conduct even if it does not directly apply to individuals (Shiffrin 2010: 117).

acquisitive. So neither is asking for more resources or primary goods than the other; the worst-off will do neither better nor worse in either case. The only basis of criticism would have to appeal to some independent moral criterion: that the artist–surgeon is getting the extra-reward because of a more laudable reason (to compensate for her forfeiting the life of art), whereas the selfish surgeon is getting the extra-reward without having to forfeit a morally comparable pursuit.

But one can see how this would be rather controversial. After all, the acquisitive may couch her demands in terms of her rational conception of the good. From the standpoint of justice it is hard to say that that conception is less just than the other, although for the ethical perspective one can surely comment on each of these life plans. Social justice does not give us the means to discriminate between a person who makes certain demands because she has artistic interests and another who makes demands because she has crass interests. Recall Rawls's remarks with respect to conceptions of the good that "within the limits allowed by the principles of right, there need be no standard of correctness beyond that of delibera-tive rationality" (Rawls 1971: 564). Thus a more nuanced incentive provision that is able to take account of persons' intentions is not an option. As Freeman writes, there "is no way to prevent this [selfish choices] compatible with maintaining individuals' freedom" (Freeman 2006a: 140–1).

In a sense the worry can be stated as a free-rider problem in the following way: even though the difference principle is not conceived to accommodate the demands of the selfish, the selfish nonetheless *get a free ride*, so to speak, on this principle and use it to make selfish claims on society. And so we can respond to this free-rider problem the way we would normally respond to other free-rider problems: as problems that society can handle and tolerate for the sake of preserving other ends (that of protecting non-selfish personal choices). The difference principle is hardly the only principle under any conception of justice that is susceptible to exploitative individuals free-riding on it.

Let me tie the above remarks back to Cohen's challenge. In the earliest presentations of his criticism, the gist of Cohen's arguments appears to fault as unjust not only the selfish surgeon or also the artist–surgeon. That is, the thrust of the early critique that a professed egalitarian ought to regulate her day-to-day decisions against egalitarian commitments appears to convict the artist–surgeon. If this is right, then this reveals an implausibility of the

critique in that it fails to acknowledge the relevance of value pluralism.
Cohen's conception of justice would be too restrictive and must
be acknowledged by him to be so in light of his own concessions to
prerogatives as mentioned above. But in his final formulation of the
criticism (urged on by responses such as David Estlund's), Cohen makes
it clearer that his objection is directly solely at the selfish surgeon and not
the artist–surgeon within some limits: limits based on personal prerogatives
(G. A. Cohen 2008: 205 ff.). So his target is now in fact a much finer one.
But as a consequence it is also now harder to locate his precise claim. It is
hard to see by means of what incentive provision Cohen can criticize the
selfish surgeon without also implicating the artist–surgeon. In short, the
option for Cohen cannot be to reject extra-incentive provision wholesale,
for this would provide no maneuvering space for the artist–surgeon, which
Cohen himself (as the more worked out versions of his criticism suggest)
wants to accommodate. So unless he thinks that there is a more nuanced
principle that can distinguish the artist–surgeon from the selfish surgeon
based on their intentions, he has to accept the permissiveness of the
difference principle as a better alternative than one that would restrict
cases like the artist–surgeon. Any concession to the artist–surgeon doctor
also, regrettably, admits the selfish surgeon.[8]

Cohen might say something like this as a final retort: "Well, in the
Rawlsian scheme, we can't call the selfish surgeon unjust; but in my
scheme, we can." But what is the basis of calling the selfish surgeon unjust?
And what is gained substantively? First, notice that, even on this point,
Rawls has the resources to proclaim the selfish surgeon unjust. As he
writes, "Many different kinds of things are said to be just and unjust: not
only laws, institutions, and social systems, but also particular actions of
many kinds including decisions, judgments, and imputations. We also call
the attitudes and dispositions of persons, and persons themselves, just or
unjust" (Rawls 1971: 7). The point is that principles concerning the
dispositions of persons, their actions, and so on, on the one side, are
distinct from principles regulating the institutions of society on the other
(as well as most likely distinct among themselves). The difference between
Cohen and Rawls diminishes even on this matter of moral condemnation.
To be sure, however, the selfish doctor need not be unjust from *the*

---

[8] Cohen also has an internal critique of the difference principle, namely that it is inconsistent with Rawls's underlying luck egalitarian commitments (Cohen 2008:106 ff.).

*perspective of social justice.* Another way to express this point is that political philosophy says nothing about the doctor's conduct, even though from some other moral perspective, by some criteria of personal as opposed to social justice, the doctor could be decried as unjust. But all this is semantic quibble: the key point is not how we describe our moral disapproval of the selfish doctor but whether it is appropriate to evaluate her conduct by reference to principles the institutional egalitarians take to be specific to institutions.

Even if the critical difference between Rawls and Cohen is diminished, it need not be eliminated altogether, one might think. Presumably it still matters whether we can say that the selfish doctor's decision is socially unjust or not socially unjust (even if wrong on some other moral criteria). We expect demands of social justice to have a certain weight and, as mentioned, allow that they have a certain normative primacy. Moreover, it is taken that demands of social justice are demands that are subject to social enforcement of some kind in principle. Yet, since Cohen himself is in fact reluctant to conclude that the egalitarian ethos is one that the state can try to enforce even in principle, and that in fact there can be moral reasons for overriding the demands of egalitarian justice (thereby opposing the primacy claim), it is unclear if the substantive disagreement between Cohen and Rawls is not eliminated altogether.[9]

Seana Shiffrin has argued that personal endorsement of egalitarian principles for institutions will require personally endorsing "the justificatory underpinning" of these egalitarian principles and the underpinning justifications can have bearing on individual conduct. For instance, if the principle of moral arbitrariness, that is, "the claim that talents are arbitrary from a moral point of view" (Shiffrin 2010:121), is the underpinning justification of the difference principle, then, Shiffrin argues, endorsing the egalitarian principle implies acceptance of the moral arbitrariness principle. Accordingly, individuals who assent to egalitarian principles for institutions will moderate their personal choices against this underpinning principle.

If Shiffrin is arguing that the underlying principle must be understood as a principle applicable to the whole of personal life, then she asserts what the institutional approach exactly denies (and as argued for in the previous

[9] See Cohen's considerations against forced labor in G. A. Cohen 2008: 220–1.

chapter), which is that the underlying principle for the egalitarian principles itself cannot be understood to apply beyond institutions. Persons make appeal to the underpinning principle of, say, moral arbitrariness only when they are addressing the question of the justness of their social institutions, but not when they are making decisions about how to act within the rules of these institutions. To take the underlying principle as a general moral principle that governs the whole of life, from which issue distinctive and more specific principles for institutions, personal conduct, and other areas of social life, presumes a value monism that I have said is at odds with the basic assumption of the institutional approach. Again, my claim here is not that value monism has to be rejected, but that a decisive rebuttal of the institutional approach will first have to make the case for value monism. In as far as the institutional approach is meant to present an understanding of the bounds of justice on the presumption of value pluralism, it is not enough to show that value monism will show the inadequacy of the institutional focus.[10]

It is useful in this regard to consider an argument that Shiffrin makes about the moral arbitrariness of race and how that is analogous to the moral arbitrariness of talents (Shiffrin 2010: 126–8). Shiffrin argues that if one holds that social institutions ought not to permit discrimination against persons based on race, and if one main justification for this is that race is morally arbitrary (and hence ought not to determine persons' prospects in life), then it is hard to see how one can consistently allow racial prejudice to influence her conduct within the rules of race-neutral institutions. Thus, just as there is a certain inconsistency in affirming that institutions have to be race-neutral without also wanting to limit personal conduct by the justificatory underpinning of the institutional requirement, so too it is inconsistent to say that institutions ought to be neutral about talents without also accepting that within the rules of institutions talents cannot have unlimited bargaining advantage.

But this analogy with race inequality fails because, unlike in our evaluation of racial injustices, there is no necessary comprehensive moral commitment underlying our evaluations of talents and inequalities. Our defense of race-neutral institutions is typically informed by a more basic moral view about the objectionability of racism across the board. How we

---

[10] I believe the criticism of the institutional approach in Murphy (1999) takes the same form, and can be responded to in a similar way.

want our institutions to respond to the matter of race reflects a deeper
moral commitment with regard to race inequality in a range of different
spheres of life. Thus, there is certainly an oddity when someone professes
to support race-neutral institutions but is willing to take racial advantages
in personal life. But just because some institutional principles have comprehensive moral justificatory underpinnings (like the objection to racism)
does not mean that all institutional principles are that way. If it is the case
that inequalities due to talents are to be seen as morally objectionable
across the board in most areas of human activity, like the way most of us
regard racism, then yes, the justificatory underpinning of talents-neutral
institutions should also inform personal conduct. But that inequalities due
to talents should have that kind of across-the-board moral objectionability
is of course the issue at debate here. Thus the analogy with racism does not
help, because in the case of racism it is largely accepted that, unlike the case
of talents and inequality, racism is morally objectionable in most spheres
of human activity. To put the point schematically, racism is morally
objectionable, and hence we create institutions that reflect this moral
stance; inequalities due to talents need not be morally objectionable, and
we create institutions in order to determine conditions under which they
are acceptable and under which they are objectionable.

## 3.3 Freedom of occupation

The above discussion takes personal pursuits to include the freedom to
determine one's occupation. It is this freedom of occupational choices that
allows for society to offer incentives to persons in order to reconfigure
their occupational preferences and so motivate them to take on freely
occupations that benefit society most. Thus, on the grounds of occupational freedom, it is appropriate and not contrary to egalitarian justice to
offer the surgeon–artist special incentives to remain a surgeon instead of
switching to art, her all-things-being-equal occupational preference. Indeed to try to compel her to be a surgeon otherwise seems to recall a
version of the problem of the slavery of the talented, so I argued.

In *Rescuing Justice and Equality*, Cohen considers the argument from the
freedom of occupational choices and fails to find that argument persuasive.
Consider a talented individual (with doctoring skills that will benefit
society) who also likes gardening and in fact, income being equal, would

prefer to garden. Yet gardening will do less to benefit the worst-off in society. So granting this individual extra-incentives so that she would freely choose to doctor (and thereby benefit society) instead of gardening preserves freedom of occupational choice for that person while benefiting society. The argument is presented as a <u>trilemma</u> of the following form, using Cohen's own schema (G. A. Cohen 2008: 185):

1) To doctor at £50,000
2) To garden at £20,000
3) To doctor at £20,000

Option 1 is the most preferred option in terms of both job satisfaction and income, option 2 is the next preferred one since the reduced wage is compensated for by increased job satisfaction, and option 3 is the least desirable since the less preferred job is not accompanied by compensating pay. As a basic background condition, it is presumed that no matter which options the doctor–gardener adopts, her life quality is still superior compared to her average fellow citizens. That is, doctoring is not (to her) particularly arduous but indeed is less so compared to many other jobs, and to be paid £20,000 is not to be paid below the average or socially acceptable wage.

Now the <u>occupational freedom</u> argument, in Cohen's explication here, alleges that to compel the doctor to practice medicine at £20,000 (option 3) which best serves equality undermines occupational freedom <u>since she</u> would rather be gardening at that unenhanced wage. Taking <u>occupational freedom seriously would thus rule out option 3, the egalitarian option</u>.

Cohen's first response is that this argument presents a false trilemma. <u>The doctor need not be doctoring at £20,000 at the cost of her own occupational freedom if the doctor sees that this would be the right thing to do and does so freely.</u> That is, if the doctor were a professed egalitarian and accepts some analogue of the difference principle as a principle of egalitarian justice, then she ought to choose freely to doctor at £20,000 in light of her commitment to egalitarianism. Cohen is thus unconvinced that occupational freedom cannot be preserved without extra-incentives for the doctor. He refers to this as the "ethical solution" to the alleged trilemma.[11]

---

[11] See Macleod's observation that "[i]t is often no small feat to establish that this or that determinate inequality in the distribution of resources is in fact needed in given circumstances for the provision of incentives" (A. Macleod 1985: 184). This is an important challenge that I will leave aside *ex hypothesi*.

But does the doctor not lose out here? As an egalitarian, she ought to want to doctor freely at £20,000 when, other things considered, she would rather be gardening. Does egalitarianism on Cohen's conception not impose a strong demand on her with regard to her occupational choice? Compare this doctor with another person, also a professed egalitarian who cares for gardening, but who lacks (in this case luckily so) doctoring skills and talents. So no social demand is placed on this person's occupational choice, and he is free to garden (at £20,000) without having to confront and respond to social expectations and his own egalitarian conscience. Unlike the doctor, the gardener's egalitarian commitments do not set demands on his occupational choice as the egalitarian commitments of the doctor impose on hers.[12]

To be sure, Cohen is explicit that the doctor–gardener is not to be forced to doctor at £20,000. If this were not so, he would be vulnerable to the charge of "enslaving the talented."[13] But still Cohen is claiming that the doctor, given her egalitarian commitments, should freely want to doctor at £20,000 (even though gardening moves her more). The problem is that there is no guarantee that this moral resolution is without costs to the doctor–gardener's personal pursuits: she cares deeply about gardening, but she surrenders this aspiration to the egalitarian demands which she also cares about. Her seemingly free choice of gardening at £20,000 is not really cost-free then, contra Cohen. Society can feel that this person has let the disadvantaged down, or if she has a deep egalitarian conscience she may feel that she has let society down. She will suffer some egalitarian angst, so to speak, at the very least. It therefore seems unfair in that egalitarianism has imposed a stronger demand on the doctor compared to say the untalented gardener for whom egalitarianism makes no such imposition. This perhaps is not a case of the "slavery of the talented" in a blatant form; it is nonetheless a slavery of the talented of a sort, one might say, for the talented is required to make sacrifices that the untalented is not.

[12] One might suggest that tempering egalitarian ideals understood to be applicable to personal choices by personal prerogatives avoids the purported "over-demandingness" placed on the talented doctor. But, as mentioned in the previous chapter, the question is how to demarcate the requirements of egalitarianism from those of admissible prerogatives.

[13] See Fabre (2010) who argues that Cohen has to force the doctor–gardener to doctor given his own egalitarian commitments; compare with Otsuka (2008) who accepts Cohen's view that egalitarianism does not require forced labor, but only, says Otsuka, by appeal to the idea of self-ownership, which Cohen does not do.

EVADING THE DEMANDS OF JUSTICE? 69

The talented is held to a higher moral standard: she is criticized as being a hypocritical egalitarian if she does not freely opt to doctor at £20,000 while the untalented is left free to pursue gardening.[14] At the very least, on Cohen's idea of egalitarian justice, the talented egalitarian should be nagged by her conscience should she pursue the less useful job but one that she prefers; the untalented does not suffer such pangs.  *Negative connotation. Not pursued by egalitarianism; benefited by it*

Cohen will suggest that if doctoring is not particularly arduous to our gardener–doctor, and that in fact she gets a normal level of satisfaction being a doctor except that she would rather garden, then there is nothing untoward about holding the doctor to the above evaluative standard. After all, she is simply expected to do what persons are normally expected to do (G. A. Cohen 2008: 207–8). So in this "standard case," in which the talented could with ordinary effort and no extraordinary dislike for it do the socially useful job, there is no higher burden imposed on the doctor.  Yet this does not seem right. Suppose that there is also another person who, like the first, does not find doctoring unpleasant but also has an equivalent higher preference for gardening. The difference between this individual and the gardener–doctor is that the former has no special talents for doctoring. Thus, unlike the talented, the untalented now gets to realize his stronger desire for gardening without any moral qualms. It is right that, in this standard case, being a doctor is not so unpleasant for the talented individual; but unlike her less talented compatriot with whom she shares a passion for gardening, she has no morally-tainted free option of becoming a gardener.

In light of these considerations, it is clearer why the incentive provision protects occupational freedom. The ethical solution to the occupational freedom problem is not without some costs, and the extra-incentives can be seen as compensation for these costs. Of course it is compensation only in kind as the extra pay does not make up for her gardening deprivation, but it is a form of compensation nonetheless. *

Indeed, Cohen's ethical solution to the trilemma not only entails a form of slavery of the talented in the specific sense I noted above, but it in fact lies in some tension with his expressly "anti-Stalinistic" commitment. As

---

[14] The discussion does not deny what Cohen refers to as "the standard case": the doctor enjoys doctoring; it is just that she cares more about gardening. Similarly the gardener but untalented doctor cares more for gardening than doctoring even if counterfactually he could doctor. Yet egalitarianism places a greater burden on one than the other.

he notes, what he condemns is the demand of the doctor for £50,000 in order to continue to practice medicine, not that she prefers to do some other job if she isn't to be paid well enough. Cohen needs to allow for this to avoid the charge that his understanding egalitarian justice makes no room for occupational freedom. (For if he were to say that egalitarian justice must demand that the doctor doctors at £20,000, then occupational freedom is indeed undermined and there will be no possible way of arguing around this.) Thus he has to, and he does, accept that in the name of occupational freedom the doctor may opt to garden; what egalitarian justice rejects is that she gets to doctor at enhanced pay.[15] Yet this necessary concession is not entirely in line with the proposed ethical dilemma that imputes that the doctor ought to want to doctor at reduced pay on pain of having her egalitarian commitments called into question. The ethical solution holds out the possibility that as an egalitarian the doctor can *freely choose* to doctor at reduced pay; yet the concession to occupational freedom (that holds that the doctor is only required not to demand extra pay to doctor) suggests that it is not objectionable for the doctor to opt to garden instead. Thus there is a tension: on one hand, Cohen *expects* (and indeed the doctor is perceived to be morally flawed in some ways if she feels that in opting to doctor at £20,000 she is *not* acting freely) the doctor freely to want to doctor at £20,000 (as required by his ethical solution); on the other, he *denies* that he is denying occupational freedom.

A trans-institutionalist might put aside the ethical solution, accept that there is a trilemma, and affirm the following view: there is no violation of occupational freedom absent the incentive provision because the doctor is still free to garden; what she is not occupationally free to do is to doctor at £50,000. (Unless one wants to say implausibly that occupation freedom includes not just the work you do but that the work be rewarded

---

[15] There is a certain ambiguity in Cohen's position on this matter. On what Shiffrin calls the "canonical formulation" of Cohen's view (Shiffrin 2010: 118), even though the state ought not to force the talented to do the useful job without enhanced pay, there is a failure of justice if the talented does not freely choose to do the needed job. Yet, departing from this canonical formulation offered by Shiffrin, Cohen also says that we can reply "Fine" if the talented refuses to do the socially useful job without enhanced pay. What we are really "aggrieved" by is this person's bargaining her way into that job with enhanced pay (G. A. Cohen 2008: 212). This suggests a reading on occupational freedom and equality closer to Shiffrin's own, that is, that the talented may without blame opt to do the less useful job. See note below.

in an enhanced way.) The trilemma is acknowledged because there is no denial here that freedom of occupation is at odds with equality. What is denied, however, is that occupational freedom necessitates enhanced incentives. Thus the incentive provision in the difference principle cannot be defended on grounds that it is necessitated by respect for occupational freedom.[16]

But this formulation of the criticism acknowledges only part of the story and hence fails to see how the Rawlsian incentive structure is supposed to invoke the idea of occupational freedom. The claim of those who advance the idea of occupational freedom against Cohen's rejection of incentives is not that occupational freedom is served by enhanced incentives, which would be clearly false as shown above, but rather this: *in light of pressing social needs, these social needs can be served consistent with occupational freedom only via a scheme of incentives.* The problem being addressed is not "how can occupational freedom be protected?" but "how can equality be promoted by improving the situation of the disadvantaged *while* protecting occupational freedom?" The incentive provision recognizes in the first instance that it is entirely legitimate for the doctor to want to garden. What it is also committed to in addition is to reduce inequality by improving the condition of the disadvantaged, and by hypothesis in this case this means the gardener has to doctor. There is a conflict of commitments, then, between the combined goal of pareto and equality on the one side and occupational freedom on the other. The incentive provision provides a means of demarcating the bounds of justice and personal pursuits, and thus a means of balancing these commitments by attempting to reorder the doctor's preferences. The problem confronting the institutionalist is not that alone of how to secure occupational freedom; nor that alone of how to achieve equality (e.g. by improving the situation of the worst-off); nor how to compromise justice for the sake of occupational freedom. The problem of justice confronting her is the *combined* one of *how to achieve equality* and improving the situation of the disadvantaged while *protecting occupational freedom.* Yes, occupational freedom is not violated if the doctor

---

[16] Shiffrin holds that accepting the justificatory basis of the difference principle will require that the talented not take advantage of her special position to enhance her income and wealth should she accept a socially beneficial occupation; but she is not morally required to accept the post. Thus occupational freedom is maintained. She writes: "declining in itself does not involve treating one's talents as though they were personal assets to generate income" (Shiffrin 2010: 130).

gets to garden at £20,000; but the dual goal of equality and pareto is. The institutional approach, in this case the incentive provision that it grants, presents a way of bringing these goals together.

Indeed, the institutional approach presumes a different view of justice from its critics like Cohen. The institutional approach takes it as a given from the very outset that a conception of justice has to be attuned to these matters of personal pursuits. Cohen's account presumes, however, that in conceptualizing the demands of justice there is no need to take account of these personal pursuits (though he allows that in practice justice may be compromised for reasons of efficiency—but then we call this a compromise of justice and not justice). Justice ideally would have the doctor doctoring at £20,000, and any departure from this ideal is a deviation from justice. Even though we are not to coerce the doctor to practice without the enhanced pay, justice is met only when the doctor freely opts to do this job at non-enhanced pay. The problem with this, again, is how consistent that is with the idea of value pluralism.

## 3.4 The demands of egalitarian justice

Let me turn to a more general question: Does the institutional approach represent an evasion of egalitarian justice? This will depend on what egalitarian justice does demand of individual agents. And how we conceive the proper demands of egalitarian justice will depend fundamentally on why we think distributive equality matters. Two dominant views of why equality matters are the position known as "democratic equality" and that known as "luck egalitarianism." On democratic equality, very simply, some form of distributive equality matters because democratic equality among citizens requires it. That is, without some distributive equality, democratic ideals such as fairness in political processes etc. cannot be satisfied. Moreover, the ideal of shared democratic citizenship entails that inequalities between citizens be limited in some ways. On this view, distributive equality has only indirect value: it is either a means of meeting other valuable ideals, or is derived from other commitments. On the luck egalitarian view, distributive equality matters directly in that equality in distribution is taken to be the benchmark from which only departures due to personal choice and effort are acceptable, but not departures due to luck and circumstance. I will elaborate on these two positions in the next two chapters and defend the luck egalitarian view. But for the moment, adopting an ecumenical view on why distributive equality matters, I want to argue that whether we adopt democratic equality or luck egalitarianism, the demands of distributive equality do not include the regulating of personal choice and decisions within the rules of institutions justly regulated.

### 3.4.1  Democratic equality

Consider, first, the democratic equality argument for distributive equality. A common way of justifying distributive egalitarianism on democratic grounds invokes the ideal of reciprocity, an ideal taken to be characteristic of democratic relations among citizens. As Rawls has put it, the gap between rich and poor in a democratic society "cannot be wider than the criterion of reciprocity allows" (1999a: 114). Under the ideal of reciprocity, citizens may impose only those social arrangements on each other that each can reasonably accept, and any arrangement that permits too great an inequality will fail this reasonable-acceptance test. Accordingly, in this derivative argument for equality, egalitarians want an egalitarian basic structure because this is one necessary condition under which a shared social arrangement meets the criterion of reciprocity, thereby gaining legitimacy in the eyes of its members. Rawls takes his difference principle (which offers the talented extra-rewards for their contribution on the condition that the worst-off benefits) to express the ideal of reciprocity, in that the inequality resulting from the talented being rewarded extra for their contribution must be seen as reasonable from the point of view of the worst-off (Rawls 2001: 64, 76–7).

But does this derivative argument for equality require citizens to do more than establish an egalitarian basic structure? That is, does the criterion of reciprocity call on egalitarians not only to impose social arrangements on each other that all can reasonably accept, but also to act as egalitarians in their personal interactions with each other?

It is not clear that it does. In a society with unjust institutions, the idea of reciprocity is clearly not realized because those unfairly disadvantaged could reasonably object to the institutional arrangements that the well-off are helping to impose on them. Thus personal pursuits that feed off or sustain this injustice should be of concern to egalitarians. But in an ideal society where the terms of justice are fully and appropriately met by the basic structure, there is no reason why personal non-egalitarian pursuits need be objectionable to egalitarians motivated by the ideal of reciprocity. A society that has fully met the requirements of institutional justice may still have lingering inequalities due to personal choices within the rules of institutions, but these lingering inequalities need not violate the principle of reciprocity. The ideal of reciprocity will require that our shared social scheme—the background rules within which we pursue personal ends—is as egalitarianly informed as possible; such a scheme, and only such a scheme, would be accepted as reasonable by participants of that scheme. But the ideal of reciprocity would allow for personal pursuits within the rules of the egalitarian scheme even if these result in some inequalities.[17]

This last point does not mean that the ideal of reciprocity does not apply to interpersonal choices and actions but only to institutional arrangements. It is compatible with my argument that the ideal of reciprocity is an ideal that is basic to morality as such, and so applies in interpersonal moral situations as well (Scanlon 1998). My point is that reciprocity enjoins different kinds of commitments in different contexts. Reciprocity with respect to the kinds of institutions we may impose on each other would require that we advance and support only those institutional arrangements that give equal consideration to the interests of all. However, reciprocity at the personal level need not necessarily require an impartial egalitarianism of this sort, but can in fact allow for deviations from such egalitarian considerations. As T. M. Scanlon has noted, an interpersonal morality that does not provide space for personal concern, for example, the partial concern between friends, would be one that reasonable people may reasonably reject (Scanlon 1999: 160; also Kelly 2000: 117–18). That is, impartiality across the board would fail the requirement of reciprocity. A morality that demands egalitarian motivation or justification for each one of an individual's choices and actions will not allow the kind of space that ordinary morality grants for special concern to relationships and personal projects. A morality grounded on reciprocity must, therefore, interpret reciprocity in such a way as to be able to accommodate different kinds of special concerns.

---

[17] To the extent that individual attitudes, such as, say, racist ones, can impact the basic institutions of society, e.g. by the exclusion of a minority from public spaces (taken here to include enterprises normally open to the public such as private commercial spaces), these clearly undermine the democratic ideal of reciprocity and would be condemned as unjust.

Thus, the main claim is that the ideal of reciprocity generates an obligation to secure a certain kind of institutional arrangement, not that this ideal applies only to the question of institutions. Reciprocity as an ideal would apply to personal conduct as well, but the duties that reciprocity would generate in the sphere of personal interaction are different and need not be duties that require impartial egalitarianism as the norm of conduct. Thus, while it does not violate the ideal of reciprocity to favor one's kin or friends more than strangers in one's genuinely personal dealings within the context of just institutions, it would violate the ideal if institutions are arranged so as to favor specific individuals over others.

The argument from democratic reciprocity requires that our institutions, in order to be just, be as impartial as is possible with respect to individuals' conception of the good, their personal ties, preferences, and so on. But reciprocity does not require impartial conduct within the rules of just institutions. So, if the ideal of reciprocity is what grounds egalitarian justice, the institutional approach does not represent an evasion of the demands of justice.

### 3.4.2 Luck egalitarianism

Consider, next, the luck egalitarian defense of distributive equality. The main idea, as noted, is that persons' life prospects should not be unfairly limited by circumstances beyond their control; hence the motivating goal of egalitarian justice is to mitigate the effects of such contingencies. As Cohen himself has put it elsewhere, "a large part of the fundamental egalitarian aim is to extinguish the influence of [differential] brute luck on distribution" (G. A. Cohen 1989: 931). In this direct argument for equality, we care about equality not because equality facilitates, or is a necessary condition for, a higher moral objective (e.g. that of democratic reciprocity), but because inequality is bad in itself when it is due not to choice but to circumstance outside a person's control. We can call this view "luck egalitarianism" following the standard usage.

But if we are concerned about equality because of a direct concern with mitigating the effects of contingencies on persons' life chances, there is no immediate reason why such a concern must take us beyond the basic structure. The belief of institutional (luck) egalitarians is that an appropriately ordered basic structure will come close to annulling the effects of chance and brute luck on people's lives without intruding on people's liberties to pursue their ends. If our institutional scheme appropriately eliminates "disadvantage[s] for which the sufferer cannot be held account-able" (Cohen 1989: 916), our society has lived up to its commitment to equality as a direct goal. Such a society, even if lingering inequalities persist due to choices people make (but not luck), need not be troublesome from a luck egalitarian viewpoint.

The reason why institutions are the direct target of this account of equality is that, to borrow Rawls's words, the "effects [of institutions] are so profound and present from the start." The social positions of people, and their ex-pectations, are determined to a large degree by the institutions of society (Rawls 1971: 7; also 1993: 259). Natural facts in themselves need not have any implications for justice; what matters is what institutions make of these facts. As Rawls writes: "A further essential distinction is between the unequal distribution of natural assets, which is simply a natural fact and neither just nor unjust, and the way the basic structure of society makes use of these natural differences and permits them to affect the social fortune of citizens, their opportunities in life, and the actual terms of cooperation between them" (Rawls 1999b: 337). Institutions are what turn natural contingencies into crucial determinants of a person's life prospects, and hence justice would require that institutions be appropriately arranged so as not to convert natural contingencies into actual social disadvantages for individuals.

The goal of luck egalitarian is to minimize the effects of luck on persons' life chances. And arranging social institutions in the appropriate ways provides a strategy for realizing this end. But what about the impact of luck within the rules of institutions on personal pursuits? Surely luck also affects the outcome of individuals' personal choices within the rules of institutions? For instance, some people may be luckier (perhaps due to their temperament, appearance, or simply timing) with respect to the ability to make meaningful friendships than others. Should luck in the personal sphere not also be of concern to the luck egalitarian, given her goal of mitigating the impact of luck on individuals' life prospects?

An immediate response here might be to stress that luck egalitarians are concerned with mitigating the effects of "brute luck" but not "option luck," to use Ronald Dworkin's distinction (Dworkin 2000: 73–4).[18] The

---

[18] The distinction between brute and option luck is a subject of debate in the contemporary literature. See Vallentyne (2002) for one discussion. But while luck egalitarians disagree over where the cut lies, they accept that there is a basic moral distinction between (brute) luck and choice. I return to this question in Part II.

outcome of most freely and fairly undertaken business ventures (within the rules of just institutions), for instance, are often luck-dependent to a degree. But this is option luck, in that it pertains to choices that individuals have freely made. On the other hand, the inheritance one acquires, the ability or disability that one is born with, and so on, are due to brute luck in that they are not chosen at all. So, while an institutional approach does not nullify the effects of option luck, neither does it aim to nullify such effects, given that these are fundamentally the results of the choices people have made. The institutional approach aims only to mitigate the effects of brute luck. Brute luck pertains to the background conditions within which people make choices, and background inequalities are the sorts of inequal-  ities (one's natural abilities, social class, etc.) that institutions can address.

But, more importantly, an institutional approach preserves the other twin tenet of the luck egalitarian position, namely the ideal that distributive justice ought to be sensitive to the choices of individuals. Luck egalitarianism is premised, fundamentally, on the idea that distributive principles ought to be luck- or circumstance-insensitive, but choice-sensitive in that people should be held accountable for their choices (though not for the unchosen situations that they happen to find themselves in). Indeed, one might say that one of the starting premises of luck egalitarianism is that people ought to be free to choose and pursue their goals, and to take responsibility for their choices and pursuits; this is precisely why conditions that compromise people's ability to choose that are not themselves the result of choice are to be resisted. A distributive arrangement that reflects people's unchosen circumstances is unjust; but so too is a distributive scheme that does not adequately reflect people's  choices, for this would have the effect of subsidizing people who have made bad choices by penalizing those who have made good choices.

The institutional approach, I am suggesting, allows us a means by which to identify the relevant background circumstances that ought to be equalized with respect to luck, while preserving, at the same time, space for individual choice and responsibility. It identifies the basic structure of society as this background condition within which individual choices are made, and so the impact of this on persons' life prospects should not be subject to luck. Individual choices within the rules of the basic structure are, however, not defined as matters of luck on this view, and luck egalitarians would not wish to mitigate the effects of these on distributive outcomes. The institution/personal choice divide is meant to parallel in a

*MAJOR POINT IN NOTES*

feasible way the circumstance/choice divide that is basic to luck egalitarianism. It provides a means of operationalizing this luck egalitarian distinction.

So, while it is certainly plausible that luck may affect a person's options even in the personal sphere, to nullify the effect of luck in this context by imposing egalitarian requirements on personal conduct will be at the high cost of sacrificing the commitment to choice-sensitivity. As long as the effects of luck can be sufficiently (even if not completely) mitigated by institutional means, any attempt at countering the effects of luck in personal conduct by interfering with personal pursuits within the rules of just institutions will be overly broad.[19] The residual inequalities of luck on personal life are acceptable given the greater costs of attempting to eliminate these inequalities.

*Are the costs necessarily greater??*

The institutional approach, in other words, provides a practicable means of balancing the luck egalitarian core ideal, namely, that distributive justice should be circumstance-insensitive but choice-sensitive. It is better able to identify and preserve the choice/circumstance distinction than an ethos-based approach to justice (such as Cohen's). In short, it is not implausible that luck egalitarianism as an account of egalitarian justice can affirm an institutional view of justice.

Let me gather the strands of the arguments made in this section. On the view that equality matters because of the ideal of democratic reciprocity, egalitarian institutions are required, but not necessarily egalitarian interpersonal conduct as such.

*Good Summary*

Indeed, the ideal of reciprocity should allow for non-egalitarian personal pursuits within egalitarian rules. On the alternative view that equality matters because inequalities due to bad luck are unacceptable, egalitarian institutions can go a long way towards mitigating

---

[19] Cohen has argued that she who is simply unlucky to be born with expensive needs, e.g. to be a photographer, is unlike he who has an expensive taste for champagne because he "schooled himself into it" (G. A. Cohen 1989: 914, 923). From Cohen's view, the former (though not the latter) ought to be compensated somehow for her "bad" luck because she was "stuck" with her tastes, unlike the latter who freely chose to acquire his. In Dworkin's reply to Cohen, he writes that Cohen's recommendation does not track "ordinary people's ethical experience", to wit, that people take responsibility for the personalities that they have (even if these are a matter of brute luck) (Dworkin 2000: 289–90). My response is a different one: that once we begin compensating the aspiring photographer for the expensive pursuit that she is (unfortunately) stuck with, we cannot avoid also compensating the champagne lover for the habit that he has trained himself to have. There is no way of telling the two apart. The institutional approach, I am proposing, attempts to reflect this idea; it is willing to permit brute luck to impact on people's lives in this limited way because any interference with this would undermine the importance of respecting choice altogether.

the effects of bad luck; but going beyond this institutional focus risks compromising the other luck egalitarian ideal, namely, that inequalities due to personal choices must be respected. An institutional focus is thus necessary but also sufficient for the purpose of egalitarian justice. It is necessary because establishing the right kinds of institutions is required as a matter of reciprocity; or it is required for mitigating the effects of luck on persons' life chances. But it is also sufficient because going beyond institutions and requiring egalitarian conduct across the board in society will undermine the ideal of reciprocity; or it will have the consequence of annulling the effects not just of luck but also those due to individual choices and ambition.

## 3.5 Non-ideal conditions: Injustice and personal pursuits

The above discussion of incentives assumes that the incentive schemes are offered in a society with more or less just and stable institutions. That is, the issue was whether a just society has to have more than just institutions; and the institutional approach holds that when there are just institutional rules, persons are free to pursue their own ends within these rules. But this relationship between personal pursuits and justice is altered when there are no just institutions and institutional rules to speak of, or when existing just institutions are under clear and present threat. In such cases, the natural duty that persons have to establish, support, and maintain just institutions  may mean that individuals will have to forego personal pursuits that they would otherwise be free to enjoy under more propitious circumstances. For instance, a society whose basic structure is under threat because of unjustified outside aggression may plausibly conscript its members to contribute in different ways to the just cause of defending society and its basic institutions. Or, to take another case, an outlaw society, whose basic institutions are severely unjust, may be one in which its members can be expected to put personal pursuits on hold while they work towards restoring justice in their society. Finally, to use the above example of the aspiring artist cum surgeon, consider a state of medical emergency in which the surgeon's services are urgently needed. Here it would be a strain to say that this artist–surgeon remains within her rights to refuse to serve unless given appropriate incentives. A just person would see in these cases that the urgent needs of society, namely that of securing the basic preconditions of justice, have priority over her own personal ends, and the primacy of justice that defines the terms of acceptable personal conduct will also require certain personal sacrifices when justice itself or its preconditions are under threat.[20]

So the claim that a just society may allow persons freely to pursue ends within the rules of its institutions is a claim that applies within "ideal theory," that is, where there exist just institutions that are stable and secure and where there is compliance. Under non-ideal conditions, where these institutions don't exist or where their existence is under threat, this claim need not hold. For example, in societies marked by severe distributional inequality because of the lack of appropriate institutional commitments, it is harder to say that persons may freely pursue non-egalitarian ends and still profess to be committed egalitarians. Given these existing unjust inequalities, one would expect real egalitarians to be more willing to take on more personal sacrifices for the sake of promoting egalitarian justice in their society. This is where the force of Cohen's criticism is really felt, and since the real world is far from meeting ideal standards, Cohen's contribution to our understanding of real world justice is significant. But this concern with real world justice, what Cohen calls the "vernacular" context (G. A. Cohen 2008: 68), is consistent with the institutional approach to justice, which accepts that there is a primary duty on all persons to support and maintain just egalitarian institutions. It is only when such institutions are antecedently in place that persons may go on to do as they wish within the rules of institutions and be secure in the knowledge that background justice is preserved. Even though Cohen's critique is propelled by facts of vernacular injustices, he takes himself to be making a conceptual point about ideal justice (ibid.: 68 f.).

Yet, even with regard to non-ideal situations, the institutional approach and its understanding of the division of labor between justice and personal life under idealized conditions, I contend, provides useful guidance for

---

[20] To the extent that the maintenance of just institutions presupposes some basic material and favorable social conditions, a natural disaster can have the result of threatening just institutions, thus compelling a "recalibration" of justice and personal pursuits. A doctor in a society devastated by an earthquake can have a duty of justice to put aside personal pursuits for the sake of providing basic assistance to her compatriots, since just societal institutions presupposes that most persons are able to participate and contribute to the institutional life of society, a requirement potentially unmet in a society facing serious natural disaster.

how we are to understand personal responsibility. The primary responsibility of individuals even under unjust conditions will be the collective one of establishing just institutions within which personal ethical ends may be realized. It is just that this primary responsibility may require significant personal sacrifices under seriously unjust conditions, but it is still distinct from saying that persons will have to adopt an ethos of egalitarian justice as a way of life through and through. As Dworkin notes, "When injustice is substantial and pervasive in a political community, any private citizen who accepts *a personal responsibility to do whatever he possibly can* to repair it will end by denying himself the personal projects and attachments, as well as the pleasures and frivolities, that are essential to a decent and rewarding life" (Dworkin 1992: 236, my stress). It will seem that the institutional approach does not require persons to forfeit all of their personal lives in the name of combating injustice, but they are expected to do at least their fair share in restoring just institutions in their society (ibid.; also Murphy 2000). But, to add to Dworkin's comment, we should note that the space for legitimate personal pursuits varies according to the extent of background injustice.

The mitigation of injustice requires, as it were, a division of labor in the classical sense: it will involve not just deliberation about justice, but mobilization, lobbying, protesting, and in extreme cases perhaps even rebellion.[21] Where the injustice in question is severe and its removal urgent—imagine that a society is confronting tyranny—then quite naturally the space for legitimate personal pursuits will be much more limited than in a reasonably just society. The institutional approach takes it that legitimate personal pursuits are possible only under conditions of just institutions. In the name of preserving space for personal pursuits, the institutionalists limit the site of justice to institutions. But the significance of personal pursuits, whose free and equal pursuit is the *raison d'être* of justice, entails that where there are no just institutions to speak of, or where just institutions are under imminent threat, the space for personal pursuits has to be recalibrated. The primacy of justice can require that personal pursuits be put on hold quite extensively and the pursuit of justice be given full priority, depending on the severity of social injustice.

---

[21] See Walzer (2007) for an insightful discussion on the various (non-deliberative) actions the pursuit of justice and political action require.

## 3.6 Conclusion

The dispute between the institutionalist and her critic seems in the end to turn on the metaphysical question "What is justice?" and related questions concerning its domain. If one holds that conceptually justice is equality across the board, across the whole of society, and, all else being equal, a society where the actual distribution of resources is more egalitarian than another is also more just, then a departure from equal distribution across the board is a departure from justice. It seems that Cohen holds a view of this sort when he says that the difference principle is not a principle of justice (because it admits of inequalities for the sake of efficiency) but a compromise of justice, what he calls a "rule of regulation." It is not that a principle of regulation is per se indefensible; sometimes other values (such as efficiency, etc.) demand consideration. But let's not call it a principle of justice, says Cohen (G. A. Cohen 2008: 277).

If this is at bottom the real dispute, it is important to note that it is not merely a semantic one. On Cohen's view, one can proclaim that a Rawlsian society is less just than another that exhibits an egalitarian ethos (and therefore admits of lesser actual inequalities). But given the critical force of "justice," to say of a society that it is less just, as opposed to merely selfish or uncharitable, is not just a manner of speaking but carries normative implications. For one, it entails a strong corresponding obligation that the unjust society be directed towards justice. This is a substantive issue, not a semantic one. I have tried above to suggest that this more demanding idea of what justice requires compromises the freedom of personal pursuits.

The Rawls–Cohen dispute also reflects, I think, a deeper disagreement as to what political philosophy aims at. In its normative rendition, political philosophy is concerned with social justice (among other things), and if social justice has the broader site that the trans-institutionalists say it has, covering personal conduct, then political philosophy has to take an interest not only in institutions but also in personal interaction and potentially even personal conscience or character within the rules of institutions. This makes political philosophy indistinguishable from other matters of morality, such as personal ethics. For, on this reading, political philosophy has to be concerned also with matters of personal choice.

Indeed one might say that the difference between Cohen and Rawls is that Rawls has a distinctively modern notion of political philosophy and what its purview is, whereas Cohen seems to have a view of political philosophy that we more commonly associate with the ancients, that justice has to do also with character, with the state of one's soul.[22] For moderns like Kant, justice is possible even in a nation of devils. With the right laws and institutions in place, justice can be achieved <u>without the need to address the character of citizens directly</u>. It is precisely because people "have different views on the empirical end of happiness and what it consists of, so that as far as happiness is concerned, their will cannot be brought under any common principle nor thus under any external law harmonizing with the freedom of everyone" (Reiss 1991: 73-4). To make vivid the contrast, we might say that the just state does not need just individuals.[23] <u>For the ancients, however, justice requires not merely just institutions but individuals with the right character, i.e. just individuals.</u>[24]

*directly bcis the opening word. Institutions by nature, affect individuals and mold them. ✗✗✗*

One of the implications of Part I of this book is that the more we accept the idea of the legitimate plurality of personal ends, the less appealing do we find the ancient conception of political philosophy. To the extent that it is the case that modern political philosophy is a response to the recognition that there are a plurality of values and conceptions of the good life in spite of the special primary of justice, and that the purpose of justice is to set external constraints on the kinds of ends persons may have and how they can realize them, one cannot return to the ancient conception without rejecting this idea of individual freedom.

---

[22] Cohen is of course basically concerned with personal conduct, but he also notes the importance of attitudes, sentiments of persons, and suggestively claims that true egalitarian justice will require possibly a "revolution in the human soul" (Cohen 2000: 3).

[23] Kant writes famously: "It only remains for men to create a good organization for the state, a task which is well within their capability . . . so that man even if he is not morally good in himself, is nevertheless compelled to be a good citizen. As hard as it may sound, the problem of setting up a state can be solved even by a nation of devils (so long as they possess understanding)" (Reiss 1991: 112). Also: "we cannot expect their [absent] moral attitude to produce a good political constitution; on the contrary it is only through the latter that the people can be expected to gain a good level of moral culture" (ibid.: 113). One might ask Kant how just institutions can be reasonably sustained if humans are indeed devilish through and through. Is "understanding" only enough? But the key point here is the negative and more modest one: that the workings of just institutions do not require any revolution in the human soul. Justice is to be conceived for humans as they are, not just for angels (for whom, in fact, it is superfluous).

[24] For one distinction between political philosophy and moral philosophy more generally, see Rawls 1993: xvii ff.

# PART II
# Luck

# 4

# Luck Egalitarianism:
# A Modest Account

In Part I, I defended the institutional approach to justice, namely the view that principles of social justice are primarily for the purpose of regulating the basic institutions of society, within the rules of which persons interact. With regard to the specific issue of distributive justice, it means that the primary locus of any distributive principle of justice is the basic social institutions of society. Principles of distributive justice regulate the design and operations of the basic institutions of society, and one important consequence of the institutional site of justice is that, within the rules of these institutions, persons are free to pursue their respective ends in life. One of the arguments I offered in defense of the institutional approach earlier was that independently of whether we take the ground of equality  to be based on luck egalitarianism or democratic reciprocity, that approach is sustained. In this part of the book, I will elaborate on the luck egalitarian position.

As I will attempt to explicate below, luck egalitarianism rests on an intuition about the moral equality of agents and what this entails for commitments of distributive justice. This intuition is not without plausibility or moral appeal, thus accounting for the position's popularity among some contemporary prominent egalitarian theorists. Yet the luck egalitarian ideal, and its basic intuition, has come under severe criticisms in recent debate. My central goal in this part of the book is to sustain the intuitive appeal of luck egalitarian ideal in light of these influential criticisms. These criticisms together allege that luck egalitarianism is from the outset an implausible account of equality. I do not claim to provide a complete defense of luck egalitarianism. Several difficult matters concerning this ideal will be left aside in this discussion, including that of settling on the proper cut between choice and luck. But this and other questions concerning the

Very Interesting

refinement of luck egalitarianism can be fruitfully debated only if it can be shown to be not wholly implausible as charged. Thus my defense of luck egalitarianism, although limited, is I hope a necessary first step towards its more complete defense.

In this chapter, I will recollect some key features of luck egalitarianism, including its basic assumptions and motivating purpose, and I distinguish luck egalitarianism from democratic equality. In particular, I will clarify what I take to be the proper domain, site, and justificatory role of luck egalitarianism and the notion of choice it presupposes. One thing to note is that the institutional approach defended previously is summoned to support what I will call *institutional luck egalitarianism*. Thus one key aim of this part of the book is to suggest the appeal of adopting an institutional approach to luck egalitarianism. In addition, I will propose a more moderate conception of luck egalitarianism, not just with respect to how it understands the site of justice, but also with respect to its domain and justificatory role. I will suggest that we can understand luck egalitarianism in this less ambitious way while retaining its significance and distinctiveness as an account of why distributive equality matters. I will argue in the next chapter that this more modest conception of luck egalitarianism escapes some of the powerful objections that have been raised against it.

## 4.1  Luck egalitarianism: The basic claim

Luck egalitarianism has been defended by several egalitarians and admits of several variations in formulation. While my objective in this chapter is to propose a modest account of luck egalitarianism, I will first explicate some of the central tenets that are basic to any luck egalitarian view.

We might start by saying that luck egalitarianism offers one grounding reason for why distributive equality matters (e.g. Arneson 1989, 2000; G. A. Cohen 1989; Dworkin 2003: 200). That is, it is conceived as a response to the specific question of the ground of distributive equality. For luck egalitarians, the idea of the moral equality of persons requires that each person take responsibility for her choices and assume the costs of these choices. Conversely, it holds that no one should be worse-off because of her poor luck. For some luck egalitarians, the aim of a distributive principle is to forestall or pre-empt the effects of luck on persons' opportunity for well-being (Arneson 1989 and, in a qualified way, G. A. Cohen

1989); for others, the aim is to mitigate the effects of luck on the social distribution of goods and resources among persons (Dworkin 2000; Kymlicka 1990). But however differently luck egalitarians work out its implication, the basic idea that they all share is that persons should not be differentially disadvantaged or advantaged on account of their bad or good luck. This general ideal is expressed by G. A. Cohen, who writes, "there is  injustice in distribution when the inequality of goods reflects not such things as differences in the arduousness of different people's labors, or people's different preferences and choices with respect to income and leisure, but myriad forms of lucky and unlucky circumstance" (G. A. Cohen 2000: 130). Put another way, distributive justice should be fundamentally choice-sensitive but luck-insensitive. This distinction between luck and choice is basic to the luck egalitarian position, and I will for convenience refer to it as the *luck/ choice principle*.

Luck egalitarians are thus motivated by the belief that there is a morally fundamental difference between luck and choice, that is, a difference between things that happen to people on the one side and, on the other, things that they freely choose to do; *and* that it is wrong to hold persons accountable and responsible for things not of their doing, but appropriate to hold them to account for their choices. This fundamental difference between luck and agential choice gives content to the ideal of moral equality of persons within luck egalitarianism (an ideal that is presupposed by any egalitarian theory or for that matter any plausible ideal of justice as mentioned in Chapter 1). The moral difference between luck and choice, along with the presumption of the moral equality of persons, suggests to luck  egalitarians a moral default of equality in distribution, and that any departure from this benchmark of equality is justifiable only when it is the result of agential choices and decisions, but not when it is a matter of pure luck. Thus characterized, luck egalitarianism is an egalitarian distributive ideal in the way we described in Chapter 1: an equal distribution of economic goods is taken to be a benchmark from which any departures have to be justifiable. For luck egalitarians, a distributive arrangement that reflects not agents' free decisions and choices but the circumstances that are forced on them, such as  their good or bad luck, fails to treat them as moral equals.

In explicating what I take to be the implicit starting point of luck egalitarianism, that of equal moral agency and how that ideal is interpreted to support equal distribution as a default independent of luck but subject to choice, I have not provided any argument for it. I take this ideal of equal moral agency and its egalitarian entailment to be a basic and starting *intuition* common to most accounts of luck egalitarianism. My purpose is to see how a plausible account of the ground of distributive equality can be developed from this presumed starting point. The idea is not to defend luck egalitarianism from first principles, so to speak, but to begin with its basic assumptions and ideas, and to try to develop a persuasive account of equality from there. Since luck egalitarianism has been criticized in the literature for being fundamentally flawed *in spite of* its seemingly intuitive starting assumptions—for example, that its starting assumptions generate morally unintuitive outcomes—I hope my mode of proceeding and framing the discussion can have some philosophical pay-off.[1]

As mentioned, luck egalitarianism rests on a fundamental intuition about the moral equality of agents and an inference as to what this presumption of agential equality entails. This is an appealing intuition and hence the popularity of the luck egalitarian ideal amongst several prominent egalitarian theorists. After all, it is a morally attractive view that, from the perspective of distributive justice, persons should not enjoy better life opportunities or prospects simply because they happen to be luckier than others. Such luck includes being born to rich families or a high economic class, being endowed with special native abilities that are valued by society, and so on. Echoing Cohen's remarks quoted above, a distributive arrangement is more just when it is ordered by a distributive principle that *reflects* the real choices and actions of persons than their good or bad luck of these kinds.

It is also worth noting that it is the commitment to equality that moves luck egalitarians in the first place. As I see it, luck *egalitarians* need not start off with some independent obsession with luck and the importance of neutralizing differential luck per se. They are foremost egalitarians agitated by social and economic inequalities, and concerned with identifying a standard by which *inequalities* may be condoned as just or condemned and in need of redress. Their basic idea of the *equal* moral agency of persons grounds the egalitarian default, that is, the idea that all persons as a general principle should be in a position to enjoy equal life prospects. Their notion of moral *agency*, additionally, specifies when departures from this benchmark of equality are acceptable. Specifically, it takes departures to be

---

[1] This does not rule out the possibility that one can use the basic luck/choice principle to ground non-egalitarian theories such as prioritarianism etc. My concern is whether it can coherently ground an egalitarian theory.

acceptable when they result from or are expressions of agency; departures from the egalitarian default are not acceptable when they are due to circumstances outside agential choice.

Luck egalitarianism need not, therefore, begin with the idea of luck neutralization for its own sake. It can endorse luck neutralization as a response to existing inequalities. Recognized as the more complex idea that persons presumed as moral equals are entitled to equal life chances unless personal choice and not luck dictates otherwise, luck egalitarianism is in this sense capable of providing a grounding for the egalitarian default as well as specifying what egalitarianism is, what equality should aim for. Luck neutralization is an integral feature of luck egalitarianism, but it is a feature to be understood within its basic egalitarian agenda. The luck/ choice principle, in other words, is a tool for evaluating and responding to inequalities, not a basic principle in itself. Luck egalitarianism, therefore, does not entail that an equal distribution which is due to luck be altered on the ground that this arrangement is due to luck, as a basic reading of luck neutralization principle taken outside the context of egalitarianism might suggest. As an egalitarian ideal, one that attempts to justify the commitment to an egalitarian default, there will be no compunction for it to deviate from equality for the sake of neutralizing luck. Thus the vision of luck egalitarianism I am proposing can perhaps be more accurately described in this more qualified way: where there is inequality (i.e. where there is deviation from the benchmark of equal distribution), this inequality is acceptable when it is solely the result of the relevant agents' choices, but not if it reflects their good or bad luck.[2]

## 4.2 Luck and choice

Given the centrality of the luck/choice principle, it will be useful to make some remarks on the ideas of luck and choice.

### 4.2.1 Luck as circumstance

We tend to reserve the term "luck" for the fortunes or misfortunes of nature, and use the term "social circumstances" to refer to socially imposed

---

[2] See Hurley's criticism along this lines (Hurley: Ch. 6), and G. A. Cohen's (2006) response. See also Segall (2010) for more discussion of this point.

conditions on persons outside their choosing.[3] Thus, we might ordinarily call the person born with a debilitating illness unlucky, whereas a person born into a lower social class in a rigidly stratified society is described as one who is facing disadvantageous or discriminatory social circumstance. But from the above description of luck egalitarianism, we can see that the notion of "luck" utilized by luck egalitarians is a broader category meant to capture any situation outside the choices and control of individuals, including the constraints of social circumstances that have an impact on her. Luck egalitarians, that is, are not narrowly concerned only with natural misfortunes, but are compelled by the background social circumstances outside of persons' control that affect their life prospects. A luck egalitarian is as moved by the social disadvantages a person faces because of her socially "ascribed" place in a particular social class as by the fact of another person's congenital illness that compromises her life prospects. For luck egalitarianism, these are both examples of bad luck that issue in inequalities which egalitarians should confront. I will argue later that a more plausible account of luck egalitarianism is not concerned directly with inequalities directly caused by nature misfortunes as such, but with what institutions and shared social practices make of these natural facts. But the main point here is that the key distinction that moves so-called luck egalitarians is not the non-exhaustive one of natural misfortune versus personal choice, this being non-exhaustive for there are things outside of persons' control that are not imputable to nature but to embedded social conditions, but the broader one of unchosen circumstances versus choice. To be more accurate, the basic distinction in luck egalitarianism is between circumstance (including social circumstance) and choice.[4] But the catchy term "luck egalitarianism," coined by Anderson in her criticism of the position, captures the essence of the position, and has been co-opted by several of Anderson's targets themselves. And this is not inappropriate, as these egalitarians do talk extensively about the vagaries of luck or fortune in relation to egalitarian justice.

[3] See Nagel's "Moral Luck" (1979) for a discussion of the problem of luck in moral philosophy.
[4] Kymlicka (1990: Ch. 2) thus notes that distribution should be ambition-sensitive but endowment-insensitive.

### 4.2.2 Choice: Social not metaphysical

Luck egalitarians need not rely on some metaphysics of choice. If this were not so, then luck egalitarianism would be as controversial as the conception of metaphysical freedom on which it is predicated. What is sufficient for luck egalitarianism understood as a conception within social justice, it seems to me, is that there are some workable socially accepted standards as to what counts as personal choice and what does not. Luck egalitarianism can begin from some pre-theoretical (non-philosophical) and socially accepted understanding of individual choice and of the conditions under which persons can be said to be choosing freely. There is no need to invoke any particular metaphysics of choice for us to be able to distinguish, say, a willing gambler who has to take responsibility for her poor decisions from a person who is born disabled, for the purpose of social evaluation.

This independence of luck egalitarianism from the metaphysics of freedom is expressed by G. A. Cohen's remarks: "We are not looking for an absolute distinction between presence and absence of genuine choice. The amount of genuineness that there is in a choice is a matter of degree, and egalitarian redress is indicated to the *extent* that a disadvantage does not reflect genuine choice. That extent is a function of several things, and there is no aspect of a person's situation which is wholly due to genuine choice" (G. A. Cohen 1989: 934). We don't, for example, need to ask what "amount of information" a person must have in order to have genuine choice. "All we need to say, from the point of view of egalitarian justice, is: the more relevant information he had, the less cause for complaint he now has" (ibid.). Similarly, Dworkin, speaking specifically of the difference between option and brute luck, accepts that "the difference between these two forms of luck [option and brute] can be represented as a matter of degree . . . If someone develops cancer in the course of a normal life, and there is no particular decision to which we can point as a gamble risking the disease, then we will say that he has suffered brute bad luck. But if he smoked cigarettes heavily then we may prefer to say that he took an unsuccessful gamble" (Dworkin 2000: 74–5). These remarks suggest that choice is largely a matter of degree. But the more basic point that can be gleaned from them, as I see it, is that what counts as option luck (choice) or brute luck (chance) is not determined metaphysically but against a set of reasonable background conventions and social assumptions. That is, we do and can make sense of the distinction between choice and chance in ordinary life (and the differences in degrees of choice), and luck egalitarianism need not rely on anything more controversial than some shared understanding of the distinction.

To be sure, there will be areas of disagreement as well as shifting conventions about individual and social responsibility (as when we are more prepared to take socialization into account in sentencing decisions at present than in the past), but these disagreements and shifts in ideas of individual responsibility do not count against the luck egalitarian dependence on the choice/luck distinction. On the contrary, they affirm that the luck/choice distinction is a socially given one as this changes with the times, and some basic socially grounded distinction between choice and luck affects our views of responsibility.[5]

### 4.2.3 The luck–choice cut

Much of what humans do is subject to luck in varying degrees, especially if luck is defined broadly in the way suggested above to include social circumstances outside affected agents' control. Luck is pervasive in human affairs. Whether a gamble freely undertaken turns out well for the gambler is determined to some extent by luck. Because of the pervasiveness of luck in human affairs, luck egalitarians need to be able to distinguish the kinds of luck that matter for egalitarians and those that don't. Here, it is worth recalling Ronald Dworkin's distinction between brute and option luck. Option luck, as Dworkin puts it, "is a matter of how deliberate and calculated gambles turn out." Brute luck, on the other hand, is luck that befalls a person independently of any deliberate gamble on her part (Dworkin 2000: 73). To illustrate, if I buy a stock that falls in value afterwards, I suffer from bad option luck; in contrast, if I am struck by lightning while going about my day-to-day business, I suffer bad brute luck. It is an instance of option luck (and a bad one) because I chose to engage in this gamble. Because option luck is at bottom a matter of choice, luck egalitarians are concerned only with brute luck. Thus luck egalitarians

---

[5] That the idea of choice and its lack thereof is not metaphysical, but social, does not mean that it has to be necessarily non-normative. To the contrary, how society makes this distinction is often normatively informed: because we think it is appropriate to hold a person morally responsible for X, we take that to be the result of her choice; and vice versa with regard to luck. Luck egalitarianism can certainly operate on some prior normatively based account of choice and luck. My point is that luck egalitarianism need not itself be responsible for furnishing such an account, but can ride on existing accounts of luck and choice.

do not implausibly take all human affairs that are subject to chance or luck to fall under its range of concern, even though in a sense these activities are influenced by luck. That is, it does not attempt to compensate people for their poor option luck. Rather, luck egalitarians are specifically concerned that brute luck not be turned into social advantages or disadvantages for persons. Most luck egalitarians accept this Dworkinian distinction between option and brute luck, even though they may disagree with him and each other over where to draw the line. That is, even though luck is perhaps pervasive, most luck egalitarians do accept that there are some types of decisions which persons can be said to have chosen and thus be held responsible for, even if the outcome is subject to chance, and others which they cannot be said to have freely adopted and hence ought not to be held responsible for (Dworkin 2000: 73–4; also Nagel 1979: 103–4).

As indicated above, there is no consensus as to the precise cut between what is luck and what is choice, or between brute luck and option luck, and there is a lively ongoing debate among luck egalitarians on what luck is, and how to place the cut between luck and choice. The general luck egalitarian ideal, that persons' life prospects should be affected by choice rather than circumstance, has been developed and fleshed out in different ways by different egalitarians. Richard Arneson, G. A. Cohen and Ronald Dworkin, for instance, while all endorsing the general distinction between luck and choice (or Dworkin's basic distinction between brute luck and option luck), disagree over how that "cut" between is to be drawn.

Consequently, Cohen and Arneson on one side and Dworkin on the other disagree over what it is that a distributive theory based on luck egalitarianism should strive to "equalize" or what the currency of equality ought to be. Cohen and Arneson hold that it is opportunity for welfare, while Dworkin holds that it is resources, construed to include not just social and economic resources but also what he calls "personal resources," that is, the talents and native abilities that persons have.[6]

---

[6] For more examples of this internal debate, see Otsuka (2002), Lippert-Rasmussen (2001), Vallentyne (2002), and Sandbu (2004). Some of these debates concern whether option luck should not also be discounted under luck egalitarianism; that is, whether the basic distinction should be between luck on one side (including option luck) and choice on the other. See Segall (2010) for helpful discussion on this specific point. This internal debate about where to draw the line: whether it should be between option luck and choice on the one side, with brute luck on the other (and here there can be disagreements as to where this line is to be drawn); or whether it should be between real choice on the one side, and optional luck and brute luck on the other, does not affect my discussion here. What matters for me is that luck

So luck egalitarianism does not present one united front against alternative conceptions of equality. What is relevant is that luck egalitarianism is unified around the core ideas noted above, even as there are disputes over how these may be refined.

Moreover, on the issue of the luck/choice cut, it seems to me that there is sufficient agreement not just among luck egalitarians but also most egalitarians in general concerning the typical cases with which distributive justice is historically concerned as to whether luck or choice is causally determinant for the luck egalitarian project to get off the ground. For instance, most people—not just luck egalitarians—would accept that a person who is now worse-off because she freely squandered opportunities presented to her is worse-off largely due to her choice, whereas a person who is made worse-off because of an unexpected illness or accident that she couldn't have reasonably avoided is worse-off mainly on account of bad luck. Or, to take another example, most egalitarians accept that the social class into which one is born is a matter of luck, whereas the offices or economic positions one acquires through ambition and hard work under conditions of fair equal opportunity can be largely credited to personal choice and effort. With regard to these standard cases, I think there is sufficient agreement among interlocutors in the egalitarian debate.

There is no denial that there is more work to be done within luck egalitarianism to clarify its basic ideas, including specifying more precisely the basic luck/choice distinction. But luck egalitarianism does sufficiently  identify a prospective and distinctive account of why equality matters, and its luck/choice principle, although in need of refinement, is adequate with regard to the standard cases in the egalitarian debate. One might say that one longer-term objective of this work is to encourage further refinement of the luck egalitarian ideal by defending its basic plausibility as a distinct position on equality against certain external criticisms.

Moreover and more importantly, it seems to me that any plausible egalitarian theory must make use of the luck/choice distinction at some point in its account of distributive justice. It is hard to imagine a defensible theory of distributive justice, particularly one predicated on the capacity of individuals to make decisions and to take responsibility for these decisions,

egalitarianism of any stripe accepts some basic distinction between luck and choice. My concern in this work is with external criticisms, and my response to these criticisms is neutral with respect to the internal debate.

as liberal conceptions are, that does not recognize the difference between  matters over which persons can exercise some meaningful choice and those which are beyond their control. (This is a point that I will return to later in this chapter.) If this is right, the philosophical responsibility to refine and develop the luck/choice distinction further is not borne by luck egalitarians alone. Accordingly, if the ambiguity between luck and choice is really troublesome for luck egalitarianism, most non-luck egalitarian theories will be in trouble as well.

## 4.3 Democratic equality: A contrasting account

To have a better appreciation of the distinctness of luck egalitarianism as an account of why distributive equality matters, we can contrast it with an alternative position broadly called "democratic equality" (e.g. Anderson 1999; Scheffler 2003a; Freeman 2006a; also Rawls 2001). As a general account of why equality matters, democratic equality holds that equality is the benchmark, not because persons as such stand in some general relationship of moral equality, but because of the political relationship between members of a democratic political order. In short, distributive equality is not a moral ideal but a political ideal, one which derives from the more fundamental ideal of democracy.[7]

The democratic equality justification for distributive egalitarianism can perhaps be formulated in this way. A democratic society is ideally conceived as a system of fair social cooperation among members of that society, and the ideal of fair social cooperation entails that members must live with each other on terms that each can reasonably and mutually accept. The last point introduces the ideal of reciprocity, and the ideal of reciprocity will require, among other things, that a given social economic arrangement be reasonably acceptable to all participants. Simply put, then, reciprocity will require that the gap between the rich and poor of a democratic society not be wider than can be justified to all members,

[7] The term "democratic equality" has been used by some to denote an alternative to luck egalitarianism (e.g. Anderson), but not all those whom I describe as democratic egalitarians actually use that term to contrast their egalitarian position with luck egalitarianism (e.g. Scheffler and Freeman). I am adopting the term for a broader usage, to cover a family of views that takes distributive equality to matter because of democratic relations among citizens. Different democratic egalitarians will specify the character of that relationship differently and draw different egalitarian implications from that.

especially those disadvantaged by it. Hence, on grounds of democratic reciprocity (as I will call it), a distributive principle is demanded for the purpose of regulating admissible inequalities between members of a democratic polity. Thus Rawls, in accounting for the justificatory basis of his distributive principle, the difference principle, says that "democratic equality properly understood requires something like the difference principle" (Rawls 2001: 49; 1971: 65–6, 319).

Accordingly, we can see how luck egalitarianism and democratic equality account for why equality matters in different ways. For democratic egalitarians, distributive equality matters because democracy matters. For luck egalitarians, distributive equality matters because the moral equality of persons demands it. For democratic egalitarians, the point of a distributive principle is to regulate inequalities among members so as to satisfy the criterion of reciprocity, and this matters because of what it means, normatively speaking, to stand in a true democratic relationship with each other; for luck egalitarians, the point of a distributive principle is to regulate distribution in society so that inequalities in distribution reflect agential choices and not the luck that befalls agents, and this matters because of the presumption of the moral equality of individual agents. Thus, they each explain the motivation and point of distributive equality differently.

For this reason, it is perhaps not inappropriate to say that, under democratic equality, distributive equality is a political value, since it is confined to members of a democratic polity on account of what it means to be an equal member of a democratic association; whereas it is a moral value for luck egalitarians, since it is taken to apply to all agents antecedently presumed to be moral equals. This last point has immense implications for how we are to understand the reach or scope of equality, the question of Part III of this book.

It is worth noting that it does not follow from the contrast between democratic equality and luck egalitarianism that democratic egalitarians do not make use of the luck/choice distinction at all. Indeed, I suggested earlier that it is implausible for them not to, once the commitment to equality is motivated, in order to flesh out what that motivation would require. One can imagine the following position: once democratic reciprocity gives rise to the commitment to regulate inequalities, it remains an open question how to regulate these which inequalities to be admitted and which not on terms that all members can reasonably accept. In this regard, it is possible that members will give some weight to the luck/choice difference and say that certain inequalities due to choice of persons are mutually admissible, though certain ones due to pure luck are not to be accepted.[8] But this invocation of the luck/choice principle alone does not turn the position into a luck egalitarian one, because although the luck/choice principle is invoked in working out what distributive egalitarianism requires, it is not used to motivate the commitment to equality in the first place. This point will be explained in greater detail in the discussion to come.

## 4.4 Luck egalitarianism: Its domain, site, and role

I have so far offered a general description of the luck egalitarian ideal and contrasted it with democratic equality. As I have presented it, luck egalitarianism rests on a basic plausible intuition about the moral equality of persons. It is motivated by the belief in the fundamental difference between the doings and choices of persons on the one side, and on the other side circumstances and conditions not of their choosing. Its basic ideal that distribution should reflect choice and not luck is *grounded on* the ideal of the moral equality of persons. This suggests that equality in distribution should be the moral default unless agential choice determines otherwise.

What I will attempt to do next is to offer a conception of luck egalitarianism that is more modest than most luck egalitarian accounts. My account will be more modest with respect to how it specifies the special domain, site, and limited justificatory role of the luck egalitarian ideal. I will elaborate on these points in turn below. The task at hand here is to suggest that this modest luck egalitarian account is plausible and not without appeal. I will argue that what is attractive about luck egalitarianism is not forfeited when we limit its domain, site, and justificatory role in the way I am proposing.

---

[8] For example, Rawls invokes the luck/choice distinction when working out what equality, once committed to as an ideal, demands (Rawls 1971: 100–1). For this reason Rawls is sometimes characterized as a luck egalitarian. But if luck egalitarianism is understood specifically as an account of why equality matters, we can see how Rawls, his references to the luck/choice distinction notwithstanding, is not a luck egalitarian. I will return to this interpretative question below.

### 4.4.1  Its domain: Distributive justice

First, concerning its operational domain, luck egalitarianism should be seen strictly as an account of *distributive* justice, or more precisely as a response to the question as to why *distributive* equality matters. It should not be seen to be speaking for an account of justice broadly conceived, let alone an account of the whole of morality. I understand distributive justice to be concerned with how persons fare in relation to each other above a threshold of sufficiency. A distributive principle is thus comparative, but also operational on the presumption that basic needs (however defined) are being met. Questions of distributive egalitarian justice are distinct from questions of assistance or rescue, and luck egalitarianism need not attempt to provide answers to questions about the conditions under which a person who is lacking urgent and basic needs is entitled to social assistance or rescue. Instead of claiming such a broad domain, luck egalitarianism should, and can, claim for itself a more limited domain of application. Its purpose is to explain and justify why some distributive equality with respect to resources, over and above those that persons need for basic subsistence, is required as a matter of justice. This is distinctively a concern of distributive justice as opposed to that of humanitarian rescue or assistance. If this limited domain of luck egalitarianism is acknowledged, then its choice/luck principle cannot be invoked to determine whether a person who is lacking basic goods, without which she could not live a minimally decent human life, is entitled to social assistance. The luck/choice principle is meant only to determine the distributive entitlements of persons above the threshold of a basic minimum (however that minimum is defined), and is irrelevant for the purpose of determining whether a person who is floundering due to a lack of basic goods ought to be rescued. In such a case, the more appropriate considerations are those pertaining to human rights or humanitarian decency.

Good def of DJ

In short, a social order in which all members' basic and urgent needs are accounted for will still have the social mission of deciding how to distribute social resources fairly among its members, beyond what basic needs demand. This is the question of *distributive justice*, and in a productive social order it remains a morally salient question even when persons' basic needs are met, for there are fairer and less fair ways of distributing remaining available resources. As an account of distributive justice, luck egalitarianism is fundamentally concerned with this question. It is only with regard to the distribution of resources in the space above the threshold of basic needs that the luck/choice principle takes effect.

This division between the domains of distributive justice and humanitarianism required by my understanding of luck egalitarianism is neither eccentric nor arbitrary, but is in fact a commonplace in contemporary political philosophy. For example, Rawls in *The Law of Peoples* holds that there are reasons of basic rights to ensure all "people's basic needs are met" (reasons that have global application for Rawls) that are distinct from reasons and requirements of distributive justice that do not have global application (Rawls 1999a: 38, 65; cf. 113–15).[9] Thomas Nagel has also stressed the distinction between duties of humanity and duties of distributive justice for the purpose of arguing that, while there is a global duty of humanitarian assistance to ensure that persons' basic subsistence needs are met, there is no global duty of distributive egalitarian justice. As he writes, "there is some minimal concern we owe to fellow human beings threatened with starvation or severe malnutrition and early death from easily preventable diseases." But these "basic duties of humanity" are distinct from the duties of distributive justice and rest on different considerations (Nagel 2005: 118).[10] Both Nagel and Rawls here operate on the presupposition that duties of distributive justice and duties of humanity or duties of assistance belong to different categories of moral duties.

Moreover, it is generally taken for granted that distributive justice considerations become salient only when persons' basic needs can be met. Here it is illustrative to recall Rawls again, this time his reaction to the criticism that his prioritizing of basic liberties (under his first principle) fails to appreciate the fact that, without meeting their basic subsistence needs, individuals cannot begin to exercise their basic liberties properly. Rawls responds by noting that it is understood that any principle of basic

---

[9] Rawls, of course, goes beyond global humanitarianism as his duty of assistance calls for helping and supporting people to ensure that they can support well-ordered functioning institutions, which clearly involves providing people with more than the resources to meet very basic humanitarian ends. See also Rawls (1971: 542) where it is noted that "reasonably favorable conditions" are presupposed for the operation of the priority of liberty, and hence by implication for justice as fairness as a whole.

[10] As Nagel also puts it, "Humanitarian duties hold in virtue of the absolute rather than the relative level of need of the people we are in a position to help" (2005: 119). I note here Nagel's general claim that reasons for distributive equality are distinct from reasons for humanitarian compassion. As we will see, the luck egalitarian position I am proposing would suggest that distributive equality can have global application.

liberties must presuppose some prior principle of basic needs, "at least insofar as their [basic needs] being met is necessary for citizens to understand and to be able to fruitfully exercise those rights and liberties" (1993: 7).[11] That is, there is a basic needs principle that has lexical priority over Rawls's principle of basic liberties, which in turn has lexical priority over his second distributive principle. Rawls takes it to be simply obvious that some unspecified basic needs principle has to be assumed when conceiving and applying his two principles of justice. Considerations of basic liberties as well as distributive equality rest on the presumption of a prior principled commitment to persons' basic needs.

That I refer to one domain as "distributive justice" and another as "humanitarian" is solely for the purpose of identifying two distinct domains in which different principles apply. My point is not the conceptual one that the concept of justice must necessarily be understood in the exclusive way as described, but a substantive one that is not altered if we insist on calling humanitarian duties "duties of distributive justice." What I am claiming is that these duties can be different (and with different basis) in form and substance from duties belonging to the category I call distributive. Nor is it my purpose here to establish the case for a basic right to subsistence, or to provide some other grounding for the humanitarian duty to provide persons with basic needs.[12] My claim is a structural one about the plural character of the moral order, namely, that distributive egalitarian considerations are distinct from humanitarian considerations, and that  distributive considerations become operational on the presupposition of a commitment to persons' basic needs (however that is defined). The central idea is that luck egalitarianism can accept this general division of moral domains and this priority of basic needs. There is nothing in the fundamental idea of luck egalitarianism that must oppose this division of moral domains and its limited application to the domain of distributive justice. Indeed, understood specifically as an explanation for why *distributive* equality matters, it cannot but be confined to this specific domain.[13]

---

[11] See also the instructive remarks in Rawls's *The Law of Peoples*: "By basic needs, I mean roughly those that must be met if citizens are to be in a position to take advantage of the rights, liberties, *and opportunities* of their society" (1999a: 35, my stress; 38 and 65).

[12] For the landmark account of a basic right to subsistence, see Henry Shue (1980).

[13] Segall (2007, 2010), N. Barry (2006), and Casal (2007) have advanced luck egalitarian positions that hold that luck egalitarian principles aren't the only relevant principles, and

### 4.4.2 *Its subject matter: Institutions not nature*

Rawls writes that natural facts in themselves are neither just nor unjust; what is just or unjust is "the way the basic structure of society makes use of these natural differences and permits them to affect the social fortune of citizens, their opportunities in life, and the actual terms of cooperation between them" (Rawls 1999b: 337). On this view, social justice is principally concerned with the basic structure of society, that is, its main political and social institutions, and does not deal directly with natural facts as such. Luck egalitarianism, in my view, can and should accept this important point about the subject matter of social justice. Luck egalitarianism ought not to be in the business of mitigating all natural contingencies (due to luck) that people face. As an aspect of social justice, luck egalitarianism is only concerned with how institutions deal with such natural contingencies. Its goal is to ensure that institutions are not arranged so as to convert a natural trait (a matter of luck) into actual social advantages or disadvantages for persons. So, only those natural contingencies that have an institutional consequence in this way fall within the scope of luck egalitarianism.

For example, as a simple illustration, it is purely a matter of luck whether one is born with blue or brown eyes. And, normally in our society, this contingency in itself does not raise questions of justice, because our social institutions are not such that the color of one's eyes determines one's life opportunities. So arbitrariness of eye color is not the sort of luck that exercises luck egalitarians. But if, counterfactually, social and political institutions are designed such that persons with brown eyes are favored with more opportunities or resources and those with blue eyes are discriminated against, a matter of luck has become a matter of justice. But this is not because one's eye color in itself is a matter of luck that demands the attention of luck egalitarians, but because institutions have, in this counterfactual, turned this natural fact into a matter of (in)justice. Luck egalitarians can sensibly say, in this imagined case, that the luck of people's eye color is a matter of justice and demand that institutions be reformed such that this natural fact does not disadvantage or advantage people. But

indeed can be defeated or constrained by other competing moral principles. I will discuss in the next chapter how my account differs from some of these.

they say this, again, because of how existing institutions are treating this contingency.

Thus, it is the justice of institutions that remains the primary objective of luck egalitarians, in that institutions should not be designed in ways that turn natural facts about persons into social advantages or disadvantages for them. But this institutional focus is still a *luck* egalitarian position, because it is fundamentally concerned with how institutions respond to matters of luck.

 On this institutional approach to luck and justice, it is also clear that luck egalitarians do not need to strive to make the (unlucky) disabled person as whole as possible and thus devote vast social resources to this end. This would probably be counter-productive, and in any case in light of other social commitments potentially morally absurd. Rather their aim is to create (or to reform) social and political institutions so as to not render this person's disability into actual social disadvantage for her. This can take the form of instituting greater accessibility in public spaces, educational accommodations, additional health care support, etc. Or it may require the establishing of new and complementary institutional mechanisms to mitigate the potential unjust effects of existing institutions on these natural contingencies (e.g. by providing a special educational curriculum and opportunities for the disabled). These institutional responses are not wrong-headedly inspired by the goal of wanting to make the disabled person fully able or to compensate her as far as is possible for her natural misfortune, but by the recognition that as an equal member of society she is entitled to a social order in which she is *not* socially disadvantaged  compared with others *just because* of some natural facts about her when alternative forms of social arrangements are available.

So when luck egalitarians speak of neutralizing the effects of differential luck, this should be read as a shorthand for saying that institutions should be reformed or supplementary institutional mechanisms implemented so that natural facts about people do not become real social disadvantages for  them. And when luck egalitarians seem to "compensate" a person for her natural deficiencies, not by making her whole but through institutional adjustments and corrections, this is not to be seen as a second-best solution. That is, it is not that ideally luck egalitarians would want to make the unluckily disabled person whole, and that because they cannot they have to settle unhappily for a less-than-ideal solution by focusing on institutions, and attempt to repair institutions rather than to cure the unfortunate person. Rather, reforming institutions so that a disabled person's options are not institutionally limited is just what justice demands from the institutional view of justice. Accepting this view of justice, luck egalitarianism is precisely concerned with institutional design and how that affects people socially, rather than with mitigating the effects of any luck per se.

Another way of putting the point across is this: the stipulation that social justice (which includes distributive justice) is primarily institutional, that is focused on institutions, and whose principles' application is limited to institutions, is one which luck egalitarianism can accept without undermining its distinctiveness as an account of why distributive justice matters.

### 4.4.3 Its justificatory role: Why distributive justice matters

Luck egalitarianism must be seen specifically as a response to the question "why does distributive equality matter?" and, relatedly, the question "what is the purpose of a distributive principle?" It is important to recognize that these are distinct questions from the question "equality of what?" and that of "how to distribute?" (Sen 1992). Luck egalitarians are not forced to say, for example, that it is equality of welfare that is fundamental (which has to do with "equality of what?"). This might be a tempting (though false) inference, because its concern with making up for a person's bad luck may suggest to its critics that luck egalitarianism is ultimately concerned about making everyone equally happy within the constraints of their free choice, or to feel equally lucky. But this would be an unwarranted inference, because a luck egalitarian could as well be concerned specifically that the social and economic *resources* with which people have to pursue their ends not be distributed as luck dictates.[14] It is a distinct question as to whether luck egalitarians should be welfare egalitarians of some stripe or resource

---

[14] I don't suggest that many, if any, critics of luck egalitarianism explicitly make this inference. But that some luck egalitarians are also interested in welfare—like Arneson ("equality of opportunity for welfare") for example, and Cohen in an importantly qualified way ("equality of access to advantages")—may perhaps prompt some readers to apply arguments against welfarism to luck egalitarians as a group. Still, Anderson's discussion (Anderson 1999: 331–4) seems to me to be a critique of luck egalitarianism via a critique of equality of welfare. For example, Anderson writes that luck egalitarianism, or "equality of fortune," has to rely controversially on "subjective measures of welfare or the worth of personal assets" (ibid. :333); and that luck egalitarians would want to compensate deaf people for their "less happy" lives (ibid.: 332–3). Anderson's target luck egalitarian here is Arneson (1989). This slippage illustrates my comment at the start of the book, that it is important to distinguish the different questions of equality and not run them together in our assessment of egalitarian theories.

egalitarians, and so on. That the point of equality is to mitigate the effects of luck on persons' life options does not immediately generate an obvious and direct response to the question about what it is that society should seek to equalize.

Likewise, luck egalitarianism does not immediately on its own offer a pattern of distribution (i.e. an account of how to distribute). That is, the luck egalitarian ideal that the point of distributive justice is to ensure that distribution in society reflects persons' choices while discounting the effects of luck may ground a substantive distributive principle, with a pattern of distribution, that at the level of implementation directly adjusts for luck and choice. But it need not, and luck egalitarians might say that another distributive pattern is more reflective of the basic luck egalitarian goal. This will have to do with how a particular luck egalitarian identifies the cut between luck and choice, how she thinks this distinct is best operationalized, and how general she thinks her operative distributive principle ought to be. It should not be ruled out of court that a luck egalitarian could consistently conclude that something like Rawls's difference principle is most reflective of the luck egalitarian goal, if she accepts the need for a general principle to regulate the basic structure of society along with the inseparability of luck and choice. I will discuss this possibility in the next chapter.

To put the above point in a more general way, we might say that the luck/choice principle of luck egalitarianism is offered as a *grounding principle* for distributive equality and not as a *substantive principle* of distributive equality itself (which will have to cover both *what* to distribute and *how* to distribute).[15] That is, luck egalitarianism aims to provide a principle that grounds some substantive distributive principle. On my account, luck

---

[15] I believe my distinction between a grounding and a substantive principle of equality is in line with distinctions also made by G. A. Cohen (2008) and Shiffrin (2010). Cohen contrasts "principles that justify" with "a rule of regulation" (like the difference principle) and proposes that luck egalitarianism be seen as a justifying rather than a regulating principle (G. A. Cohen 2008: 271). Shiffrin takes the principle "that talents are arbitrary from the moral point of view" to be a "justificatory underpinning" of the difference principle (Shiffrin 2010: 121). Now Cohen's and Shiffrin's purpose for the distinction is to show that even if the substantive principle is institutional in focus, accepting the institutional principle entails accepting the implications of its grounding principle for personal conduct. (In the case of Cohen, it is also to show as a conceptual matter that the difference principle is not really a principle of justice.) In contrast, I deny that the grounding principle must regulate personal choices as well. As discussed in the previous chapter, it is not incoherent to regard a grounding principle or the "justificatory underpinning" principle as a principle exclusive to institutions.

egalitarianism holds that institutions should not be designed such that persons are advantaged or disadvantaged with respect to each other on account of their good or bad luck, and that the point of a distributive principle is thus to pre-empt or counter such discriminatory distribution of social resources. But what distributive justice entails, that is, what the substantive distributive principle itself is, will have to be worked out through further interpretation of the fundamental luck/choice principle, as well as other considerations, such as the plausibility of candidate metrics of equality on their own terms.[16] The luck/choice principle itself is not a distributive principle, on a par (and competing) with, say, Rawls's difference principle. Rather, it belongs to the same category as the ideal of democratic reciprocity (that grounds the difference principle for Rawls). And as democratic reciprocity itself does not express a substantive distributive principle, neither does (nor should it be so assumed) the luck/choice principle. And like luck egalitarians, democratic egalitarians do not all agree on what the substantive distributive principle is that democratic equality grounds. Thus, while Rawls concludes that the difference principle with its focus on primary goods (such as income and wealth broadly defined) best satisfies the requirements of democratic equality, Anderson concludes that "[d]emocratic equality . . . aims for equality across a wide range of capabilities," thus departing from Rawls on both *how* to distribute (not the difference principle, but an ideal of adequate democratic capability) and *what* to distribute (not primary goods, but capabilities *pace* Sen) (Anderson 1999: 317). What the substantive distributive principle is for luck egalitarians, as it is for democratic egalitarians, will have to be developed from their respective grounding principles, and it seems to me that the internal debate within each camp is still ongoing. (Thus, luck egalitarians should hardly be singled out and faulted for not coming into any agreement as yet with regard to these substantive matters.) This observation that luck egalitarianism has a very specific justificatory

---

[16] Thus, see the debate as mentioned earlier between luck egalitarians like Dworkin, G. A. Cohen, and Arneson, and also Sen (to the extent that Sen could be read as a luck egalitarian) concerning what Cohen calls the "currency of egalitarian justice." My point is not that there is no right answer to the "equality of what?" question within the luck egalitarian perspective, but that the starting premise of luck egalitarianism in itself does not directly furbish an answer, hence the internal dispute we witness among luck egalitarians in spite of their shared starting point. So, while the questions "why equality matters?" and "equality of what?" are interrelated, in that the reasons why we take equality to matter will inform what we think the metric of equality should be, they are nonetheless distinct questions.

purpose, that is, that of showing *why* distributive equality matters, and does not directly address the questions of *how* and *what* to distribute, is worth bearing in mind because, as I will argue in the next chapter, some criticisms of luck egalitarianism target it as if it were meant to be a substantive principle of distributive justice.[17]

Let me summarize the key features of the luck egalitarian position I have sketched. (i) Luck egalitarianism is an account of distributive justice and not the whole of justice or morality. The luck/choice principle serves to determine persons' distributive entitlements, assuming that their basic urgent needs are met. This is its moral domain. (ii) Its subject matter is the basic structure of society; its aim is to ensure that social institutions do not convert matters of luck into social advantages or disadvantages, not to equalize persons' natural luck. (iii) Luck egalitarianism aims primarily to provide a justificatory basis for distributive equality and is not itself a substantive distributive principle. Put another way, luck egalitarianism offers a grounding principle for, not a substantive principle of, distributive justice. Relatedly, it explains what the purpose of an egalitarian distributive principle is, but does not by itself say what and how to distribute.

## 4.5 Rawls and luck egalitarianism

I will digress briefly to elaborate on an interpretative advantage in treating luck egalitarianism as a grounding principle of equality, a principle that motivates the commitment to equality, and not as a substantive distributive principle. The advantage, as indicated earlier, is that it offers a tidy and elegant explanation of why Rawls is self-consciously not a luck egalitarian in spite of his comments about the moral arbitrariness of the distribution of talents, family status, and the like.[18]

---

[17] That luck egalitarianism is best seen as an account of why equality matters, rather than as a substantive account of how to distribute equally, is an important point that is not sufficiently clarified by proponents and hence not sufficiently appreciated by its detractors, some of whose objections treat luck egalitarianism as a substantive account of equality. Anderson, whose criticisms of luck egalitarianism I will later try to counter, at least got the question right when she presented luck egalitarianism as a response (albeit a wrong response in her view) to the question, "What is the Point of Equality?" That is, luck egalitarianism is an attempt at explaining what the purpose of an egalitarian distributive commitment is, and why that should matter.

[18] While there can be room for debate surrounding Rawls (1971) as to whether he endorses luck egalitarianism, there is less ambiguity with respect to Rawls (2001). There

As mentioned, for Rawls the luck/choice distinction is a relevant one in determining what equality requires. Rawls is explicit that the purpose of the veil of ignorance at the original position is to factor out contingencies that are morally arbitrary. Some commentators have taken such references  as indications that Rawls is a luck egalitarian, whereas others who read Rawls as a democratic egalitarian, I believe, downplay the significance of these references to moral arbitrariness (Freeman 2006a).

In my account of luck egalitarianism, Rawls's multiple references to moral arbitrariness are in line with his non-luck egalitarianism because, simply, while he holds that mitigating the effects of contingencies is a guiding idea when working out what equality requires, the mitigation of contingencies is not the reason why society should care about equality in  the first place. For Rawls it is explicit in his later writings that equality matters because of democratic reciprocity.[19] Understanding luck egalitarianism as an account of why equality matters thus allows us a tidy way of reading Rawls as a non-luck egalitarian.

The general point of these remarks is this: if luck egalitarianism is a label accorded to any theory of equality that invokes at some stage of its construction the distinction between luck and choice, then it ceases to be a very distinctive account of equality because it captures most accounts of equality (including Rawls). Understood specifically as an account of the ground of equality, however, it identifies a distinctive position.

## 4.6 Luck egalitarianism and the difference principle

If luck egalitarianism is a grounding principle and not a substantive distributive principle in the sense described above, what substantive principle can luck egalitarianism ground? Just as democratic egalitarians can

Rawls is quite explicit that it is democratic reciprocity that motivates the commitment to equality in society, not luck mitigation (Rawls 2001: 49, 124). See Hurley's reading of Rawls as a nascent luck egalitarian (Hurley 2003: Ch. 5), and Freeman's and Scheffler's understanding of Rawls as not (Freeman 2006a: Ch. 6; Scheffler 2003a).

[19] See also the discussions of how Rawls's egalitarian commitment connects with the moral arbitrariness principle in Nagel (2005) and Sangiovanni (2007). In Sangiovanni's case it is not clear if he takes this to show that Rawls adopts a form of luck egalitarianism or that Rawls is not really a luck egalitarianism. This may seem an idle semantic point, but it is significant because it relies on what we take luck egalitarianism to be a response to. As said, if we read it, as I am and will be proposing, as a response to equality's ground, democratic equality and luck egalitarianism are mutually exclusive types.

disagree with one another as to what substantive principle of distributive democratic equality commits them to, so luck egalitarians will disagree about what substantive distributive principle best reflects the luck egalitarian ideal. But just as we don't dismiss democratic equality just because there is internal disagreement among democratic egalitarians, so there is no ground to dismiss luck egalitarianism just because at the moment luck egalitarians disagree with each other on this point. What is important, if it there is to be confidence in its plausibility, is that luck egalitarianism can provide some indication as to what form of substantive principle it could ground. Thus let me briefly consider how luck egalitarian could ground something like Rawls's difference principle.

To start, the difference principle, as a substantive distributive principle, even though distinct from its grounding principle, must of course reflect in some way the grounding principle. In Rawls's later writings as presented in *Justice as Fairness*, even though the luck/choice distinction is not irrelevant in working out the difference principle, what is central are considerations of reciprocity. The difference principle, as Rawls there notes, expresses "the reciprocity condition: those who are better off . . . are not better off to the detriment of those who are worse off" (Rawls 2001: 123; also 49, 76–7). But things were less clear cut in his earlier writings. In *A Theory of Justice*, Rawls allows that the difference principle could be derived from a luck egalitarian basis, and in parts of that work suggests how the difference principle in fact reflects a luck egalitarian starting point.[20] I will exploit this point by proposing how the difference principle could be derived from a luck egalitarian grounding principle. I will suggest that the unavoidable ambiguity between luck and choice makes the difference principle a plausible derivation of the luck egalitarian ideal.[21]

[20] In *A Theory of Justice*, Rawls allows possible "ethical variations," as he puts it, in specifying the original position, and explicitly notes that the nullification of contingencies could be the key consideration of the parties in the original position, which he contrasts with the argument from reciprocity. He writes: "For example, one might assume that the parties hold the principle that no one should be advantaged by unmerited assets and contingencies, and therefore they choose a conception of justice that mitigates the effects of natural accidents and social fortune. Or else they may be said to accept a principle of reciprocity" (Rawls 1971: 585). This luck egalitarian alternative is also present in Rawls's *Political Liberalism* (id. 1993), as I will note in the text. That Rawls's early arguments in *Theory*, on his own understanding, allows for a luck egalitarian interpretation explains the prevalence of reading Rawls (1971) as a luck egalitarian.

[21] I think my outline here is consistent with Rawls's reasoning, though I am not claiming to do a reconstruction of Rawls's luck egalitarian arguments for the difference principle.

First, recall the egalitarian default as given by luck egalitarianism: equal distribution is the default and this means no inequalities due to luck (as per the luck egalitarian ideal); and that departures from this default have to be justified. How are inequalities to the advantage of the worst-off justified under this condition without undermining the luck egalitarian ideal? After  all, why should the one luckily in possession of the needed skill benefit extra at all?[22] It is here that the ineliminable vagueness between what is really luck and what is choice becomes relevant and a virtue (so to speak): if we accept this imprecision, then it seems that something like the difference principle might be the best that we can and need to have. Assuming a society of two classes, advantaged and disadvantaged, the justification for the inequality has to be to both: to the disadvantaged class, we need to explain why the residual inequality is acceptable (why, that is, the talented should be given the extra-reward if the worst-off benefits most when society does this). To the advantaged class, we need to explain why the inequality has to be limited, why inequalities are acceptable only if the worst-off benefits from them.

First to the disadvantaged, the response is that we have to permit some inequalities (i.e. extra-rewards for the skilled) because we do not know  with sufficient definitiveness when luck ceases and effort kicks in with regard to the advantaged members of society. In general, we presume that some of the gains have to be due to luck, that the fruition of his talents are due to various happenstance besides personal application, hence we do not hold that the talented person is really entitled to all that he can get by virtue of the exercise of his talents (see Rawls 1993: 282–4; 2001: 51). Yet we also know that some has to be due to effort, including the effort of cultivating talents, of applying the talents once cultivated, and so on, and so we have to permit the talented to keep some of his extra earnings. Nothing so far is at odds with luck egalitarianism. What we need next then is a device for finding the appropriate balance, between what the talented may keep and what he has to give up. While as a matter of social convention we hold that a person's natural talents, or social class by birth, is a matter of luck, while choice and effort is not, it nonetheless remains indeterminate in evaluating a person's success how much of it exactly is due to luck (of talent, say) and how much to choice (of effort).

---

[22] This is one of Cohen's problems with Rawls's difference principle (G. A. Cohen 2008: 156–61).

Since there is no prior convention for determining this, the original position procedure can be invoked as a means of coming to an agreement on this matter. Note that this has to be only a device for arriving at an agreeable balance, not a device for arriving at a true or correct answer. The difference principle arrived at via the original position provides an agreeable way of balancing these competing considerations.

The justification for the talented proceeds similarly, although this time we need to explain to them why it is acceptable that they have to relinquish some of what they take to be their entitled earnings. Again the presumption here is that some of the talented's earnings have to be due to luck rather than choice effort, and so on luck egalitarian requirement, those part of the earnings due to luck have to be foregone. But which part and how much? Again, there can be no right answer here, but egalitarianism demands some way of operationalizing the cut; and the original position procedure can offer a method of settling this matter. The difference principle that is derived reflects the luck egalitarian ideal that persons are not entitled to gains due to luck but are entitled to gains due to effort. The difference principle does this not by claiming that it truly reflects the cut between choice and luck, but by providing a way that can be agreed on for normatively approximating the distinction.

Hence the inescapable vagueness of the luck/choice distinction allows an explanation as to why the difference principle is not inconsistent with luck egalitarianism. The principle allows for a way of splitting the difference in light of the acknowledged indeterminacy of choice versus luck. As Rawls notes (in his more luck egalitarian rendition of his principle), the difference principle *gives expression* to the idea that while the person contributing more to society deserves more because she has expended more effort (somewhere along the line), her ability is also influenced by "happenstance" (Rawls 1993: 283, 283–4).

One might think that luck egalitarians would find the difference principle too ham-fisted a principle, because after all there are clear-cut cases of advantages accruing purely to luck that we could isolate and should target. Take the most obvious case, such as a person's inheritance. Why should any luck egalitarian allow the terms of legitimate inheritance to be governed at some point by the difference principle, rather than insist that this is all due to luck and so no one has the right to any of her inheritance? The response to this problem can parallel that suggested above with regard to talents and effort. This time the competing ideas to be balanced are that of personal freedom versus some ideal of equality starting point. That is, a person's inheritance is morally arbitrary under luck egalitarianism (just as one's natural endowment is); yet the passing on of a heritage is an expression of choice to a degree on the part of the benefactor. After all, it can be assumed that she opted to save her (by hypothesis, just) holdings for her descendants instead of indulging herself. So just as the difference principle, as outlined above, can be seen as a principle by which an implementable agreed-upon split between talents (luck) and effort (choice) can be arrived at, so too can the difference principle be seen as a principle by which to arrive at an agreeable split between inheritance (luck) and freedom of benefactor (choice).

One might ask: "In what way is an egalitarian principle a luck egalitarian principle if the pattern of distribution it entails bears no formal resemblance to the luck/choice principle? What is the point of luck egalitarianism in this case?" This question challenges the normative contribution of reading luck egalitarianism more narrowly as a grounding principle of equality than as a substantive distributive principle itself. That is, what difference does it make, then, it we were to adopt luck egalitarianism or democratic equality? In reply, the point of luck egalitarianism is that it offers a distinct understanding of the point of egalitarianism and why it should matter, and this distinctive understanding remains even if the substantive distributive principle it arrives at could coincide with one that (some) democratic egalitarians also endorse. More to the point of  the question, even if a luck egalitarian arrives at a distributive pattern (i.e. a substantive principle) identical to one that democratic egalitarians endorse, this does not mean that there is no substantive normative difference between the two. Because of their different grounding of equality, they could potentially differ over the scope of equality. They may agree on the difference principle as the substantive principle, but disagree over its reach. This will be the subject of Part III.

A substantive distributive principle (in this case, the difference principle) must of course reflect the ideals of the principle that justifies or grounds it. But this does not mean that it has to mimic the formal character of the grounding principle. It reflects the grounding principle by living up to the  ideals expressed by the grounding principle; but it does not mean that it has to mirror exactly the grounding principle. I am suggesting that the difference principle can be understood as a substantive expression of a more basic luck egalitarian principle. Luck egalitarianism can be read as a grounding principle for the difference principle, not because the difference principle takes the formal character of a luck neutralization principle (it clearly does not), but because it can be seen to express the ideals of that principle.[23]

## 4.7 Conclusion

My account of luck egalitarianism is at variance with some dominant accounts. It treats luck egalitarianism explicitly *not* as a doctrine about the whole of justice, let alone the whole of morality, but as a explanation for why *distributive* equality matters, that is, strictly as an explanation for why economic and social inequalities between persons ought to be mitigated by some distributive principle. Moreover, luck egalitarianism does not by itself offer a substantive distributive principle or an account of the currency of equality; rather its purpose is to provide a justificatory basis for why there must be some distributive commitments among individuals. That is, it is strictly a response to the question as to why distributive equality is of value, and is not in itself a complete response to the questions of what and how to distribute. Finally, luck egalitarianism can retain the institutional focus of social justice. Thus luck egalitarians need not implausibly hold that nature is itself just or unjust; rather, it is the way institutions  translate natural facts into advantages and disadvantages for persons that presents questions of justice for the luck egalitarian. If a label can prove useful, I can call my position *institutional luck egalitarianism*.

Yet institutional luck egalitarianism is still distinctively a *luck* egalitarian position and fundamentally different from democratic equality. First, even though it is limited to the domain of distributive justice, within that specific domain it takes the luck/choice principle to be fundamental. Second, even though it takes the subject matter of distributive justice to be social institutions rather than natural facts, it is still a *luck* egalitarian position in that it holds that institutions ought not to turn natural contingencies into social advantages or disadvantages. Finally, it offers a very

---

[23] Shiffrin has put this point well: to accept the "moral arbitrariness of talents" principle as a justificatory principle for our substantive distributive principle does not mean that the substantive distributive principle has to be an "isomorphic 'correlate'" of the grounding principle" (Shiffrin 2010: 121).

different (direct) defense of distributive equality as of value in itself as compared with democratic equality.

In the next chapter, I will argue that this modest conception of luck egalitarianism has the advantage of evading or deflecting certain objections to which more standard accounts are vulnerable.

# 5

# Defending Luck Egalitarianism

Luck egalitarianism, in spite of its initial appeal, has come under some severe criticisms in recent debate. Some of the prominent objections may be stated as follows: (i) luck egalitarianism is a morally implausible account of equality given the absurd moral implications of its luck/choice principle; (ii) luck egalitarianism is an implausibly asocial account of equality given its fixation on mitigating the effects of luck on persons' life chances while failing to pay attention to the social relations among persons; and (iii) luck egalitarianism is a philosophically implausible account because of its reliance on the philosophically imprecise if not dubious distinction between luck and choice.

These objections attack the fundamental ideas of luck egalitarianism, objections that if left to stand will render luck egalitarianism, however developed in other respects, fatally flawed. Thus, any attempt to refine a luck egalitarian account of distributive equality will be moot unless these basic objections can be responded to. My goal in this chapter is to see how these objections can be countered. I will argue that some of the objections are repelled once we get clear on the special justificatory purpose of luck egalitarianism and also the notion of luck/choice it relies on. Other basic objections will be deflected, I claim, if we are able to understand the contours of luck egalitarianism in the ways I have proposed earlier, that is, as having a special domain and site of operation. Since my account of luck egalitarianism may seem too revisionist to some luck egalitarians (thus able to evade objections only at the cost of giving up the central idea of the defended position), I will close with some comments to alleviate this concern.

## 5.1  The objections

Let me start by spelling out the objections outlined above. The first objection is that luck egalitarianism is morally implausible because of the implications of its luck/choice principle. The objection thus has the form of a reductio argument: the core principle of luck egalitarianism, it alleges, actually leads to morally absurd and intolerable conclusions. Accordingly, any initial intuitiveness or appeal of the luck egalitarian ideal is only illusionary; on further reflection it is in actuality, so it is alleged, rather counter-intuitive. The following cases are commonly presented as evidence of its implausibility. First, it is argued that luck egalitarians have to hold that one who has chosen poorly and who has consequently squandered everything and is in dire straits is not entitled to social assistance (Anderson 1999; Scheffler 2003a, 2005). But this would be morally counter-intuitive.[1] Second, luck egalitarians will have to be in the business of compensating persons for all of their good and bad luck, including, for example, providing publicly-funded plastic surgery for the unlucky ugly person; this is clearly an absurdity (Anderson 1999: 335). Lastly, it is argued that luck egalitarians have to imply that the person whose life is not going so well because of bad luck has a less worthy life, and so even when luck egalitarians come to the assistance of victims of poor luck, they hold that person in contempt or pity (Anderson 1999: 302 ff.; Wolff 1998: 109–13). In general, the first objection takes luck egalitarianism to be morally implausible because of its implied harshness toward the imprudent, its over-commitment to the naturally unlucky, and its disrespect for those it aims to assist.

---

[1] See Fleurbaey for an earlier discussion of these problems (Fleurbaey 1995: 40–2). As Scheffler puts it, "[m]ost people do not insist, as a general matter, that someone who makes a bad decision thereby forfeits all claims to assistance" (Scheffler 2005: 15). He calls this luck egalitarianism's "tendency to a rigid and unsympathetic moralism" (ibid.: 16). With reference to Dworkin's distinction between "brute" and "option luck," Anderson has argued that luck egalitarianism fails to show respect to "victims of bad option luck" (Anderson 1999: 303–7). Recall that option luck pertains to the outcome of gambles freely chosen (so a person who freely speculates on the stock market and loses all suffers from bad option luck), whereas brute luck concerns luck in matters over which an agent has no choice at all (so a person who is born disabled suffers bad brute luck) (Dworkin 2000: 73–4). In either case, that of the makers of a bad choice or victims of bad option luck, the thrust of the objection is that luck egalitarians do not show moral concern for people who are suffering some calamity that they could have realistically avoided by choice at some point. For discussions on the distinction between brute luck and option luck, see Vallentyne (2002) and Lippert-Rasmussen (2001).

The second objection seeks to expose the mistaken understanding of equality underlying the luck egalitarian project. It takes luck egalitarianism to task for being wrongly asocial and hence missing the whole point of equality. Because of their fixation on mitigating the effects of luck on persons' lives, and so given their fixation on how people relate to their own bad or good luck, luck egalitarians fail to appreciate properly that equality is a social ideal. The point of equality is to regulate the relationship between persons in a social order, and once this point is correctly acknowledged, it will be seen that mitigating the effects of luck on persons' lives is quite beside the point (Anderson 1999: 312–16; Scheffler 2003a: 21–4; 2005).

As a symptom of this problem, a further criticism can be raised, which is that luck egalitarianism is an incomplete account of distributive justice. Distributive justice is concerned with the background rules of society that determine persons' entitlements; yet the luck egalitarian principle has only the form of a principle of redress (Freeman 2006a: 132–5). That is, instead of seeking to regulate the social background conditions against which persons' entitlements and ownership rights are to be determined, it seeks only, so it is charged, to compensate persons for their misfortune while taxing others for their good fortune, and says nothing about the social or background conditions of ownership in society. One might say, with the objection, that luck egalitarianism is not truly a distributive principle in that it does not pay heed to the antecedent conditions that determine persons' entitlements, but is only merely *re*distributive in the sense that it applies only post facto as a corrective principle, that is, serving to reallocate resources after an initial distribution has been made.

The third objection is that luck egalitarianism must either contentiously presuppose some account of metaphysical libertarianism, or its luck/choice distinction cannot have the "across the board make or break significance" that is expected of it. In other words, luck egalitarians face a dilemma: either they venture perilously into the metaphysical deep waters of the freedom versus determinism debate and demonstrate the reality of personal freedom; or they cease and desist from giving the luck/choice principle such a prominent normative role as they appear to do (e.g. Scheffler 2005).

In the next three sections of this chapter, I attempt to respond to these charges—that luck egalitarianism is implausible, mistakenly asocial, and philosophically dubious. No doubt there are other philosophical burdens that a complete defense of luck egalitarianism will need to bear, such as clarifying further the notion of luck, providing arguments for its ideal of moral equality that I mentioned is its presumed starting point, and so on. But in addressing the above objections, my goal is to try to restore initial plausibility to the luck egalitarian ideal, thus motivating and encouraging and justifying continuing discussion and refinement of that ideal of why equality matters.

## 5.2 Why luck egalitarianism is not morally implausible

### 5.2.1 Harshness toward the imprudent

As mentioned above, one argument in support of the moral implausibility charge is that luck egalitarianism is indifferent to the suffering of people whose plight is due to their own poor choices. The person who has made a bad choice freely and is now severely suffering from it is not entitled to social assistance. The objection appeals to our moral intuition that a person facing serious deprivation is entitled to assistance or rescue from society. The reductio argument relies significantly then, for its force, on the severe nature of the situation confronting the person who has made the impru-  dent choice freely. The objection will not put the same pressure on luck egalitarians if it is not presumed that the imprudent, on account of her bad choice, is in dire straits, as opposed to merely having less compared to others with which to pursue her ends.

But once the source of the objection's force is properly located, we can see that it does not touch luck egalitarianism, if its limited domain is appreciated in the way I have proposed. The objection attributes to luck egalitarianism a more spacious operative moral domain than luck egalitar-  ians need to claim. Luck egalitarianism is an account of the grounds of distributive equality, and nothing about luck egalitarianism so understood rules out other moral considerations in favor of assisting or rescuing persons in dire straits. The luck/choice principle provides guidance for how resources and goods, above the basic minimum people need, are to be assigned, but it can defer to other principles when the case at hand falls under the domain of basic needs. Assuming a division of moral domains, luck egalitarians can easily accept arguments based on, say, basic rights. They could, consistent with their luck egalitarian ideal, hold that persons deprived of basic needs retain a principled claim to assistance in spite of their own bad choices. These basic rights considerations do not clash with the luck/choice principle that persons are to be held responsible for their choices, because they apply within different domains.

The relevant contrast between duties of assistance and duties of distributive justice is not that the former is not enforceable whereas the latter is. To the contrary, a duty of assistance can be institutional and (hence) also enforceable. Institutional principles are not limited to principles of distributive justice. The contrast here is the different forms of the principles: a duty of assistance is not comparative, whereas a duty of distributive justice is (see Chapter 1). That is, luck egalitarianism, I am proposing, is concerned with comparative allocation of goods to individuals and need not be regarded as a general principle of allocation.

In short, there are moral reasons for assisting persons in distress that are distinct from considerations of distributive justice. Principles of basic rights or human decency can require that a person deprived of basic needs be rescued or assisted, even if the deprivation was due to her own imprudence. And it will indeed be considered a moral duty owed to these victims rather than mere charity. We may even insist on calling such a duty a duty of justice broadly conceived, but this is still distinct from the more specific duty of *distributive* justice. The luck/choice principle, designed for the domain of distributive justice, does not kick in here to oppose considerations in favor of rescue.

So by understanding luck egalitarianism strictly as an account of the grounds of *distributive justice* as opposed to an all-encompassing moral principle or a general principle of resource or goods assignment, we can see that it need not rule out other moral arguments (based on basic rights, for example) for a duty to provide for people's basic and urgent needs that have nothing to do with the luck/choice distinction. What it insists on, more modestly, is that when it comes to distributing resources and goods among individuals above the minimum threshold (as determined by basic rights, for example), the luck/choice principle becomes salient. There is nothing in the basic principle of luck egalitarianism that suggests that individuals are to be held responsible for their choices but not their luck, which inherently rules out this confined application of the principle. A person who has been rendered severely disabled because of some activity that she willingly undertook is entitled as a matter of right or human decency to some social assistance, without which she cannot live a remotely decent human life. That it was her choice (or her bad option luck) that led to her disability is immaterial, for the luck/choice principle is simply an inappropriate principle to call on here. Indeed, as I noted earlier, it is commonly accepted that distributive justice presupposes a prior basic needs commitment, and so, instead of ruling out basic rescue to the severely needy, luck egalitarianism as a doctrine of distributive equality must in fact operate on this presumption.

It is in fact curious that democratic egalitarians do not think that an analogous *reductio ad absurdum* could be turned against them. Critics of democratic equality can charge that democratic equality is counter-intuitive because it is not responsive to the severe suffering of non-members of a democratic order. For instance, it seems compelled to say that foreigners deprived of basic needs are not entitled to any assistance at all from us since we don't stand in reciprocal democratic relation with them. To avoid this embarrassing implication, democratic egalitarians too must presuppose some division of moral domains, and stake the democratic equality principle only within the domain of distributive justice. They must accept something along the lines that although distributive equality commitments apply only among members of a democratic order, there are obligations based on other moral principles to meet the humanitarian needs of all persons.

Indeed, if democratic egalitarians do not accept some division of moral domains of the sort described above, it will be unclear how democratic egalitarians who tie their account of distributive justice to membership in a democratic society can justify providing assistance to foreigners deprived of urgent needs. Democratic egalitarians may affirm the duty of assistance as a global principle (which many do) while denying a duty of global distributive justice (as many also do) only if they accept, as Nagel for example does, the distinct domains of the morality of assistance and that of distributive justice, and accept that there are (globally applicable) reasons to assist persons in dire needs that are distinct from (societally limited) reasons of distributive justice.

It can be seen then that the objection that luck egalitarians neglect the imprudent in need of rescuing rests on a category mistake of sorts. It mistakenly applies the luck egalitarian principle to a category of cases (for example, cases of urgent and basic needs) to which it is not designed to apply. Not surprisingly, then, the principle is easily (but wrongly) shown to result in absurdity. The reductio objection has to invoke cases of severe deprivation (that luck egalitarians allegedly neglect) in order to demonstrate the alleged absurdity. Yet precisely because of this, the objection misses the target entirely. By shifting the discussion from that of distributive justice to that of basic needs, it changes the subject.

It is correct that some luck egalitarians quite expressly intend the luck/choice principle to have a general across-the-board application, and so accordingly society has no obligation at all to persons suffering severely because of their own bad choices (or option luck).[2] To be sure, this "hard-line" version of luck egalitarianism (as Anderson labels it) concedes that luck egalitarianism allows for the withholding of any assistance from people in dire straits because of their poor choices, and accepts the burden of explaining why this is not an absurdity (Anderson 1999: 298). My contention is that it is not necessary for any luck egalitarian to assume this burden, nor should any want to. The core of the luck egalitarian doctrine and its distinctiveness as an account of the basis of distributive equality can be preserved even as we confine the luck/choice principle to the domain of distributive justice (thus evading the charge of absurdity). Luck egalitarianism, I have suggested, can be understood specifically as a response to the question "What is the ground of *distributive equality?*" and not an account of morality in general. When the question that luck egalitarianism is supposed to address is framed narrowly as a question about the ground of distributive equality, there is no reason why luck egalitarians should be tempted to claim a larger moral domain of application than the question requires. Luck egalitarianism can be constructively interpreted in this more morally modest way without losing its important distinctiveness as an account of why distributive equality matters.

Some luck egalitarians, in defense of the hard-line view, may claim that the luck/choice principle should have an across-the-board application *even in the domain of basic needs* and thus take issue with my attempt to limit that principle to the domain of distributive justice. For instance, they may point out that when there are not enough basic goods to go around, it would seem plausible that the persistent maker of bad choices not be given the goods over the person who had been really unlucky.

But my account can accept this intuitive point, so long as the claim here is not anchored on the premise that the maker of a bad choice is *as a matter of principle* not entitled to these goods. What my account can accept is that

*Reject the hardline version*

---

[2] For example, Rakowski 1991: 153.

the maker of a bad choice in this case will unfortunately not get what she is in fact entitled to as a matter of humanitarian principle because of other considerations (such as abject scarcity), that her claim is overridden by the claim of another. This does not mean that she is no longer as a matter of principle entitled to assistance; she remains entitled and this entitlement is not invalidated. It is just that, under the circumstance, it is possible that her principled claim is overridden by other considerations.[3] Recall that the objection that we started out with was that luck egalitarians have to say that the maker of a poor choice forfeits any social assistance to even basic needs as a matter of principle. We can deny this objection while maintaining that social circumstances can be such that, tragically, sometimes persons don't get what they in principle have a claim to. Choice can be a tie-breaker even in the domain of basic needs in tragic situations *without* implying the premise that a person who has made a bad choice forfeits all claim to assistance.

In other words, it does not seem to me that there is much to be gained by giving the luck/choice principle across the board significance; yet there is much to lose. The purported advantage of the hard-line approach, that of guiding the allocation of resources under conditions of severe scarcity, is also available to my account. My account does not lead to the absurdity that agents' imprudence carries no consideration when society is determining the allocation of scare resources in cases of humanitarian needs.

A luck egalitarian could claim with the hard-line approach that the luck/choice principle has across-the-board application while denying that it falls into the alleged absurdity as claimed in the moral implausibility objection. One dominant account of this sort is in Dworkin, and it is worth looking briefly at Dworkin's view to see how my account differs. Dworkin (in responding specifically to Scheffler's forceful challenge) argues that on his egalitarian theory people "deprived of urgent needs" because of their own past decisions would not be left out in the cold, *pace* Scheffler, because "equal concern requires that everyone be given the benefit of a hypothetical insurance regime that would meet the 'urgent needs' [Scheffler] has in mind" (Dworkin 2003: 192). That is, rational and prudent individuals would want to insure themselves against being

---

[3] Consider Dworkin's well-known point that principles can be overridden without being invalidated (Dworkin 1977: 25–7).

deprived of urgent needs (presumably even as a result of their own poor choices), and so a just society should replicate the distributive allocation of an imaginary society in which persons enjoy initial equality of resources and in which they have the option of taking out such an insurance policy. Thus, a just society has the collective responsibility to provide for persons thus deprived, and so, contra the charge, Dworkin argues, a society regulated by his luck egalitarian principles does not leave makers of bad choices to their seriously dire fates.

As is clear, Dworkin responds to the charge (that luck egalitarianism is disrespectful of victims of poor choices or bad option luck) not by limiting the domain of the luck/choice principle (as my account does), but on the contrary by invoking the luck/choice principle, and showing how the luck/choice principle coupled with his ideal of an insurance market can justify social support for persons in destitution even if this is due to their own bad choices. My account, on the other hand, pre-empts the Scheffler-type charge altogether by denying that the luck/choice principle has any application in such cases, and defers these cases to some other principle (e.g. a principle of humanitarian assistance). By delimiting the application of the luck/choice principle, my account leaves it open for other principles to be invoked to ground some duty to rescue the makers of bad choices from dire straits. While Dworkin's approach has the advantage of unity— his luck egalitarianism aims to account for both cases of *distributive justice* and *basic needs*—its success ultimately depends on the acceptability of his argument that a hypothetical insurance market would provide insurance coverage for persons' basic needs regardless of past personal choice.

Yet Dworkin's argument is controversial, it seems to me, because on Dworkin's own understanding and description of the insurance market it is not obvious that persons will indeed have the benefit of such a policy. Though it is, plausibly, rational and prudent for persons to want to take up insurance coverage against severe deprivation regardless of past choice, it is doubtful that it would be rational and prudent for any insurance provider to offer such a coverage, for this policy effectively guarantees the basic needs of persons with no consideration whatsoever of their personal conduct. Such a coverage would be either too costly for insurance providers to offer; or, if insurance providers were to offer this coverage without loss, its premiums would be too high for the average rational person to want to purchase. Considerations of what insurance policies providers in the hypothetical insurance market would find profitable and prudent to offer are hugely important to Dworkin's theory of egalitarian justice, for they are appealed to in order to set the upper limits on the levels of coverage that are available to individuals in his imaginary world. For example, in the hypothetical insurance market, there can be no policy guaranteeing a person a "movie-star's wage" and no policy for "highly speculative and marginal" healthcare because, Dworkin argues, such policies will either be too expensive for rational persons to want to buy or too unprofitable for providers to want to sell (Dworkin 2000: 88–98, 345). Because these kinds of coverage would not be available for any rational person to purchase in the hypothetical insurance market, individuals in the real world will have no claim against society for such guarantees. So, analogously, one can argue that an insurance policy guaranteeing people their basic needs without regard to their habitual conduct would not be available under Dworkin's hypothetical insurance market, and so in the real world individuals cannot have any claim against society to cover their  basic needs *without regard to their own past conduct*. Thus, it is not clear if Dworkin succeeds in showing that the luck/choice principle can be invoked to ensure that persons are not left to perish because of their own bad decisions. His insurance idea, invented originally for the purpose of protecting persons against *bad luck*, cannot be extended to protect persons against their own detrimental *bad choices*, and hence does not successfully, it seems to me, deflect Scheffler's challenge which has to do with protecting people against their own bad choices. My account of luck egalitarianism, even if not all-encompassing in the way that Dworkin's aspires to be, is not only consistent with the commonly accepted division of moral domains between the realms of humanitarianism and distributive justice, as mentioned earlier, but has the added advantage of being able immediately and straightforwardly to deflect Scheffler's objection without having to invoke controversial arguments about the workings of a hypothetical insurance market by appealing uncontroversially to the background division of moral domains.

Another luck egalitarian, Shlomi Segall, has defended luck egalitarianism against Scheffler-type objections by presenting the luck/choice principle  as a defeasible principle, that is, as a principle that can be overridden by other moral principles (Segall 2007: 177–98; also 2010). In Segall's account, there is no need to limit the luck/choice principle to the domain of distributive justice; it can still apply across the board to cases of basic needs as well as distributive justice so long as it can be potentially overridden also across the board. For Segall, the principle of solidarity comes to the rescue of the severely impaired imprudent, for in such cases solidarity with the imprudent outweighs the requirements of the luck/choice principle. Thus Segall allows the luck/choice principle to have across-the-board application by qualifying this broad application with the provision that it is a defeasible principle.

This is an insightful conceptualization of the luck egalitarian principle. But Segall's model rescues luck egalitarianism by weakening its status throughout, and so offers a Pyrrhic victory. The significance and distinctiveness of luck egalitarianism as an account of equality is eliminated, if even within the domain of distributive justice the luck/choice principle is defeasible. Indeed, given the significance Segall accords the principle of solidarity in his account of justice, one might wonder what real role is left to the luck/choice principle in this approach. Couldn't the principle of solidarity be invoked to account for distributive equality in addition to the rescuing of the imprudent? Indeed, Segall's account of solidarity seems to be another specification of democratic reciprocity, and thus accordingly his solidarity-qualified luck egalitarianism seems to collapse into democratic equality. The luck/choice principle risks becoming redundant in this rendition. Some ideal of democratic equality, the ideal of solitary for Segall, appears to be more basic than the luck/choice principle. My approach in contrast, and advantageously, maintains the primacy of the luck/choice principle within the domain of distributive justice.[4]

### 5.2.2 Compensates for all natural misfortunes

Consider next the argument that luck egalitarianism has to be in the absurd business of providing social compensation for any of a person's natural bad luck. For example, Elizabeth Anderson argues that luck egalitarians must counter-intuitively compensate ugly people who find their bad looks distressing, "perhaps in the form of publicly subsidized plastic surgery" (Anderson 1999: 335).

---

[4] Now solidarity for Segall is not contingent on shared citizenship, as he makes clearer in his later writings (Segall 2010). But if this notion of moral solidarity as opposed to democratic solidarity prevents his position from becoming a democratic equality position, it still makes it not basically a luck egalitarian position; for even on matters of distributive justice, what is ultimately doing the work is the ideal of solidarity, not luck mitigation. See also Casal's notion of "sufficiency-constrained luck egalitarianism" (Casal 2007: 35). My account is perhaps closer to Casal's constrained luck egalitarianism, although Casal's rationale for her "hybrid" view is based on the costs/benefits of (not) compensating severe situations versus less severe ones, whereas mine is based on the distinction of moral domains (ibid.: 36).

If this absurdity is indeed what luck egalitarianism is forced into, one  should be prepared to concede that it is an implausible account of distributive justice. The example of ugliness seems trivial, but it is of course deliberate and is what gives the reductio argument its supposed force, that luck egalitarians are preposterously forced into responding to trivialities of this sort.

But luck egalitarianism need not be committed to this kind of absurdity. First, as mentioned, luck egalitarianism is not necessarily a welfarist position. So, just because a person scores poorly on a welfare scale because of his (real or perceived) bad luck of, say, being born ugly does not mean that luck egalitarians must compensate him for his lower welfare. A luck egalitarian who is an egalitarian about resources, for instance, will not be fazed by the person's ugliness so long as that person does not get less than his fair share of resources on account of his ugliness. So, at the very best, the objection strikes only luck egalitarians who are also welfare egalitarians.

More significantly, a luck egalitarian need not be a resource egalitarian to escape this charge of absurdity.[5] There is a more generic point about luck egalitarianism that immunizes it against this charge independently of how luck egalitarians understand the currency of distributive equality. On the *institutional* luck egalitarian view I have proposed, luck egalitarians will not take it to be their concern to correct for every natural misfortune that comes along. What luck egalitarianism is concerned with, on my account,  is *how institutions deal with* luck, not luck per se. A person who is ugly may truly be unlucky, but luck egalitarians have nothing to say about this unless it were the case that social institutions were such that ugly people were in fact put at a social disadvantage. Adopting a luck egalitarian position within institutional justice straightaway limits the types of cases of bad or good luck that would excite the luck egalitarian. Luck impinges on the whole of our lives. Within the rules of just institutions, the friends and personal relations we forge are subject to luck. But luck egalitarianism as an institutional view of justice is silent about these matters so long as they do not distort persons' institutionally mediated entitlements.[6]

Most of us can accept Anderson's intuition that it would be absurd to compensate people who are ugly because, or so we would hope in any

---

[5] Thus, though I am partial to resource egalitarianism, my defense of luck egalitarianism is I believe neutral with respect to the currency of equality.

[6] I take this point to hold even if we presume institutional *welfare* egalitarianism, if it is not institutions as such that have diminished the ugly person's welfare.

case, ordinary ugliness is not a natural trait that institutions in our society turn into actual social disadvantage for persons. Such people may be less happy, but this is not necessarily an issue of justice for distributive egalitarians (unless we presupposed some form of direct welfare egalitarianism). So it would possibly be absurd if society were obliged to provide those who deem themselves ugly with publicly funded plastic surgery. But our moral response to the matter surely changes if it were the case that society did disadvantage ugly people. In this case, luck egalitarians would take ugliness as a concern of justice and this would be far from counter-intuitive. They would want institutions and social norms about appearances to be reformed (through education, legislation, etc.); or if (counterfactually) social institutions could not help disadvantaging somewhat people perceived to be ugly, then they would want existing institutions to be supplemented by additional arrangements to compensate the ugly for their institutionalized disadvantage. Under this scenario, a matter of natural luck has, because of institutional intervention, become a matter of actual disadvantage and luck egalitarians would, and not absurdly so, be exercised by this, because of how institutions or background norms are treating this brute natural fact, and not because of persons' ugliness per se. Yet this is still a staunchly *luck* egalitarian position, because the concern is with how institutions handle the natural fortunes or misfortunes of persons.

Some luck egalitarians like Richard Arneson will insist that "the natural fact that people are susceptible to disease, accident, and natural catastrophe" themselves does present issues of social justice (Arneson 2000: 346). Yet not only must this view of social justice be defended against the institutional approach (as argued for in the previous section), but more relevantly for our present purpose, this trans-institutional approach falls prey to Anderson's fatal objection without any compensating advantages over the institutional alternative. My version of luck egalitarianism which ties natural facts to institutions preserves the attractive central intuition of luck egalitarians, like Arneson's, that the social disadvantages faced by, say, the unfortunate disabled person constitute an objectionable social injustice. The difference is that on my account, contra Arneson, the locus of this injustice lies not in nature or the cosmic order but in institutions, that is, in what institutions make of persons' disabilities. So my account, by maintaining an institutional focus, advantageously side-steps the charge that luck egalitarians absurdly treat the natural order as a subject of social

justice while preserving the core intuition of luck egalitarianism, namely
that persons should not be socially disadvantaged because of bad luck.

### 5.2.3  Disrespect for the unlucky

The claim here is that when luck egalitarians come to the aid of the
unfortunate, the motivating premise is that the victim is living a life that
is less worthwhile (as the result of her misfortune). Rather than expressing
equal respect for persons, this reflects some kind of contempt, pity, or
disrespect for the unlucky (Anderson 1999: 302–7; also Wolff 1998: 109–12).
From the preceding paragraphs, we can perhaps anticipate how the first
part of the worry should be dealt with. First, on one interpretation, the
objection seems to assume falsely that luck egalitarians must necessarily be
egalitarians about welfare, and so has to impute to the unlucky that her life
is going so poorly (perhaps even in spite of her own perception) as to be
less worthy. But if luck egalitarianism takes the form of a resource egalitarian position, then it need not make such judgments about the quality of
a person's life. In this case, its concern is with a person's legitimate resource
entitlements, not whether her life or her conception of the good is worthy
or not. Conceived as a form of resource egalitarianism, luck egalitarianism's central point will be that persons' entitlements as defined by the
institutions of their society should not be determined by arbitrary natural
factors. The guarantee to all persons of their legitimate entitlement is a
mark of equal respect, not disrespect or contempt, and the focus is on
persons' legitimate entitlements, not the worthiness of their life as such.

Moreover, the institutional approach evades this worry at a more
fundamental level. From the institutional approach, the question becomes
not how worthy or pitiful a person's life is, but whether the social order is
according to this person her fair share. Luck egalitarians are moved to act
when the institutions of society are ordered such that some persons obtain
a lesser share simply because of some arbitrary facts, not because they think
the lives of these persons are poorer and hence they are to be given
charitable hand-outs, but because they have not been given their fair
share from the beginning. And this is a mark of respect for persons, rather
than of contempt and disrespect.

Finally, the objection seems to presume that luck egalitarianism is
merely a compensatory theory, that is, entirely about giving hand-outs
to the less fortunate. I will comment more on this worry in the next

section, since I think it is due to the failure to recognize the specific role of the luck egalitarian principle. But for the moment, it suffices to note that this charge is at odds with the institutional understanding of luck egalitarianism. On the institutional luck egalitarian view, the goal is to identify the background conditions of rightful ownership, not just about identifying the conditions for receiving hand-outs and social assistance. It is as concerned as any distributive justice account is with antecedent justice rather than justice *ex post*. That is, to use the terminology introduced earlier, the objection charges that luck egalitarianism is simply a redistributive principle, serving only to correct an existing distributive allocation. But as an institutional account, it is in fact concerned with background justice and the antecedent social conditions that determine persons' entitlements.

In sum, the charge that luck egalitarianism is morally implausible because of its absurd implications—such as indifference toward the imprudent in deep waters, its ready compensation for any bad luck, and its contempt for those at the receiving end of distributive benefits—is deflected once we properly appreciate the domain and institutional focus of luck egalitarianism.

## 5.3  Why luck egalitarianism is not implausibly asocial

Let me turn to the objection that luck egalitarianism is unacceptably asocial as an account of why equality matters, and the related charge that luck egalitarianism is only a principle of remedy or redress. According to the second line of criticism, luck egalitarians fail to appreciate the social aspect of equality and so have "lost touch with the reasons why equality matters to us" (Scheffler 2003a: 23). Luck egalitarians are allegedly fixated on the notion of the equal moral worth of persons, failing thus to see that equality has to do crucially with the "structure and character" of personal relationships (ibid.: 33). But the "purging of the influence of [differential] brute luck from human relations," Scheffler argues, is not the motivating point of distributive equality. The point of equality is to ensure that relations among persons are of the sort that ought to be expressed in a society of equals. Similarly, Anderson argues that democratic equality is a "relational theory of equality: it views equality as a social relationship" (Anderson 1999: 313; cf. D. Miller 1999). Unlike luck egalitarianism,

Hierarchies and oppression formed by/predicated on people been ask to capitalize on arbitrary endowment that undeservedly elevate their position, thereby making others subservient

Anderson points out, democratic equality has the objective of ensuring that relations between persons are non-hierarchical and non-oppressive.

But luck egalitarianism need not be blind to the inherently social and relational quality of equality as charged. On the contrary, it recognizes that the motivation of distributive justice is to secure the relationship among persons that best reflects their equal status vis-à-vis each other. Its luck/ choice principle is not meant as an (asocial) alternative to the social account of equality, but is rather an alternative interpretation of what social equality among persons demands. Luck egalitarianism holds that to relate to each other as equals precisely is, among other things, to hold one another accountable for our choices but not for our luck in matters of distributive justice. It is precisely because of the importance of maintaining a relationship of equality, of respecting the social character of equality, that luck egalitarians hold that distributive allocation should not be affected by persons' luck but only by their choices. As a matter of distributive justice (as distinct from humanitarian assistance), a person should not be entitled to more than her fair share of social resources just because she has made poor choices; but neither should she be given less just because of bad luck. Allowing the latter is to fail to relate to her as a social equal. Democratic egalitarians can, of course, challenge the claim that social equality among persons means that they should not impose institutions on each other that turn *matters of luck* into advantages or disadvantages in matters of *distribution*. But this is different from saying that luck egalitarianism has neglected the social character of equality. Luck egalitarianism, I am suggesting, shares with democratic equality the starting assumption of the egalitarian dis- course: that individuals are to relate to each other socially as equals, and this is precisely why they are troubled by institutions that make some worse-off than others on account of some natural facts about them.[7]

Accordingly, we can see why the related criticism, that luck egalitarian- ism is unable to address pressing issues of social justice having to do with race, gender, and ethnicity because of its asocial character, is without basis (*pace* Scheffler 2003a: 38; Anderson 1999: 312–13). First, in as far as luck egalitarianism (as I have suggested) is also primarily concerned with the basic institutions of society—the norms and background rules of society—

---

[7] Indeed, if luck egalitarianism takes the institutional form I am recommending, and its task is acknowledged to be that of regulating the background social conditions of ownership, it cannot but have a social dimension as noted above.

it will have something to say about race, gender, and ethnicity in situations where the institutions of society discriminate against or privilege members of particular racial or ethnic groups or gender in the distribution of social and economic goods. Luck egalitarianism as an account of distributive justice surely can directly address such arbitrary advantaging or disadvantaging of persons on account of their race, gender, or ethnicity through institutional design. So in as far as oppressive social relationships are supported by norms of the basic structure of society which distribute goods and resources on the basis of arbitrary factors, such as a person's race, gender, or ethnicity, luck egalitarians can directly criticize such oppressive relationships.[8]

Second, luck egalitarianism as an account of distributive justice does not deny that issues of race, gender, and ethnicity can raise important questions of political justice, distinct from the impact of such political injustices on the justness of economic distribution. Luck egalitarians focus on distributive equality not because they think "equality is inherently a distributive notion" (*pace* Scheffler 2003a: 28 n. 26), or that distributive equality exhausts the entire domain of equality and nothing else matters, but because social equality has an inherent *distributive* dimension that has to be addressed. And it is this specific dimension of equality that luck egalitarianism is designed to address. As mentioned, luck egalitarianism is best seen as a claim about the grounds of *distributive justice*, not about the whole of justice (which includes political justice). Luck egalitarians, on my account, can agree with its critics, like Scheffler and Anderson, that "the basic reason [equality] matters to us is because we believe that there is something valuable about human relationships that are, in certain crucial respects at least, unstructured by differences of rank, power, or status" (Scheffler 2005: 17). What luck egalitarianism, as I understand it, offers is an interpretation of what such a relationship ought to consist of with respect to economic or distributive justice. But that its luck/choice principle is designed to deal mainly with issues of distributive justice does not

---

[8] See N. Barry (2006) and Navin (2011) for more discussion on luck egalitarianism and oppression. Navin makes the interesting argument that people who are not oppressed may not always be able to anticipate how their choices can lead to their being oppressed, and freely entering into oppressive relations can eliminate future choice for getting out of that relationship. See Stark and Landesman (2011) for responses. See Pierik (2006) for an interesting attempt to apply luck egalitarian intuitions to the case of reparations for past injustices.

mean that luck egalitarians must treat political justice as secondary or unimportant.[9]

This concern with background institutions also suggests that it is too hasty to think that luck egalitarianism is only a principle of redress and not really a principle of distributive justice. Freeman objects that the luck egalitarian ideal in itself does not "specify a system of distribution and all that must go with it," and does not address questions such as "who should own the means of production, how widespread the distribution of land and capital should be, limits on accumulation of resources and concentration of wealth, the degree to which private and social ownership of natural resources and real capital are each in order" and other such complex questions of background justice (Freeman 2006a; also 2006a: 134–5). But in response, in virtue of its institutional focus, luck egalitarianism is in fact concerned with how the basic political, social, and economic institutions of society combine to determine persons' fundamental economic entitlements. Its luck/choice principle is not simply a principle of redress whose basic role is to re-assign resources from the lucky to the less lucky against a fixed background institutional order that has determined who owns what, but is a principle whose role it is to determine how that background order should be regulated. Put another way, luck egalitarianism provides a principle for the social order that persons may collectively impose on each other, not just a principle of interpersonal interaction *without regard* for the background social order.

A further response to the charge that luck egalitarianism is simply about redistribution/redress and not distributive justice is available once the specific justificatory purpose of luck egalitarianism is clarified. Luck egalitarianism is meant as a response to the question "why equality matters." How equality is to matter, what the currency of equality is, and so on, are matters that will have to be further worked out. The objection that luck

[9] A similar response can be made against Sagar Sanyal's claim that luck egalitarianism trivializes the nature of injustices. He writes that in the case "of poverty caused by [say] unilaterally belligerent military action, it is odd to focus on the luck of the institutions converting the arbitrariness of birth into (and inhabitation of) a region into disadvantage. It is more compelling to focus on the lack of equality in the relations between the aggressor and the victim. In an indirect but significant sense, the poverty in this case is due to the belligerence" (Sanyal: 432). Sanyal is right that it is the lack of equality in the relations that is at issue. But why and how is this lack of equality an issue? Luck egalitarianism, I am arguing, provides one explanation. Sanyal raises other challenges in his paper that I regret I will have to address at another time.

egalitarianism is an incomplete account of distributive justice because it has only the form of a principle of redress thus mistakenly treats luck egalitarianism as a substantive theory of equality when it is meant to ground a commitment to equality. In a way, then, this objection commits a category mistake: it treats a grounding principle of equality (that is, a principle designed to explain why equality matters) as a substantive principle of equality (that is, as a principle that explains how the commitment to equality is to be best realized), and then shows how it falls short as a substantive principle. If, on the contrary, the limited justificatory function of luck egalitarianism is clarified, then the fact that it has the appearance of a principle of redress is not a shortcoming because it does not claim to be a complete and substantive principle of distribution.

Indeed the category mistake committed by the objection is reiterated when critics compare the luck/choice principle with Rawls's difference principle, and claim that the former is woefully incomplete by comparison. But this is a comparison across categories, that is, a comparison between a grounding principle and a substantive principle (and hence it is not surprising that the former comes out short). The apt comparison will have to be between two grounding principles of distributive justice, in this case, the luck/choice principle and the ideal of democratic reciprocity, and here we can see that luck egalitarianism is not more incomplete than democratic equality. Democratic equality in itself does not furnish a direct response to the questions of what to distribute and how to distribute any more than luck egalitarianism does; and indeed, like luck egalitarians, democratic egalitarians themselves debate over what to distribute and how to distribute (e.g. Anderson 1999: 317).

To be sure, there is a very particular sense in which democratic equality is regarded as social in a way that luck egalitarianism is not; but it is important to see where this difference really lies and what it amounts to. A democratic society is understood as a fair system of social cooperation between free and equal members, and for democratic egalitarians it is in this context of fair social cooperation that the ideal of democratic reciprocity applies and where distributive egalitarian considerations can take hold. Only persons engaged in fair social cooperation are in the position rightly to demand from one another certain classes of commitments, including the commitment of distributive equality. That is, only persons thus reciprocally related can ask that inequalities between themselves be those that all can reasonably accept, and that a distributive principle be collectively endorsed to regulate inequalities in light of this criterion. So for democratic egalitarians, the value of distributive equality applies only among persons who see themselves as participants in a fair system of social cooperation, which is how a democratic society is to be conceived. Luck egalitarians, on the other hand, disengage the value of distributive equality from that of social cooperation, in that they do not take social cooperation to be a necessary condition of distributive justice commitments. From my institutional approach, the existence of social engagement via institutions, when these institutions have the effect of transforming natural facts about persons into social advantages or disadvantages, is sufficient to trigger distributive egalitarian commitments. That these are not institutions based on social cooperation is beside the point.

What is important to note is that this denial that distributive equality matters only in the context of social cooperation is not a denial that distributive equality is a social ideal. Certainly it does not mean that distributive justice cannot have as its end that of regulating *social relations* between persons through the institutional structures of a social order against which they interact. It does not even mean that social cooperation is insignificant for luck egalitarians, for they can very well accept that fair social cooperation is a necessary means of realizing the ends of distributive equality, and demand that cooperative social institutions be established for this sake. Social cooperation is only one form of social engagement, and luck egalitarians deny that distributive equality is of value only among persons already participating in fair social cooperation. Rather than suggesting a mistakenly asocial conception of equality, this rejection of social cooperation as a necessary precondition of distributive justice shows that luck egalitarians have a more inclusive view of the "social" to which distributive justice commitments apply.

That luck egalitarianism takes distributive equality to be of value independently of the practice of fair social cooperation is not by itself a strike against it, for this is the very point of the debate: why does equality matter and within what social context does it matter? Does it matter only among persons engaged in fair social cooperation, or does it matter independently of the fact of social cooperation? In defending the plausibility of luck egalitarianism as an account of why equality matters, I am also then defending a position on the scope of equality. Democratic egalitarians cannot take this understanding of the scope of equality as a point against luck egalitarianism, unless it were so obviously counter-intuitive. But the conclusion that equality has scope beyond the borders of political societies is far from counter-intuitive; in fact it is a rather plausible position. But again, I am not suggesting that the plausibility of global equality supports luck egalitarianism since it leads to this ideal (though such an bolstering argument could fairly be made); rather I have defended the plausibility of luck egalitarianism on other grounds, and the global scope of equality that it supports is a resulting implication, one that I will examine in the next part of the work.

Thus, to return to the Anderson-criticism that democratic equality is relational whereas luck egalitarianism is not, the following remarks can be offered. If by relational we mean the presence or ideal of *democratic* relations of some form as a requisite ground for distributive equality, then luck egalitarianism is clearly not a non-relational theory of equality, and deliberately so. But if by relational we mean more generally how persons are to relate and stand with respect to each other, and that a relational account of equality is concerned with addressing social relations among persons, luck egalitarianism is relational.

## 5.4 The ambiguity of the luck/choice principle

Let us now consider the objection that the luck/choice principle is unfounded and therefore cannot be relied on in the way that luck egalitarians require. Critics think that the role of choice in luck egalitarianism is philosophically contentious because it assumes an unstated and undefended commitment to metaphysical libertarianism. As Scheffler notes, luck egalitarianism "tacitly derives much of its appeal from an implausible understanding of the metaphysical status of the category of choice" (Scheffler 2003a: 18). He argues that unless there is genuine choice as given by metaphysical libertarianism, why should egalitarians allow so much (morally speaking) to ride on the distinction between choice and its lack thereof?

Scheffler's objection can be perhaps presented in the form of a dilemma: either luck egalitarians take on the daunting metaphysical issue head-on, and against all odds demonstrate the possibility of real free choice; or luck egalitarians accept that the distinction between choice and its lack is not philosophically "deep" enough to bear the great normative weight that they expect it to hold. That is, either luck egalitarians throw themselves into metaphysical deep waters, or they cease giving the luck/choice principle the kind of dominance it has.[10]

Luck egalitarians, I believe, can rely on the concept of choice in a way that can side-step the first horn of the dilemma without subsequently getting impaled on the second. Regarding the first horn, I contend that luck egalitarianism can avoid getting entangled in the metaphysics of choice by making it explicit that the notion of choice it utilizes, and needs to utilize, is a social rather than a metaphysical one. All luck egalitarians need to assume is that, for practical and social purposes, members of society can plausibly distinguish between cases of persons having freely chosen to act in certain ways (and thus being held responsible for the consequences of their action) and persons not having free choice over a matter (and thus not being responsible). As mentioned in the previous chapter, luck egalitarians can begin from some pre-theoretical or pre-philosophical understanding of free personal choice and the social conditions under which a person can be reasonably described as having acted freely. Social conventions, common understandings and practices are what inform the distinction, not metaphysics.[11]

Luck egalitarians (e.g. Cohen and Dworkin) have in fact been quite explicit that their notion of choice is not a metaphysical one but a social one, and hence the doctrine of luck egalitarianism is quite independent of  the metaphysics of determinism/freedom and need not get mired in this dispute.[12] Perhaps we may adopt a Humean compatibilist approach to this

---

[10] It is worth pointing out that even if there is no metaphysical freedom, this only means, from the luck egalitarian perspective, that there has to be actual outcome equality, since on this presumption all that happens in fact happens outside individual choice and control. So luck egalitarianism as an ideal of equality stands even in the face of determinism; it is just that on its ideal no inequalities will be deemed acceptable, because on the presumption of determinism none will be freely chosen. I owe this point to Peter Vallentyne. See also G. A. Cohen (2006), where he holds that luck egalitarianism is a principle independent of the fact of whether freedom actually obtains or not. So determinism does not defeat the principle itself. Still, since luck egalitarianism's key appeal is that it is able to account for choice in its actual application, and to account for departures from equality, this response is not fully satisfactory. The principle may be saved but its purpose is defeated.

[11] Compare with Fleurbaey's discussion of "responsibility by delegation" (Fleurbaey 1998: 209).

[12] To be sure, G. A. Cohen, in considering the idea of free choice, acknowledges at one point that if metaphysical determinism is true, then luck egalitarians are really "up to their necks." That is, if it is the case that there is really no such thing as free personal choice, then the luck egalitarian ideal that individuals are to be held responsible for their choices gets no traction at all. But it is important to note that Cohen prefaces these remarks with the qualification that this is the less assuring of two available responses, and he immediately

matter, holding that we can and do make sense of the distinction between choice and constraints in ordinary social life against a set of reasonable background conventions and assumptions. Nothing metaphysically deeper need be inferred.

Thus it is not the task of luck egalitarianism to provide a metaphysics of personal freedom. It is a theory of distributive justice that operates on the presumption that there are shared assumptions about the scope of individual choice, and is itself not a metaphysical doctrine of free choice. What it does is to draw out the egalitarian implications for society, given existing understanding of personal freedom and their lack thereof. Indeed, should conventional understanding of choice/circumstance shift, our normative evaluations can shift too with regard to personal responsibility, as when we now accept that sentencing decisions ought to take into account the social and familial conditions of the convicted criminal, given that we now take these factors to have a significant role in influencing persons' conduct.

This is not to deny that a prior moral theory of responsibility can reflexively inform our understanding of the luck/choice cut. To the contrary, a commitment to what we can and cannot hold persons morally responsible for can influence our view as to what things are subject to choice and what are not. The claim that the luck/choice distinction does not presuppose a metaphysics of freedom does not mean that it is also nonnormative (unless normativity is implausibly presumed to be necessarily metaphysically grounded). Luck egalitarianism can rely on some normatively-based view of luck and choice, without itself having to furnish such an account. As an account of distributive equality, its claim about luck/choice is basically a conditional one: that if X is due to luck and not choice, then from the perspective of distributive justice a response is required. But whether X is in fact due to luck or choice is to be settled not within luck egalitarianism. It is an account of equality that presumes a reasonable way of making the distinction between choice and luck, and draws out distributive implications from this; it is not an account that needs to offer a basis for this distinction.

backs up the first response with a more reassuring one, and this is that luck egalitarians need not rely on a metaphysical conception of choice in order for their conception of equality to get off the ground. My response emphasizes Cohen's "more reassuring" response (G. A. Cohen 1989: 934; cf. Scheffler 2003a: 18; and 2005: 12–13).

Moreover, it is worth noting that being able to make the luck/choice *Good* distinction is significant not just for luck egalitarianism but for any plausi- *Point* ble conception of distributive justice. Even democratic egalitarians have to rely on the luck/choice distinction, as I noted. The democratic egalitarian, to be sure, does not call on this principle to motivate the commitment to distributive equality, but relies instead on the ideal of democratic reciprocity to justify distributive commitments. But once that commitment is motivated, democratic egalitarians cannot avoid the luck/choice distinction in working out what the appropriate distributive principle should be. Thus democratic egalitarians too have to accept that the distinction is workable at least for the range of cases that excites social equality discussions.[13]

Thus, the first horn of metaphysical challenge can be happily avoided. If we like, we can say that this is an application of Rawls's view that political philosophy be done independently of metaphysics. What is crucial for luck egalitarianism is that society can make sense ordinarily of the distinction between persons having acted freely and not having done so, independently of the metaphysical fact of the matter (if there is indeed such a fact). The notion of choice within luck egalitarianism is social, not metaphysical.

But here is where the second horn of the dilemma threatens: unlike democratic equality, luck egalitarianism relies on the choice/luck principle as a fundamental and decisive moral principle, and yet the imprecise metaphysical status of the principle is not equal to the normative task expected of it. As Scheffler writes, "unless genuine choices (both the wise and the unwise) are conceived of as metaphysically distinctive in a way that makes them privileged indicators of our true identities or ultimate moral worth, it is obscure why they should have the kind of *across-the-board,* *Strong* *make-or-break significance* that luck egalitarians assign to them" (Scheffler *Argument* 2005: 13, my stress). Thus, the choice/luck distinction is not philosophically "deep enough to bear the weight that luck egalitarians place on it" (ibid.: 17). (This is perhaps the real force of Scheffler's objection, for Scheffler does anticipate the above response in his discussion.)

---

[13] For instance, Rawls notes that inheritance, the distribution of natural talents, and so on, are arbitrary (Rawls 1971: 15, 72, 277), and does not give arguments for this. This claim, that these traits about persons are not chosen, is pre-theoretical in the sense that it is not derived from his theory of justice, but is an operating assumption of his theory.

But as I have tried to explain in the previous section, luck egalitarians need not understand the luck/choice principle to have an "across-the-board, make-or-break significance" in the way that Scheffler imagines. As we saw, the principle is not to be invoked for the purpose of determining whether a person in dire straits should be assisted. The victim's choice or its lack thereof here is morally irrelevant. The principle is not designed to answer all questions of personal responsibility in the entire domain of morality, but only in the limited and very specific domain of distributive justice. It thus has no across-the-board make-or-break significance. Understood strictly, and more modestly, as an account of distributive equality, the weight placed on the luck egalitarian principle is lighter than the objection assumes.

*Decent Rebuttal). Could be Stronger*

So, although the luck/choice principle is not admittedly a metaphysically deep one, it is not disproportionate to the normative expectations demanded of it, because it is not meant to be a deciding principle across the entire terrain of morality, but only as a deciding principle within the special domain of distributive justice. It has significance of course, in that it serves to motivate the commitment to distributive justice and plays a role in working out what that commitment should be. But it does not have the great significance attributed to it by its critics, to the extent that is disproportionate to its inevitable imprecision.

Indeed, it seems to me that Scheffler himself notes that the full force of the philosophically implausible objection relies on the charge of moral implausibility sticking. As he acknowledges, the metaphysical "objection would be easier to dismiss if the luck egalitarian account of the significant of choice were *morally compelling*" (Scheffler 2003a: 18, my stress).[14] That is, what makes the metaphysical objection bite is that the luck/choice principle is believed to be morally implausible and contrary to social expectations, and yet it is metaphysically shallow. So if we may deflect the moral implausibility charge, as attempted in the previous section, we can also smother considerably the philosophical implausibility charge.

---

[14] This perhaps lends support to my point that Scheffler's basic objection is that there is a disconnect between the great moral expectation of the luck/choice principle and its less than secure metaphysical status. Thus a response to Scheffler's worry is to lower our expectation of the luck/choice principle by confining it to the domain of distributive justice and not give it this across-the-board application.

To sum up the discussion in this section: against the objection that luck egalitarianism presupposes a certain metaphysics of personal freedom, I have suggested that luck egalitarians can remain agnostic about the metaphysics of choice, and hold that the luck/choice distinction is indeed not a deep one in this sense. Indeed, if the notion of free choice is per se metaphysically controversial, this is not a worry that afflicts only luck egalitarianism but also any account of equality that must make appeal to free choice at some point (which I believe any plausible account must). And if, by way of a counter-response, it is said that luck egalitarianism should not then allow this distinction that is not deeply enough grounded to have an across-the-board make-or-break moral significance, my response is that this worry presupposes a greater moral application and significance for the luck/choice principle than luck egalitarianism need or should claim.[15]

## 5.5 Institutional luck egalitarianism

The luck egalitarian position I have outlined, even though it departs in some respects from well-known extant accounts, is still significantly a luck egalitarian position and distinctive from democratic equality. First, even though it is limited to the domain of distributive justice, within that specific domain it takes the luck/choice principle to be fundamental. Second, even though it takes the subject matter of distributive justice to be social institutions rather than natural facts, it is still a *luck* egalitarian position in that it holds that institutions ought not to turn natural contingencies into social advantages or disadvantages. Third, it offers a different grounding for distributive equality from democratic equality, and hence specifies the conditions under which distributive equality matters quite differently. For convenience, and to signal its institutional approach, I will label my account *institutional luck egalitarianism*.

It is worth noting that my invocation of the institutional approach is not ad hoc, that is, it is not introduced simply for the purpose of constructing an account of luck egalitarianism capable of escaping an objection. As my reference to Rawls is meant to suggest, the institutional approach reflects

---

[15] Knight has a detailed discussion of the "metaphysical objections" to luck egalitarianism (Knight 2009:178–91). I believe my remarks are compatible with Knight's arguments.

one common way of understanding the site of distributive justice, and my argument is only that luck egalitarianism can accept the institutional view of justice without abandoning its key tenets. Moreover, adopting the institutional approach rescues luck egalitarianism from Anderson's charge that luck egalitarianism must be in the absurd business of compensating persons for any of their natural bad luck.

Some luck egalitarians will object that by limiting the range of luck egalitarian concerns to those cases of bad luck that have been converted by institutions into advantages or disadvantages for persons, I have rendered luck egalitarianism insensitive to instances of bad luck that most luck egalitarians would find intuitively troubling.[16] But this challenge will have to present a case of bad luck not due to institutional influence but that is also not so devastating to the unlucky person as to fall under the domain of basic needs, on the one side, and on the other, is intolerable enough that egalitarians should be moved by it. For example, even if we can say that a person who has been unluckily blinded is now at a serious disadvantage independently of any institutional cause, my institutional account of justice can nonetheless say that this person ought to be assisted on humanitarian grounds. And, again, to say that there are humanitarian reasons to assist this person does not mean that these duties are not enforceable or institutionalisable. A duty to provide for basic welfare can be an obligation which a state owes to its citizens. The point is that the presence of this duty is not determined by the luck/choice principle.

One might offer an example of a less debilitating misfortune, say, that of a person who is unluckily slightly shortsighted and so is at a slight disadvantage compared to others with normal sight. It is plausible, or at least grantable, that this person's disadvantage is not due to any institutional input; and it is plausible to hold that his misfortune is not so severe as to demand humanitarian assistance. So is my institutional luck egalitarian view defective because it seems unable to address this and other similar types of natural bad luck? Not necessarily, I would argue, for we have to ask: is the slight handicap so intolerable that any egalitarian view that cannot account for it is thereby obviously flawed? In the case of shortsightedness, for instance, I don't think that it is immediately

---

[16] The following is due to a question posed by G. A. Cohen in a personal exchange. The eyeglasses example below is his. See also Stark and Landesman (2011).

counter-intuitive from the perspective of distributive justice to say that a
society has no obligation of justice to provide corrective eyeglasses for
people (who are not legally blind but simply have less than perfect
eyesight). Now if it were the case that the afflicted person would go
blind without special care, humanitarian considerations for assisting her
would kick in. But it is far from obvious that the bad luck of having
marginally poorer eyesight than others in society must entail some form of
special social compensation, when eyeglasses are not so prohibitively
expensive that they would be out of reach for persons with the resources
or opportunities that they ordinarily would have in an otherwise just
society.[17]

So finding a case of a disadvantage arising from bad luck that is pre-
institutional, but which is not so severe as to tip over into the domain of
basic needs, and yet bad enough intuitively to move egalitarians may be
harder than it seems. Still, I am prepared to grant that there might be such
cases (so I am not denying that such cases can exist, but suggesting they are
possibly exceptions rather than the rule). But ultimately, the question for
luck egalitarians proposing a trans-institutional approach (as I will call the
approach that says natural bad luck in itself can be a matter of justice) is this:
what is the alternative? Even if my institutional account leaves certain cases
of bad luck outside the purview of justice (because there is no identifiable
institutional cause), it seems to me preferable over trans-institutional
approaches because the latter will have a hard time evading the Anderson-
type challenge that luck egalitarians have to be absurdly compensating

[17] What about a person who experiences slight but not debilitating pain in doing ordinary
things, like walking because of club-foot (a reader's example)? Is it not counter-intuitive that
these are of no concern to a luck egalitarian absent institutional influence? If the afflictions
described above involve only the slightest of discomfort, that is, below the threshold of what
we normally regard as "pain," and if she cannot convey to others that she is experiencing pain
in the way the term is socially recognized, then it is not clear in what sense we can really
describe the experiences as painful in any meaningful way. If so, it is not counter-intuitive that
there is no mitigation on account of bad luck. We do routinely and not counter-intuitively
expect, after all, that people put up with their felt discomforts (for example, some people may
bear hot weather less well than others; some may prefer to walk less than others). But if there
is indeed a felt experience that is publicly recognizable as a painful one, then what I call
humanitarian considerations kick in. A person who is flat-footed, for example, may experience more discomfort walking, but it is not contrary to common sense that she is expected to
bear this small cost, as opposed to a person who really experiences pain walking because of
club-foot. Of course, the flat-footed person may be exempt from duties that she cannot
perform because of her condition, such as military service. This is an attempt to respond to a
reader's query.

persons for all of their natural misfortunes.[18] In other words, the trade-off
is between an institutional account like mine that potentially ignores some
cases of bad luck but is immune to Anderson-type objections on the one
side, and, on the other, a trans-institutional approach that aspires to cover
all instances of bad luck (independently of institutional influence) but
precisely because of this also stands exposed to Anderson-type objections.
Given that Anderson's objection would fatally convict luck egalitarianism
of absurdity if it were to hit the mark, my institutional approach seems
overall preferable.

The elementary difference between democratic equality and luck egalitarianism is preserved on my institutional account. As mentioned, democratic takes distributive equality to matter only when democratic reciprocity
also matters. Institutional luck egalitarianism, by contrast, takes distributive
equality to matter whenever there are common institutional arrangements
that confer differential advantages to persons on account of arbitrary facts
about them. That is, distributive egalitarian commitments are activated, on
the institutional luck egalitarian view, when there are *affective institutions* that
convert natural facts about persons into disadvantages for them. It is immaterial whether or not these are institutions based on democratic ideals.

A normative consequence of this difference is in how each position
understands the scope or reach of distributive equality. For democratic
egalitarians, distributive equality is by definition confined to the social
setting where the ideal of democratic reciprocity applies. Thus while
distributive equality clearly matters within the borders of a democratic
society, it is not immediately the case that it also matters beyond these
borders. For the luck egalitarian, distributive equality has potentially wider
application in that it is not confined to the context of a democratic order
but can take hold wherever there are affective institutional arrangements
in place. In other words, our understanding of the ground of equality can
importantly influence our understanding of the scope of equality even
though these are distinct questions.

---

[18] The trans-institutional luck egalitarian might say that ugliness need not be a social
disadvantage at all, unlike myopia, and so need not be a concern of distributive justice, thus
avoiding the alleged absurdity. But it seems to me that we cannot properly understand how a
condition is a social advantage or disadvantage without reference to how institutions handle
these conditions; in the same way we do not know what persons' natural talents are worth
without reference to existing economic institutions that determine the "economic rent" of
particular natural talents.

One obvious arena where this difference over equality's ground has potentially important normative implications for the scope of equality is in international relations. For democratic egalitarians, the case for global distributive equality, if it can be made at all, is going to be indirect. It will depend on a successful demonstration that the ideal of democratic reciprocity applies globally among persons across state boundaries even in the absence of a democratic global political society. It is not coincidental that, in the current debate on global justice, many democratic egalitarians tend to be skeptical of the ideal of global distributive justice, whereas several global egalitarians tend also to subscribe to luck egalitarianism.[19] The extension of luck egalitarianism to global justice is the topic of Part III.

[19] For example, Rawls 1999a; Nagel 2005; Freeman 2006b, 2006c; Heath, Blake, and Sangiovanni 2007. For an attempt to defend global distributive equality on broadly democratic egalitarian terms, see Beitz 2001; also Brock 2009: 304–9, Sanyal, and Tan 2006.

# PART III

# Global Justice

# 6

# Global Institutions and Justice

## 6.1 Introduction

As mentioned in the previous chapter, luck egalitarianism can more straightforwardly support a global scope for equality than democratic equality. This is because, unlike democratic equality which takes equality to be a political ideal, that is, an ideal that holds only under a social order committed to particular political values, luck egalitarianism takes equality to be an ideal that applies among persons independently of their political relations. What luck egalitarians need to do is to show that the current global distribution of wealth and/or opportunities does not track persons' choices and efforts but is to the contrary distorted and influenced by the vagaries of luck. On the institutional luck egalitarian account I am proposing, however, it will not be just luck as such that issues a problem of distributive justice, but the fact that there is a global institutional practice that renders matters of luck into social advantages for some and disadvantages for others. I will elaborate on this claim in the present chapter.

The present discussion concerns global egalitarianism and not global duties as such. As mentioned in Chapter 1, an *egalitarian* distributive principle has the substantive aim of regulating economic inequality between persons. It specifies the limits to the kinds and degree of inequalities that would be admissible in a just social order. An egalitarian distributive principle is thus more demanding than what we might call a sufficiency principle. The latter enjoins the duty to help persons meet certain defined needs thresholds, whereas the former demands some regulation of inequalities between persons even when the basic needs of all relevant agents are being met. Put another way, egalitarian distributive justice is relative or comparative in character *and* it takes the comparative benchmark to be that of equal distribution from which any departure has to be justified to those affected.

The interesting philosophical disagreement between global egalitarians and those who reject global egalitarianism, call them anti-global egalitarians, is therefore not whether there are global duties of any kind toward strangers and other societies but whether these duties include a duty of regulating global economic and social inequalities. Anti-global egalitarians can accept some global "sufficientist" duties toward persons. Some of these commentators define the sufficiency threshold in terms of humanitarian or basic needs (e.g. Nagel 2005). Others may identify this basic minimum more robustly in terms of a society's capacity to support well-ordered institutions domestically (e.g. Rawls 1999a).[1] How the sufficiency threshold is to be defined is of course hugely important for our understanding of what is owed to persons at large as an absolute minimum. But I shall leave aside discussions *within* the sufficientist account here. My question is whether global justice includes an egalitarian commitment over and above a threshold-commitment (however that commitment is defined), and specifically whether luck egalitarianism can provide the grounding for such an egalitarian commitment.

The problem of global egalitarian justice is thus a distinct one, conceptually, from that of the problem of global poverty. The duty to counter poverty is a sufficientist duty: it is a duty that is discharged when the minimum subsistence level that defines poverty is crossed. A global egalitarian distributive duty, on the other hand, given its objective in regulating inequalities, is continuous and remains in play so long as inequalities are present between the relevant parties. Taking global egalitarian justice to be a conceptually distinct problem from that of global poverty does not mean that the two issues are separate and independent of each other in practice. It might be the case that global poverty cannot be properly eliminated, while significant global inequalities between persons or societies remain a fact. In this case, the commitment to eradicate poverty results in an

---

[1] Although Nagel (2005) sees himself to be defending something like Rawls's position, some commentators think that Nagel's account of humanity duty implies a more minimalist global commitment than that affirmed by Rawls's duty of assistance. See, for example, J. Cohen and Sabel (2006). But whether this is really so depends on how "humanitarianism" is defined within Nagel's framework, and it seems to me that nothing in Nagel's discussion precludes a robust definition of humanitarianism that includes living under functioning institutions of one's own. In any case, what is without dispute, and of relevance to this chapter, is that Nagel, like Rawls, rejects global distributive equality, and like Rawls holds the view that what global justice requires is that all persons are able to reach a certain developmental threshold.

instrumental commitment to limit inequalities. But it is however also imaginable that significant inequalities can persist between countries without anyone or any society being impoverished. Or, put another way, even when all persons in the world are lifted above the poverty line, it is still possible, and likely in practice, that significant inequalities remain. The question is whether these non-poverty-inducing inequalities generate a concern of justice.

The global egalitarian ideal falls under what is commonly referred to as the idea of cosmopolitanism. Global egalitarianism offers a substantive interpretation of the basic cosmopolitan principle that persons are to count equally regardless of nationality and citizenship. But as is clear from this, while global egalitarianism is an expression of cosmopolitanism, cosmopolitanism does not imply global egalitarianism. There are varieties of cosmopolitanism and not all professed cosmopolitans need to affirm global egalitarianism. Still, global egalitarianism is the form of cosmopolitanism that is much discussed in the current philosophical debates on the cosmopolitan ideal. With the above qualification in mind, I will use the term "cosmopolitanism" (and its adjectival cognates) interchangeably with global egalitarianism.

## 6.2 Global institutions and luck egalitarianism

Given luck egalitarianism's non-politically-confined account of why equality matters, it is not coincidental that several of the prominent defenders of global egalitarianism tend to subscribe to some form of luck egalitarianism.[2] Those who extend luck egalitarianism to the global domain—call them global luck egalitarians—typically argue that contingencies such as the natural distribution of the earth's resources and the place of birth of persons (which are largely matters of luck and not subject to personal choice) significantly influence the life chances of people in the world pervasively and profoundly, and because a just distribution of wealth and resources ought not to be influenced so disproportionately by people's luck, some global distributive principle is needed to correct

---

[2] This does not mean that all luck egalitarians also subscribe to global egalitarianism. Ronald Dworkin is one notable example (Dworkin 2006: Ch. 2). See Brown's attempted extension of Dworkin's theory of distributive justice to the global plane that focuses on Dworkin's luck egalitarian commitments (Brown 2009: 4–6, and Ch. 7).

for this discrepancy. A well-known example is Charles Beitz's early argument that some redistribution of the earth's natural resources, and resource-generated wealth, is required as a matter of justice because of the unequal and arbitrary natural distribution of the world's natural resources (Beitz 1979: Part III). This is often interpreted as a luck egalitarian argument. For Beitz, the distribution of natural resources globally is morally akin to the distribution of natural talents. Thus, just as Rawls took the distribution of personal talents to be arbitrary from the moral point of view and ought not to determine persons' life chances, so too, the argument goes, should the allocation of the world's natural resources be considered arbitrary and ought not to determine persons' life prospects (Beitz 1979: 138–43).[3] Another influential luck egalitarian argument has been made by Thomas Pogge. Pogge argues that if one were to adopt a Rawlsian methodology with respect to distributive justice, then as a matter of consistency the nationality of persons should be regarded to be as arbitrary as their gender, ethnicity, genetic endowment, or social class, which Rawls takes to be, and so within a Rawlsian approach to justice, one's nationality ought not to compromise or advantage one (Pogge 1989: Part III). On this luck egalitarian rendition of Rawls's basis of distributive justice, Pogge believes that Rawls's distributive principle ought to take global scope and not be confined to the national context.[4] Other, more recent, global luck egalitarian arguments have been made or presumed by Darrel Moellendorf (2002), Simon Caney (2005), Cécile Fabre (2006), and Alexander Brown (2009).

Indeed, given that persons' life prospects in the world are so pervasively a matter of luck in the different ways described above, it would seem that arguments to the contrary would be needed to show why a given luck egalitarian is not forced to endorse global egalitarianism. In making the case for luck egalitarianism as the ground of equality, one also by default, it seems, accepts a global scope for equality.

---

[3] As noted in the previous chapter, though Beitz relies on a luck egalitarian ideal to ground redistribution of natural resources, he allows that this is not the same as extending Rawls's difference principle to the world as a whole. The case for extending Rawls's difference principle will require that the global order represents a cooperative scheme; and Beitz goes on to argue that it does (Beitz 1979: Part III).

[4] As also mentioned in the earlier chapter, it has been argued in response that this luck egalitarian reading of Rawls is mistaken. My point here is merely to reference self-consciously luck egalitarian arguments for global egalitarianism (leaving aside whether this is consistent with Rawls's own view of equality).

But as appealing as this luck egalitarian approach is for global egalitarians, it relies on an understanding of luck egalitarianism that is vulnerable to certain objections (as discussed in Chapter 5). Moreover, global luck egalitarianism in this standard form has to confront a specific reductio challenge that I will discuss later.[5] The institutional approach to luck egalitarianism that I suggested is plausible and more defensible than non-institutional accounts but, in contrast, does not support global luck egalitarianism as directly. It is reliant on the presence of a global institutional order or practice that has the effect of turning arbitrary matters about persons into profound differences in their life chances. I will suggest that that the presumption of such a global order is not an unreasonable one.

The *institutional* approach to luck egalitarianism departs from the traditional accounts in how it more explicitly locates the source of global injustice. On my account, it will not be the natural fact of earth's distribution of resources or the mere fact of persons' geographical residence that is the cause of injustice, but the fact that existing social and political institutions and practices have converted these natural and contingent facts into social advantages and disadvantages for people. That is, it is not just the brute fact that someone is, say, born south of the river we conventionally refer to as Rio Grande, or the fact that some geographical regions on earth are richer in natural resources than others, that are matters of justice or injustice. What is just or unjust is how the existing global order makes use of such facts, that is, how global institutions have converted these natural facts into actual social advantages and disadvantages for individuals.

That a person is born south of a river is a natural geographical and biological fact that is in itself of no consequence from the point of view of justice; after all, it is just as natural a fact that persons can ordinarily relocate themselves. That another geographical region is richer in natural resources is also of no consequence as a matter of justice, if people from a less well-endowed region can simply move in. These are simply facts of nature that in themselves are unproblematic for justice. In a global state of nature, contingencies such as a person's place of birth, the spread of the earth's resources, climatic conditions and so on do not present issues of distributive justice. In the state of nature where there is free movement (understood here simply as a Hobbesian natural liberty), natural facts remain

---

[5] Brown refers to this as "a priori global luck egalitarianism," and identifies difficulties with it along similar lines (Brown 2009: 151–2).

natural facts and are neither just nor unjust in themselves, and distributive egalitarian considerations need not arise.

What transforms these natural facts into matters of justice is the presence of various kinds of global and national institutional norms, socio-political rules and restrictions, such as legally enforceable borders and immigration restrictions that limit people's natural mobility. The global institutional order turns a people's actual possession of territory into a right of ownership over that territory. The presence of a global legal system that restricts in effect how persons may traverse the face of the earth via legal norms and rules regulating migration of persons is a vivid example of how plain natural but arbitrary facts about individuals and the natural spread of the earth's resources are transformed into actual advantages for some and disadvantages for others. Borders are obviously artificial (i.e. social constructs), but the point is not that they should therefore have no moral significance. To the contrary, political borders have the significance of turning natural features of the world into matters of justice. The claim is not that a just world order should revert to some pretended state of nature where persons have the liberty to transport themselves where they please. The institutional luck egalitarian position does not necessarily present a case for open borders, but simply makes the claim that there are global institutional facts that have made matters of luck into matters of justice.

The example does not rely on the reductivist presumption that countries' fate are determined entirely by their respective natural resource holdings and that other factors such as domestic economic policies are irrelevant. The only presumption in the above example is the relatively uncontroversial one that what resources a country happens to sit on can correlate directly with how it performs economically, and this is consistent with the claims that other factors are important, and could even in combination offset advantages or disadvantages of natural resource holdings, such as domestic policies, trade arrangements, the global legal order, and so on. The main claim is that natural resources are arbitrary and do impact on social economic performance.

Immigration restrictions which are institutional, and how that together with the allocation of the earth's resources creates differential prospects for persons, is just one illustration of how global institutions along with natural facts can generate matters of justice for the institutional luck egalitarian. Also able to bring about this effect are international legal and political norms that turn the natural territorial distribution of the earth's resources

into actual and enforceable property holdings, or entitlements of governments of states within whose borders these resources happen to be located.
Or consider the global market and its trade rules (e.g. patent laws, free
trade laws) that restrict opportunities for people within many of their own
societies as well as outside.[6] For the individual born south of Rio Grande,
it is not the fact that she was randomly born south of a geological
landmark, along with how the globe's resources are naturally distributed,
that presents an issue of justice: what is just or unjust is the existence of
global norms (such as those governing sovereignty, resource ownership,
territorial rights), economic practices (such as trade laws, intellectual
property rights laws), and international laws and principles (such as those
regulating movement of persons across borders) that turn such natural facts
into a significant social disadvantage for her.[7]

But it is not just global institutional norms permitting the restriction of
individual movement and underpinning the idea of state territorial right
(including resource ownership rights) that have rendered natural facts into
social advantages or disadvantages. Other forms of global practices and
norms and arrangements contribute to this result: for example, a world
legal order that allows decisions to be made solely in one region of the
world or in a single country without justification to outsiders, even though
these decisions could have some spill-over impact on life opportunities in
another region or other countries (Held 1992; Gould 2004). This global
democratic deficit is an institutional failing that affects persons differently
based on happenstance. The world order also allows for what Pogge
refers to as the "resource" and "lending privileges" (Pogge 2002: Ch. 8).
Resource privilege grants any de facto regime of a country the legal right
to dispose of the country's natural resources as it sees fit and holds that any
third party which does business with it does so legitimately. Lending

---

[6] For a recent discussion on the relationship between natural resource distribution and
global institutions, see Tim Hayward, "Global Justice and the Distribution of Natural
Resources."

[7] See Moellendorf's comments that "the global economy has had a substantial impact
on the moral interests of persons in virtually every corner of the world. Due to this
association . . . duties of [distributive] justice exist between persons globally and not merely
between compatriots" (Moellendorf 2002: 37). See also R. Miller's discussion of the
various kinds of relationships (e.g. economic, deliberative, and imperial) that countries
in the world are in. Miller does not go all the way to conclude that these relationships
generate global egalitarian duties, but holds that they do ground very demanding duties of
global justice (R. Miller 2010).

privilege allows any de facto ruler of a country to borrow funds and to incur debts that are internationally recognized as debts owed by the country that successive governments are obliged to service. This applies even when the debt is incurred by a dictatorial regime and the burden of debt servicing now falls on a democratically elected government. These global norms and practices transform basic facts like persons' place of citizenship and the distributive of natural resources into matters of social justice.[8]

One might insist that it is domestic policy that is largely responsible for the fates of nations. But just as it would be a difficult to defend the reductivist thesis that the fates of countries rest solely on their natural endowment, so it is difficult to defend the claim that the fates of countries rest solely on their respective domestic policies. Pogge refers to this erroneous doctrine as "explanatory nationalism." The difficulty with explanatory nationalism, Pogge notes, is that it leaves out the crucial explanation as to why national factors such as corruption, incompetence, and poor decisions have these outcomes and not others; and more significantly it leaves out global explanations for why certain domestic decisions are made, why there is a certain level of domestic corruption, and so on (Pogge 2002: 139 ff.). Global factors like the above-mentioned "resource privilege" provide a more complete explanation for why certain resource-rich countries remain not just economically poor but political corrupt and tyrannical.[9]

The above are just some examples of how the global institutional order turns natural facts about the world into advantages and disadvantages for people. Persons as moral equals who stand to each other in relations of social equality can demand of each other, regardless of citizenship, that any common global order that they are imposing on one another begin from the default position of equality, and any departures from this have to be acceptable those adversely affected. On the luck egalitarian view, one who is disadvantaged under such an institutional arrangement simply because of how that arrangement has handled matters of luck has reasonable grounds

---

[8] Indeed, this suggests that the absence of a global democratic order doesn't make considerations of justice moot, but makes them all the more salient.

[9] See Wenar's discussion of the resource curse—the phenomenon whereby apparently being resource-rich can in fact be a disadvantage—that traces the "curse" not to the resource-richness of countries as such, but to the global institutional order (Wenar 2008).

for objecting to that arrangement. Her standing as an equal moral agent is not being respected.

In short, because the global arena is not a state of nature but an arena pervasively governed by institutional norms, regulations, and expectations, many natural facts about the world and its inhabitants do not remain innocuously facts of nature, but are being transformed by institutions into inequalities in life chances. To the extent that global institutions turn brute natural facts into actual differential distribution of opportunities or resources for persons, that is, to the extent that the global distributive set-up does not track people's effort and ambition but "myriad forms of unlucky and lucky circumstance" (G. A. Cohen 2000: 130), it is to this extent unjust. There is a case then for a global distributive commitment that is grounded on the principle that justice has to be choice-sensitive but circumstance-insensitive. Some of the institutional restrictions on persons that have global implications no doubt originate domestically, such as immigration policies. But these domestic policies are sanctioned within a larger global system and it is in this way that global institutional order gains salience.

Thus institutional luck egalitarianism can have global scope if the above remarks about how global institutions have turned matters of luck into matters of advantages and disadvantages for persons are plausible. The institutional twist I have added to luck egalitarianism need not limit its scope to the state. To the extent that states (and individuals in the world as a whole) relate to each other under a global system that has the result of rendering arbitrary matters into differential advantages and disadvantages for persons, luck egalitarian considerations on the terms I have proposed do kick in.

My global luck egalitarianism focuses on global institutions and how these handle certain natural facts. But it is nonetheless a *luck* egalitarian position, because it holds that what is unjust is when institutions are arranged such that the distribution of resources and opportunities does not track persons' effort and choice but various forms of good and bad luck. Crucially, unlike democratic equality, it frees considerations of global egalitarianism from considerations of the character of the global order, that is, whether it is or ought to be a democratic political order in some sense.

In spite of my focus on institutions, I need to emphasize that my account does not rely on institutions in the same way as democratic equality. To recall, democratic equality takes distributive equality to matter because of the value of democratic reciprocity thought to be intrinsic to the idea of fair social cooperation. That is, distributive equality matters only within institutional settings in which the ideal of democracy is endorsed. For many democratic egalitarians, this limits the ideal of distributive equality to the institutions of the state. Global luck egalitarians, on my institutional approach, do not limit distributive justice commitments to members of a (democratic) state. Institutional arrangements can influence or *affect* the interests of persons pervasively and profoundly by shaping their life prospects along various dimensions. The fact of these "affective" institutional arrangements, as we may call them, is sufficient for concerns of distributive justice to arise, regardless of whether these arrangements are also democratic in character.[10] Luck egalitarians, in my proposal, take egalitarian concerns to be activated whenever there are common affective institutions among persons, regardless of whether these institutions are based on the democratic ideal of social cooperation or not. Equality, and global equality included, remains a moral ideal in my account, and not a politically contingent one.

Thus the notion of "institution" I am using does not imply some *specific* forms of legal, political, and economic arrangements, but refers more generally to commonly recognized and formal social practices and norms that affect persons pervasively and profoundly. That is, it is not implied that there is an accepted global political democratic order or a global basic structure based on the idea of social cooperation. What is relevant is that there is a global social arrangement—consisting of specific institutional entities, and institutionally entrenched or enforced social and legal norms and expectations—that has the effect of rendering random facts about persons and the natural world into actual social inequalities.[11]

## 6.3 Institutional impact, political coercion and social cooperation

Why is an imposition of institutionalized practices sufficient for rendering natural luck objectionable should these practices turn it into differential

[10] See Goodin's discussion of the principle of "affected interest" in "Enfranchising all Affected Interests and Its Alternatives" (2007).

[11] It is also worth noting that while what I have said of global institutional impact on persons' lives finds support from Pogge's incisive discussions (Pogge 2002), my claim differs from Pogge's in that he is concerned with the problem of abject poverty. His institutional approach refers to the harms that institutions cause in this regard, whereas my project here is with distributive equality and I am concerned here with the inequalities due to institutional handling of natural facts.

advantages? Call this the institutional impact thesis. The reason for this has to do with what persons affected by the arrangement can reasonably object to. The idea is that a basic requirement of reciprocity is offended against if an imposed social order has the effect of converting arbitrary traits about persons into differential social advantages and disadvantages. This is because it is hard to see how that could not be reasonably objected to by those so disadvantaged.

The global institutional order turns mere territorial possession into property.[12] It accords moral legitimacy to holdings that can otherwise be contested. The ideas of state sovereignty and the territorial integrity of states presume a global institutional order that grants these ideas a certain moral standing, as claims that others should respect. But this respect is achievable only if the global order is not one that persons subject to it can reasonably reject. My claim is that a global order that turns arbitrariness about persons into differential personal advantages is one that some can reasonably reject.

One way to test the plausibility of the institutional impact thesis is to compare it with the main institutional alternatives. These are accounts that hold that egalitarian commitments are triggered not just by the mere fact of institutional impact, but are triggered only if these institutions exhibit certain normative features. The two disjunctive features often mentioned are those of political coercion and social cooperation. On the political coercion view, as I will call it, egalitarian commitments are generated as a response to the need to justify or legitimize the coercive authority of the state (Blake 2001; Nagel 2005).[13] On the social cooperation view, generally, distributive egalitarian commitments are generated because institutions based on social cooperation regard equal shares of the benefits of

---

[12] See, for example, Rousseau's point that social institutions turn possession into ownership rights (Rousseau 1987: 151).

[13] Barry, Ypi, and Goodin (2009) have described Nagel's argument as a "social cooperation argument" instead of as a "coercion" argument. The reason for their classification is that they put weight on Nagel's idea of the state as the joint project of its members. This might be just a matter of emphasis in the end, but it is worth noting that Nagel's position ultimately has to depend on the basic premise that the state is a coercive order, which then gives rise to the pertinent question: "How could this be legitimate to those who are also said to be authors of that arrangement?" Without the presumption of the state as a coercive arrangement, the issue of joint authorship would be inconsequential. His argument's center of gravity, as it were, lies in the notion of the state as a coercive order. See Nagel 1991.

cooperation as the default from which departures have to be justified (e.g. Sangiovanni 2007; Freeman 2006a).

These arguments may be described as democratic egalitarian arguments against global egalitarianism since they rely on broadly democratic egalitarian premises (as discussed in Chapter 4) to ground the commitment to distributive equality. Equality is limited to the confines of the state, on these arguments, because the global institutional order is not one in which the grounding ideal of democratic reciprocity applies. To evaluate these influential challenges to global egalitarianism, it will be useful to assess the strength of their fundamental claim that egalitarian justice is contingent on the salience of specific institutional ideals. I will contend that both the political coercion and social cooperation arguments, on one interpretation, seem less plausible than the impact thesis; on another interpretation, they seem to lend support to it.

Consider the political coercion argument. One version of the political coercion argument holds that since the coercive authority of the state involves the restriction of personal autonomy, this authority has to be justifiable, i.e. rendered acceptable, to individuals so affected if the coercion is to be legitimate. The state's taking on a commitment to distributive equality among its citizens is one necessary means by which this restriction of their personal autonomy can be made legitimate to them (Blake 2001). This argument, if it is meant as an argument to show that egalitarian demands are limited to the state, has to explain what is so distinctive about coercion within the state compared to coercion within the global order. The global order, after all, exhibits various forms of coercive restrictions on personal autonomy (as noted above). The response, on behalf of the coercion argument, cannot be that the former is legal and ongoing and the latter not, because there are several restrictions on individual autonomy in the global arena that are in fact legal, institutionalized, and sustained. So construed then, the coercion argument is not at odds with the institutional impact account I am proposing. The way that global institutions render arbitrary facts about persons into differential advantages can be seen as coercive in many instances, such as the case of immigration restrictions.

Another version of the political coercion argument trades not simply on the notion of political coercion but also on the ideal that citizens of a political society have the special standing to demand that their shared coercive institutions meet certain conditions to be legitimate. Thus this argument is not fazed by the response that the global order is in fact coercive by virtue of its impact on persons, because its comeback will be that there is no similar legitimizing requirement at the level of global institutions.

This argument has been made by Thomas Nagel, who claims that since individuals are to be conceived as joint authors of their shared political and legal order, they have the "standing" to require that this order not admit of arbitrary inequalities (Nagel 2005: 129; also Macedo 2007: 312–13). That is, the shared institutional order has to be justifiable to each member if this common coercive authority is to be legitimate before all. Accordingly to Nagel, this legitimizing requirement will ground some form of distributive egalitarian commitment within the state. But because there is no common global political–legal order of which individuals of the world as a whole are seen as joint members, there is no parallel need to legitimize the global political order even though it exhibits some coercive elements. Thus Nagel notes that even if a restrictive immigration law of a political society can be seen as coercive of outsiders wanting in, the outsiders do not have the moral standing to demand that this law be justified to them, since they need not be conceived as joint authors of that law.

As a first observation, it can be noted that Nagel's minor premise, that the global order is not normatively conceived as a shared system in which individuals can be thought of as joint participants, is subject to further examination (see J. Cohen and Sabel 2006). But more relevant to the present discussion is the major premise that only persons conceived as joint authors of a political–legal system have standing to demand justification for how that system is affecting them. Compared to the institutional impact thesis, this more stringent thesis seems rather counter-intuitive. It suggests that my coercion of you requires no justification when you have no say at all about what I can do to you, whereas if you are regarded as someone having some decision-making rights, I will need to justify my coercion of you. This curiously removes protection for those who are most vulnerable to my decisions and actions, namely those who are powerless and disenfranchised from my decision-making process. Joint authors, on the other hand, are by comparison less vulnerable by virtue of their role as collaborators in the design and sustenance of a given lawful system. So the normative premise seems morally untenable: it offers protection against arbitrary threats to members, but removes protection from those who are most vulnerable by virtue of their non-member status. As some commentators have pointed out (Julius 2006; Tan 2006; Abizadeh 2007), this premise seems morally perverse.

To be sure, Nagel does not say that no explanation is ever owed to persons affected by laws not made in their name. When externally imposed arrangements and laws affect persons by violating their "'pre-political' human rights" some accounting for the violation is required (Nagel 2005: 129–30). "Pre-political" rights are the rights persons have independently of any institutional arrangements, and these are for Nagel limited to basic rights that include subsistence rights, but do not cover the right to distributive equality. So where lawful arrangements merely allow for inequalities or where they only disadvantage some, no explanation is owed to those who are only subjects to the laws.

Why is an explanation owed only when people's pre-political basic rights are violated, but not when they are put at a disadvantage? Is this a morally significant distinction? Imagine a pre-political state of nature in which a community A is settled upstream in relation to another B further downstream. Each of these communities is dependent on the resources from the river. Imagine now that A elects to extend a net across the river for the purpose of improving its yield of fish. Imagine also that this net when constructed will not violate any pre-political rights of people in B; some fish and other resources will continue to slip through, so the basic needs of the community are not at threat. Still, members in B will now have a diminished quality of life; perhaps they now have to work extra hours to obtain the same amount of goods as they used to enjoy before the construction of the net. Or perhaps, even though they still are able to meet basic needs, they simply have fewer resources to work with now, thus compromising their material quality of life. On Nagel's model, members of B have "no standing to ask" why they should accept this arrangement. Their pre-political rights are not violated for they are still able to meet their subsistence needs; and the arrangement (the net across the river) was not erected in their name but in the name of people in A.

But why is no explanation or justification owed to the people downstream by those upstream? The fact that this is an institutional arrangement— it is a practice that A has authorized, put in place and is maintaining—not made in B's name or for their sake is immaterial. What is material is that this arrangement affects the people of B disadvantageously. To be sure, if the erection of the net results in the community downstream losing its means of subsistence, then a basic pre-political right to subsistence has been violated and the community upstream can be held accountable by the affected community. But why is the community to be held accountable only when basic rights are infringed? Is the fact that it has rendered another worse off not something that it has to be held accountable for? Nagel's normative premise that only persons conceived as fellow law-making members of a social order have the right to make certain moral demands against social arrangements that affect them seems hard to sustain.

Thus, the political coercion argument is either not different from the impact argument I have proposed, in which case it must have global application; or if it limits justifying coercion only to those who are considered as joint authors of an institutional order, it seems to set an implausibly stringent condition for when people can have the right to demand some accountability from social arrangements that affect them.

Consider next the argument of social cooperation. One way of understanding this argument is that since the domestic institutional order is one based on social cooperation, egalitarian demands are generated because the question of justice arises as to how to distribute the product of cooperation. Given the ideal of cooperation, this implies as a default an equal share among participants of the cooperative arrangement, unless there are grounds consistent with the ideal of cooperation to depart from this egalitarian default. Typically, in the global justice debate, the argument goes on to claim that the global order is not a cooperative order and hence distributive equality does not arise there as a commitment (Sangiovanni 2007; Freeman 2006a).[14] As with the political coercion argument, the minor premise requires more substantiation. In what sense is the global order not one based on social cooperation? Charles Beitz, among others, has attempted to identify the way in which the global economic order can be interpreted as a system of social cooperation. So, at the very least, the empirical claim that the global order is not one based on cooperation is open to further discussion. But, again here, it is the major premise with which I am more concerned. In what sense is distributive egalitarianism

[14] Sangiovanni describes his position as a reciprocity-based argument; but it is not inaccurate to class his position under the social cooperation argument, since his ideal of reciprocity derives ultimately from the ideal of cooperative social institutions. I discuss Sangiovanni's and Freeman's arguments in more detail in Tan 2010b; and also Nagel's and Blake's and Freeman's arguments in Tan 2006. See also Caney (2008), Abizadeh (2007), and Ronzoni (2009) for responses to Blake, Nagel, and Sangiovanni.

dependent on social cooperation? If the claim is that there must be an existing cooperative institutional arrangement before arguments for egalitarian commitments can take hold, this seems rather implausible. After all, domestic egalitarians are prepared to argue that, should the relevant institutional arrangements that make equality possible not be present in society, there can be a duty of justice to establish these institutions. It would seem then, if this is right, that there can be an antecedent commitment to equality, prior to there being actual cooperative institutions. Cooperative institutions might be better seen as the means to equality rather than its ground.

But the major premise can be interpreted in a different way: that it is only in a social order morally *conceived* or idealized as a system of social cooperation that distributive egalitarian demands take hold. That is, it does not matter if there are no existing institutions based on social cooperation; if ideally we ought to conceive that society as a society based on social cooperation, this will create egalitarian commitments within that society, including where necessary the commitment to create cooperative institutions to realize egalitarian commitments. If this is how the argument of social cooperation is to be interpreted, it can in fact be invoked to support the institutional impact thesis. One could argue that it runs counter to the idea of social cooperation to allow institutions to impact on persons differentially based on arbitrary factors.

Now, one might object that the global order cannot be conceived as a socially cooperative order, and hence the argument from the ideal of social cooperation limits egalitarian commitments to the state (which alone ought to be conceived as a system of social cooperation). Here it is important to locate the argument. It cannot just be that there is a centralized political authority in the case of states but none in the global context, for more must be said about what it is that the state performs that allows the domestic society uniquely to be idealized as a system of social cooperation. Is it because it makes and enforces laws, makes possible property rights and ownership, and engages in distribution of economic goods? If so, it is not obvious that these functions are unfulfilled in the global order, even if, granted, they are not performed by a central political authority. It might be noted that Rawls himself, even though he refrains from extending egalitarian commitments to the global plane, notes that the global society can be idealized as an order based on social cooperation.

If the social cooperation argument is to succeed in limiting egalitarianism to the state, it must say something about what makes social cooperation in the state special. One might say that it is in an attempt to answer this question that prompts Blake and Nagel to construct their arguments from coercion.

To sum up, the social cooperation argument either implausibly ties egalitarian commitments to existing institutions of social cooperation, or it states an aspiration about social cooperation that in fact can be relied upon to substantiate the impact thesis.

From the other side, some luck egalitarians might object that this *institutional approach* to global luck egalitarianism gives up too much: that is, in emphasizing the institutions of the global order, my account does not pay attention to natural deprivations that are independent of institutional practices. But this worry should be tempered once it is recalled that the institutional luck egalitarian approach is an account of "distributive equality" and not of morality as such. That is, since it is limited to matters of distributive justice, it does not say that basic deprivations of human needs that are not institutionally derived are of no moral consequence. As argued in Part II of this work, other moral considerations, including non-institutionally based ones, can be invoked in confronting problems of basic subsistence.

As to the worry that an institutional approach allows too much space for nations and countries to pursue their collective ends at the expense of global egalitarianism (Brown 2009: 153–4), my reply here will parallel my reply to the critics of institutional justice already discussed in Chapter 3. That is, just as a plausible conception of distributive justice has to recognize and secure space for legitimate personal pursuits, so too a plausible conception of global justice has to recognize and secure space for national pursuits or self-determination. It is not globally unjust per se if a society were to pursue certain non-egalitarian ends if it does so within the terms of a just global institutional order. On the contrary, one might say that a global egalitarian view that does not identify the proper space for legitimate national self-determination proposes an "extreme" form of cosmopolitanism (to co-opt Scheffler's 2001 term) that is potentially an absurdity (Tan 2004b). A global luck egalitarian ideal that is not institutionally informed faces this challenge.

## 6.4  Is global luck egalitarianism absurd?

Besides offering an understanding of luck egalitarianism that can deflect the common charges leveled against it, a special advantage of my *institutional* luck egalitarianism is that it avoids a popular *reductio ad absurdum* argument to which more standard global luck egalitarian positions are quite vulnerable.

The reductio argument is usually presented in the following fantastical example: should alien moral beings be discovered and be known to be doing more poorly than us (earthlings) because they inhabit a more poorly endowed planet compared to ours, luck egalitarians, so it is charged, would demand that we take on distributive commitments towards these aliens because it is after all a matter of bad cosmic luck that their planet is less well stocked than ours. But, so the argument holds, this would be patently absurd, and the standard luck egalitarian defense of global re-source redistribution seems to be forced to accept this implication.[15] It is absurd because it takes our distributive duties to be without end and predictability, subject instead to the vagaries of nature. The example is purposely fantastical in order to test the conceptual limits of the global luck egalitarian ideal. So as fanciful as the argument is, it is worth examining its asserted implications. Another way of putting the objection is in this way: that luck egalitarianism globalized is implausible. Luck egalitarianism at best can make sense only within an already prescribed scope; it itself cannot be invoked to define the boundary of distributive justice without absurdity.

Now, it would of course be a different matter if the space aliens risked death due to some episodic cosmic misfortune and, moreover, that we could without significant sacrifice do something to rescue them. In this case, it is at least arguable that earthlings do have a duty of assistance towards the aliens. The reductio argument will lose force if this were the case. We can quite plausibly accept that there is a duty of assistance to provide for basic needs where we can do so without significant sacrifice even without any prior engagement. But the reductio argument does not

---

[15] For example, Fabre mentions and rejects this objection in "Global Distributive Justice: an egalitarian perspective" (Fabre 2006: 151–2). As I will discuss, Fabre denies that the conclusion that luck egalitarianism is forced into is "utterly outlandish" (ibid.: 152); my approach denies that luck egalitarianism needs to be forced into this conclusion. Blake introduces and sustains a more down to earth version of this objection in "Distributive Justice, State Coercion, and Autonomy" (2001).

intend to challenge this claim. A limited duty of assistance is distinct from an ongoing distributive commitment for the purpose of regulating inequalities in life opportunities due to luck that is at issue here. What the reductio argument targets is the stronger (egalitarian) conclusion that global luck egalitarianism allegedly leads to: that any society of moral beings is immediately burdened with ongoing distributive commitments *to regulate inequality* the moment a less-well-off (but still thriving) society within contact is discovered.

In defense of global luck egalitarianism against this reductio argument, it seems to me that three possible responses should be considered. The first, and perhaps weakest, response is to deny the intuition that it would be absurd to have distributive commitments towards space aliens who are (merely) worse-off (as opposed to space aliens who are going to perish without our help). That is, the global luck egalitarian could simply bite the bullet and insist that it is not really a very hard bullet to bite; that there is no absurdity about having duties of distributive justice imposed on us when less-well-off societies are discovered that do not share some previous contact with us. Just as it is not plainly absurd to say that we have a duty of basic assistance when such a situation presents itself, so too we have a duty of distributive equality should the need arise. Opponents of global luck egalitarians seem to take the intuition for granted, and I just want to flag the possibility that there might be some room for debate over this.[16] But this, I will concede, is a weak response, for it simply denies the intuition of anti-global luck egalitarians by offering a counter-intuition (and not an argument) in the first instance.

The second, less weak, response accepts the intuition that something is amiss in the conclusion that earthlings now have distributive commitments to the aliens, but it clarifies and relocates the source of this misgiving. What is unacceptable is not the fact of an additional distributive obligation to moral agents with whom we have had no ongoing relations per se. Rather, what is unacceptable is the taking on of this new

---

[16] As does Fabre (2006: 152). Fabre is responding to the fictional aliens example: her claim is that as we would not think it absurd to engage in distributive commitments to a newly discovered human tribe, so we ought not to think that it would be absurd to do so in the more fantastical example. A remark about this response is that the space alien example is meant to show that it would be absurd as well to engage in distributive relations with the human tribe just for the sake of reducing inequality. So Fabre's response basically denies the intuition asserted.

duty of justice towards strangers in the context of multiple severe but avoidable failures of justice at home (on earth). So what is wrong in accepting new distributive duties to these creatures is the way we would then appear to prioritize our duties of justice (at the expense of further neglecting those at home).

So, the first response denies the intuition altogether that it is morally absurd to say that we can have duties of justice towards strangers with whom we have had no relations; and the second response accepts the intuition but brings into play the larger background context of prevailing injustices to explain what is really wrong with our taking on new duties. These are perhaps inconclusive responses to the reductio challenge that will need further defense. But they at least suggest that one ought not too complacently to endorse, without more reflection, the critics' charge that this new distributive commitment would be morally absurd.

But a third and more forceful response is available to my institutional position. This response accepts the intuition that it would indeed be absurd for earthlings to have to attend to the distributive claims of these space aliens, *but denies that luck egalitarians are committed to the absurd conclusion.* Recall that from the institutional luck egalitarian position (that I am proposing), natural facts are in themselves neither just nor unjust. It is how institutions handle natural facts, whether institutions turn these facts into social advantages or disadvantages for persons, that generates questions of justice. Thus on my institutional luck egalitarian view, the fact that a society is worse-off just because of the natural order of the universe in itself does not pose a problem of distributive justice. Again, if the events were such that some beings are going to be in severe straits without assistance, there could be considerations based on decency or humanity to assist them. But distributive justice is a different matter. Just because some others have to make do with less, where the managing with less is not life-threatening or, more importantly, at odds with any conception of human decency, does not by itself present a challenge for distributive justice. Thus, nothing in my luck egalitarian account forces the egalitarian to say that we can have duties of egalitarian distributive justice to newly discovered space aliens *just because* they are unluckily less-well-off than we are. So if we accept that it is in fact absurd that human beings ought to take on new ongoing distributive burdens whenever new moral agents are discovered, this is not a consequence that my luck egalitarian position is forced into. The *institutional* character of my global luck egalitarian view blocks this slide into the alleged absurdity.

So my account is not absurdly overly demanding, as the reductio argument claims. But, on the other hand, neither is it overly harsh. It does not say that we have no duties whatsoever to newly discovered beings. If, for example, we need to provide limited-term humanitarian assistance to these aliens because otherwise they would suffer severely, nothing in my luck egalitarian account says we could not do so. Indeed, my account also plausibly allows for the assisting of these aliens even if their dire condition is due to bad choices of their own.

Now it will of course be a different story if, continuing with the space fantasy, there are in place and in effect intergalactic institutional expectations, norms, and regulations that limit what these aliens can do to better their situation. If, for example, they are expected under this galactic institutional order not to enter earth and exploit its resources without the consent of earthlings; or if they are expected not to harvest resources in outer space in ways that can have negative impact for earthlings (say they may not redirect the sun's energy for their own benefit); in this case, then it is not just a matter of cosmic luck that these aliens are poorer than us, but ultimately the result of how affective common institutions have combined with the natural fact of the universe. But for the institutional order that they accept and that we expect them to accept, these aliens could do better (by exploiting common resources, say, to our own disadvantage). Under this institutionalized setting, where there is in place an institutional order that renders certain facts of nature into actual disadvantages for the aliens, the luck egalitarian view would support a distributive commitment. And this is hardly counter-intuitive.

What is really of significance is that the global order is more like the revised fantasy just constructed above than the one originally offered by the reductio argument. What is morally remarkable about our world is not certain facts of nature, such as the spread of natural resources, the geographical locations of people's birth and existence, but the fact of various global norms, regulations, and expectations that have transformed these natural facts into actual advantages for some and disadvantages for many persons. Thus while I claim that luck egalitarians can accept the intuition that earthlings can have no distributive commitments towards space aliens with whom we have no prior and ongoing interaction and relations, the situation on earth is far from analogous with such a scenario. So accepting this intuition does nothing to compromise the case for global egalitarianism on luck egalitarian grounds.

The alleged reductio challenge should not faze luck egalitarians who adopt the institutional approach, then, because they are not forced into the conclusion that any existing beings who are merely less advantaged are entitled to distributive claims from those who are more advantaged. Unlike non-institutional global luck egalitarians, who must either bite the bullet and accept the proposition that duties of justice can arise in cases of discoveries or reconsider their luck egalitarian principles, defenders of the institutional approach do not face this dilemma. And in affirming that distributive justice takes hold only institutionally in the way specified above (that allows them to evade the reductio claim) egalitarians do not weaken their stance on global egalitarianism, because so long as the subject remains real world *global* justice, it is highly unlikely that new human societies can be discovered that are not to some extent affected by the world order that the rest of humanity has collectively brought about.

Tying luck egalitarianism to the institutional approach provides a promising way of capturing the intuition that motivates the global luck egalitarian project: it accepts the intuition that there is a basic unfairness to the extent that persons have unequal life chances on account of arbitrary facts like their country of birth; but it also captures the intuition that global institutions and not natural facts about the world present matters of justice. Indeed, locating the source of justice in institutions not only allows the global luck egalitarian to lighten the argumentative load placed on natural facts like the distribution of the earth's natural riches, but to consider more evenly a myriad of global institution facts that have generated disparate life prospects for persons on account of random things about them such as where they happen to live their lives.

## 6.5 Conclusion

The institutional luck egalitarian account I am forwarding will support equality having a global scope, because the global order is structured in such a way as to disadvantage or advantage persons based on facts that we ought to take to be morally arbitrary. Unlike other luck egalitarian accounts that might take natural misfortunes in themselves to generate distributive commitments, the institutional account, beginning with a more modest understanding of the site and domain of equality, is limited to confronting only those inequalities that have some institutional or systemic causes. But this need not be a disadvantage of my approach, as the world we live in is hardly describable as a state of nature but is in fact a social order in which systems of rules, institutions, and common practices impose on the lives of virtually all individuals. To be sure, an institutional account like mine will not be able to address inequalities that arise simply naturally. But as the discussion above suggests, this might also be an advantage of my position rather than a weakness.

I mentioned that luck egalitarianism provides a prima facie case for global egalitarianism. But perhaps the reverse is as significant, if not more so: the case of global inequality, where persons' differential life prospects are so starkly and vividly influenced by contingencies, such as the country they live in, as these get shaped by global institutional factors, suggests the prima facie plausibility of luck egalitarianism. In the domestic context, the significance of luck/choice is harder to appreciate given the presumption of the ideal that a just social order is supposed to accord to all persons equal opportunity; and hence resulting inequalities must be due to persons' choice rather than luck. Moreover these inequalities could already also be mitigated to some extent by the state through redistributive programs. Thus the usefulness of a luck egalitarian approach might be harder to appreciate in the limited context of the state where to some extent persons' fate are already (at least presumably) collectively shared.

But in the global domain, the pervasiveness of institutional luck on persons' life chances and the great gulf of inequalities across the world seem to support the luck egalitarian ideal. Why should the mere fact that, say, one is born in a less-well-off country legitimize the fact that the person will have significantly reduced life options compared to someone in a better-off country? Should such considerations not compel an egalitarian to ask what role should luck have, if any, in influencing persons' life prospects? Perhaps as the scope of our moral world extends with our understanding and identification with the real world at large, it is appropriate that new concerns and commitments should influence how we theorize about justice, including how we understand why equality should matter.

# 7

# The Arbitrariness
# of Nationality

The global luck egalitarian argument presented in the previous chapter turns on the premise that nationality is morally arbitrary. Since persons' nationality is generally not chosen but is rather the result of circumstance, therefore falling on the luck side of the luck egalitarian equation, as it were, the luck/choice principle will require that global institutions not be designed so as to render this arbitrary matter into differential advantages or disadvantages for persons. In this chapter, I will consider objections to the claim that arbitrariness of nationality in fact yields the desired global luck egalitarian conclusion. These objections do not all directly call into question the luck egalitarian ideal but challenge its global extension. Moreover, what is basically objected to is not the supposed arbitrariness of nationality (which the objections largely grant) but that this arbitrariness in combination with the luck/choice principle generates global egalitarian commitments.

I will consider two lines of objections. One of these holds that the fact that nationality is arbitrary does not imply that it is morally irrelevant. That is, nationality, even if arbitrary, can be morally relevant in that a person's nationality can permissibly determine her set of entitlements. Another holds that the fact that nationality is arbitrary does not mean that its neutralization or mitigation will yield global egalitarian commitments. Neutralizing or mitigating the effects of nationality on persons' differential prospects entails global egalitarianism only if it is already presumed, thereby begging the question, that there is a global egalitarian default from which any departures due to arbitrariness have to be annulled or limited. I will consider these objections in turn.

## 7.1 Moral arbitrariness versus moral relevance

Luck egalitarianism takes it that a morally arbitrary factor, meaning by this a factor due to luck or unchosen circumstance as opposed to an individual's choice, ought not to have moral relevance in that this ought not to influence her distributive entitlements. But, as a challenge against global luck egalitarianism, one might argue that nationality even if arbitrary is not morally irrelevant since nationality does and can acceptably determine persons' distributive entitlements. The objection's aim is to break the luck egalitarian connection between moral arbitrariness and moral irrelevance.

David Miller presents this line of objection in his *National Responsibility and Global Justice* (D. Miller 2007: 31–4). Miller first issues a more basic challenge to suggest that in general (and not just in the case of national arbitrariness) it is far from obvious that moral arbitrariness implies moral irrelevance. Consider people with differential needs due to congenital disability. Surely, Miller points out, it does not follow that these differential needs should be deemed morally irrelevant. That is, we would not hold that persons are not entitled to extra consideration and a greater allocation of resources because their special needs are arbitrary. On the contrary, we would take their special needs to be a basis for redirecting more resources to them. Their arbitrary neediness, far from being irrelevant, is precisely the reason why we would accord them extra consideration (ibid.: 33).

But posed as a general objection to luck egalitarianism, this argument is too quick. It trades on an indeterminacy surrounding moral "relevance" or "irrelevance." To ascertain whether an arbitrary trait is morally relevant or irrelevant, we need to ask: morally relevant (or irrelevant) *with respect to what*? The idea of moral relevance or irrelevance has to be understood in relation to a *specific* criterion of entitlements. Luck egalitarians do not simply say that arbitrary factors are morally "irrelevant." What they say is that such factors are morally irrelevant when determining persons' fundamental entitlements *with respect to some defined currency of distributive justice.* When "relevance" is specified by reference to a measure of entitlement, Miller's case presents no troublesome counter-example to luck egalitarians. For a luck egalitarian also committed to welfare egalitarian, for example, a person's congenital disability ought not to compromise her welfare (the relevant currency of entitlement here), and a greater redistribution in her direction is called for precisely because the person's arbitrary condition is deemed irrelevant in this regard. On a welfare egalitarian model, the disabled person should not be enjoying reduced welfare simply because of her arbitrary condition. Thus, redistribution to make up for the person's loss in welfare is not a case of treating her arbitrary condition to be morally relevant, but on the contrary is an implication of taking it to be of *no* relevance with regard to her welfare entitlements.

This manner of responding to Miller is not restricted to welfare luck egalitarians but is independent of the currency of equality. For example, one who adopts a capability approach (as developed by Sen [1992] and Nussbaum [2000a]) can, it seems to me, argue that the restoration of a person's capability set can require some resource redistribution to make up for her congenital disabilities and attendant capability shortfalls. A person's arbitrary condition ought to be morally irrelevant in the sense that it should not compromise her capability set. To the extent that it does, redistribution is a requirement of treating her arbitrary condition as morally irrelevant, and not because, contra Miller, her disability is deemed morally relevant.

The same remarks can be made with respect to resource luck egalitarianism. The luck egalitarian who endorses a resource metric is not vulnerable to Miller's charge that she must implausibly deny the disabled more resources on account of the arbitrariness of her extra needs. It is open to the resource egalitarian to attempt to define "resource" broadly enough to include "personal" resources, that is, her personal abilities or handicaps.[1] If so, extra material resource transfers to the congenitally disabled person is a means of raising her *overall* resource level to put it more on a par with the average person's, rather than a case of giving her more. Thus, the arbitrary differential neediness is treated as morally irrelevant in the sense that it ought not to reduce a person's overall resource entitlements, and that extra

---

[1] See, for example, Dworkin (2000: 115–16, 299–303). Compare with Rawls, who holds that focusing on material resources such as income and wealth as the relevant metric of equality can account for problems of disabilities if income and wealth are defined more broadly and flexibly to include public assistance and support as part of a person's income and wealth (Rawls 2001: 172). Either way, a resource egalitarian can understand a congenital disability to be morally irrelevant and precisely because of this irrelevance support distribution in the direction of the disabled.

material transfers to her are really an effort to mitigate the arbitrariness of her resource shortfall.[2]

Thus, Miller's first argument, it appears to me, mistakenly treats any actual redistribution to a person on account of her arbitrary condition as an indication that her condition is regarded as morally relevant, when in fact this redistribution should be regarded as an effort to render the trait irrelevant with respect to a specific measure of entitlement. That is, it is because we regard the arbitrary condition to be morally irrelevant with respect to the person's entitlement that we provide her with special assistance. The arbitrary condition is morally irrelevant and hence ought not to compromise her well-being, her capability, or her life prospects.

But Miller has a more central objection directed at the morally arbitrariness of nationality. According to Miller, certain arbitrary factors like nationality cannot be considered morally irrelevant (even with respect to a specific measure of entitlements) because these so-called arbitrary factors can be taken into consideration when determining persons' entitlements. Arbitrary matters, like a person's national membership, can be sources of special obligations, that is, obligations that are owed specifically to members but not to non-members. If nationality is a source of special obligations, then surely it is not morally irrelevant, for national membership is a factor that can determine persons' entitlements. Thus the global luck egalitarian claim that nationality ought not to influence a person's entitlements is false unless we reject the idea that nationality can generate special obligations in spite of its arbitrariness (D. Miller 2007: 33, 33 ff.).

One of Miller's significant contributions to the contemporary philosophical debate on nationality and global justice is the idea that shared nationality can be the basis of non-reducible special duties and rights not generally owed to others (D. Miller 1995; also M. Moore 2001). That is, there are special national duties (duties owed to fellow members, for example) that do not derive from global moral principles or are valued simply because they are instrumental for realizing global moral ends. That nationality has a certain non-reducible moral significance in this way is a

---

[2] How about differential needs among ordinary persons: differential needs not due to disabilities but due to temperaments, tastes, and so on? Here, perhaps, the resource egalitarian can as well hold that where there are differential needs among ordinary able-bodied individuals due to things like temperament, the vagaries of upbringing, and so on, these are inclinations that people can regulate and take responsibility for (e.g. Rawls 1993: n. 185).

plausible claim, and I will grant it for the present purpose. The question is whether this disapproves the luck egalitarian idea that nationality ought not to skew the demands of global distributive justice.

Miller's underlying claim that a special relationship that generates special obligations *is morally relevant* needs some explication. The argument is, as I see it, something like this: a relationship or association cannot be morally irrelevant if, *in virtue of* certain features integral to that relationship or association, participants can come to acquire special moral claims against each other. Associations like the family, even if arbitrary in a sense, generate special entitlements and obligations for members of the unit, obligations and rights that non-members do not share. Miller seems to be arguing that to hold that family associations are morally irrelevant is to deny that family membership can generate non-reducible special rights and obligations. A similar point can be made about friendship: there may be a degree of arbitrariness in friendships, in that it is often circumstantial as to who comes to befriend whom. Yet friendship is not morally irrelevant, in that it is a relationship that can create non-reducible special claims among friends. Thus the same with the nation, Miller argues. Granting the plausible claim that one's nationality is largely arbitrary in the sense that it is (generally) not chosen, it does not follow, on this analysis, that nationality is irrelevant because nationality does generate special entitlements and duties among fellow members. The global luck egalitarian move from the arbitrariness of nationality *to* the moral irrelevance of nationality is therefore invalid, according to Miller. His argument can perhaps be outlined in this way:

1. Nationality is arbitrary in that it is not (generally) a chosen trait.
2. Yet nationality generates non-reducible special duties and therefore has a role in determining persons' entitlements.
3. That which determines persons' entitlements cannot be morally irrelevant.
4. (From 2 and 3) Nationality is therefore not morally irrelevant.
5. Therefore (from 1 and 4) nationality is arbitrary but not irrelevant, contra global luck egalitarians.

As can be seen, then, Miller's argument attempts to force global luck egalitarians into a dilemma: they can either deny the moral irrelevance of nationality or deny that nationality can create special rights and obligations. Since I have granted the plausibility of non-reducible national duties, denying the second horn is not an available option here.

The problem with Miller's argument, however, is that the proposed dilemma does not hold. A luck egalitarian can grant premise 2 of the argument, that nationality can generate special non-reducible rights and duties, without surrendering her claim that nationality is morally irrelevant in the sense salient to her argument. The problem with Miller's argument, I contend, lies in premise 3. That premise conflates two distinct criteria or levels of "entitlements": one, that which a person is entitled to *as a matter of* background justice; and two, that which a person is entitled to in virtue of special relationships or situations *within the terms of* background justice. A luck egalitarian only needs to insist that nationality is irrelevant with respect to entitlements in the first sense, but need not hold that it is irrelevant in the second.

To elaborate, consider a more familiar domestic case. Family membership is certainly relevant in the sense that it generates special entitlements through various special duties and concern among kin. This is generally presumed to mean that a person is at liberty (or even has an obligation) to care more for her kin than for a stranger. But there is an unstated precondition underlying these claims. This is that showing special concern to one's own is acceptable only when it does not violate any rightful claims of strangers. The significance of familial ties—that they can generate special duties—presupposes some *background societal justice* that, among other things, sets the parameters for what family members may owe each other. Family ties are morally relevant for the purpose of generating special obligations and rights, but only within the constraints of background justice. The real question, then, is whether from the perspective of background justice the specifics of familial ties are relevant; that is, whether we may take our particular family memberships into account when determining the terms of background justice. The typical and most plausible response to this question is that we ought not to, even though we can accept that under the constraints of justice these ties may appropriately determine persons' entitlements. Membership in an association is irrelevant from the perspective of background justice, in that it should not influence persons' background entitlements of justice. This is compatible with the belief that membership *is relevant* when determining what is owed to persons *within* the terms of background justice. The scope of moral irrelevance that luck egalitarians have in mind is thus limited, but not insignificant.[3]

Returning to the case of nationality and global justice, the global luck egalitarian does not deny that, within the terms of global justice, nationality is morally relevant and persons' entitlements can vary according to their nationality when the constraints of background global justice are respected. What they will hold is that nationality is irrelevant *from the perspective of global justice,* in that nationality should not be considered when determining persons' fundamental entitlement from that standpoint. On a global institutional view, global institutions that assign basic rights and responsibilities ought to be impartial with respect to persons' nationality. The arbitrariness of nationality precludes it from having any influence on how the global background order allocates persons' rights and responsibilities.

Thus global luck egalitarianism, or for that matter global egalitarianism in general, need not make the implausible claim that national membership and national commitments have no moral relevance and significance whatsoever. The global egalitarian or the global luck egalitarian is not forced to the view that nationality cannot influence at any point persons' distributional entitlements. What global egalitarianism holds is that, from the standpoint of global distributive justice, a person's national membership has no special significance. That is, in determining the background global institutional order within which persons and their nations on their behalf interact globally with other persons and nations, we ought not to take into account national affiliation. And denying the relevance of nationality in this way, precisely because it is arbitrary, is hardly implausible. Just as from the standpoint of domestic justice we do not take specific familial ties into consideration (but in fact would require that these be deliberately discounted) when determining what persons are entitled to as a matter of domestic institutional justice, so too we do not take into account specific national members when determining persons'

---

[3] This does not mean that how we conceive of the bounds of justice can ignore the significance of familial relations (or other similar relationships) as a general matter. See Tan 2005. As discussed in Part I, the institutional approach aims at approximating a plausible and reasonable means of demarcating distributive justice commitments from other moral commitments that people have. The point is that the *particularities* of family relationships even though significant (although arbitrary) ought not to affect the institutional assignment of economic entitlements. For more on family partiality and background justice, see C. Macleod (2011).

entitlements from the perspective of global institutional justice. And, more to the present point, just as this does not imply that familial ties have no significance at all across the board, but that, on the contrary, within the terms of the domestic basic structure, individuals are free to favor their familiar commitments and concerns; so too, within the terms of a just global structure, persons and their nations are at liberty to promote domestic ends and national justice.

That natural resources are not like "manna from heaven" in that they have to be appropriated to be "transformed" into things of value, and that modes of appropriation are often nationally determined, does not undermine the national arbitrariness thesis and accord national claims priority over global justice (cf. Moore 2010: 139). For this will simply mean that what nations may take from nature and how they do so have to be restrained by considerations of background global justice. The luck egalitarian's national arbitrariness claim operates at the earlier background stage; it sets the antecedent background conditions under which national claims over resources can have standing. This priority of background global justice with respect to natural resources also allows that nations may understand their relationship to resources in different ways (cf. Moore 2010: 139–40). That a people may find land-use more valuable than mineral extraction, or vice versa, does not contradict the priority of background global justice, for global justice only sets the parameters of how peoples may understand their own relationship to the natural world. Within the terms of global justice, we can expect that there will be sufficient space for national cultural variations with respect to resource use and valuation.

Miller might respond that the very notion that global justice itself should be impartial to nationality is what he is rebutting. But the argument that is discussed here does not make this point. The argument against global luck egalitarianism as stated only claims that nationality is a source of special obligations, and this claim is, I am arguing, compatible with the ideal that background justice should itself be impartial with respect to nationality. The idea that nationality is a basis of non-reducible special obligations is compatible with the idea of the priority of global justice over national obligations.

Nonetheless, Miller can invoke other arguments to deny the priority of global justice. One argument would be that the special obligations of shared nationality are often obligations of *justice*, and hence the conflict between national obligations and duties of global justice is a conflict between competing claims of justice. For instance, the question whether to attend to the health care needs of one's co-nationals or instead to support foreign aid pits two claims of justice against one another. Thus the simple resolution I offered above—granting priority to global justice over national claims—is not available since justice factors on both sides of the dispute (D. Miller 2000: 167). Accordingly, nationality is perhaps relevant with respect to justice if the special entitlements due to nationality are in fact grounded on claims of justice.[4]

But this argument, that there are competing national and global *demands of justice*, and hence not subject to easy reconciliation, fails to see that these are demands of justice operating at different institutional levels. Consider demands of local justice understood here to mean demands of justice within associations within the state, and contrast these with the demands of domestic justice understood here to mean justice in the state. These are justice demands directed at different aspects of society, and it is not counter-intuitive, but indeed rather commonplace, to hold that domestic justice has priority over local justice should these come into conflict. The reason is that what rightful claims individuals in a local association have against each other have to be constrained by rightful claims persons in the larger society have against each other. That is, an association cannot claim to be rightly discharging its obligations of local justice if to do so requires that it use more than its fair share of resources as determined by the terms of domestic justice. The following deliberately preposterous example illustrates the structure of this point: a criminal organization cannot claim that demands of just distribution among its members need not be constrained by the demands of justice in society at large. That is, it is obviously absurd for a criminal gang to claim that it has to violate domestic justice because local justice (among the gang membership) cannot be realized otherwise. So, even though there are distinct "claims" of justice, it is reasonable to hold that some claims of justice have precedence over others. This applies to the claims of global justice and national justice. To the extent that national justice presupposes some background global justice, the priority of global justice over national justice is maintained.

---

[4] Armstrong raises a similar concern against global luck egalitarianism, that nationality can "influence entitlements" based on justice (2010: 330–1).

The priority of global justice does not mean, dubiously, that societies are always to dictate their policies with an eye towards bettering or maximizing the condition of the global worst-off. Indeed, on the institutional approach, the favored global distributive principle will be an institutional principle, and this provides space in the global arena for the pursuit of national commitments. Global egalitarians, on the institutional view, are committed to a global basic structure of a certain kind, and will hold that individuals and their nations have the duty of justice to strive to bring about and to sustain this institutional scheme. But within the space provided by this global basic structure, national self-determination and national pursuit of justice can be exercised.

To summarize: Miller's argument for the ethical significance of nationality, that it is the source of non-reducible special duties, including duties of justice, rightly reminds us that nationality is not wholly morally irrelevant. But global luck egalitarians can accept that there can be special duties, even duties of justice, owed specifically to co-nationals, and hence accept that nationality is morally relevant in this way. What they deny, and this Miller does not succeed in showing, is that nationality is morally relevant as well when determining the terms of background global justice.

## 7.2 Neutralizing national arbitrariness and global egalitarianism

The second class of objections against global luck egalitarianism says that even if nationality is arbitrary, its neutralization or mitigation does not yield global egalitarian distributive commitments. The neutralization of nationality can generate global egalitarian principles only if global equality is already the presumed distributive default.

Andrea Sangiovanni has advanced a series of carefully constructed arguments along these lines. One of these arguments is that neutralizing differences in persons' prospects due to unchosen circumstance does not imply "global equality in prospects" because it is not necessarily the case that the relevant global comparative baseline is an egalitarian one. Why should it follow that neutralizing the effects of nationality will in fact result in global equality if there is no antecedent global commitment that persons' life prospects should all be equal? Suppose that the global distributive default is not egalitarian but utilitarian, that is, distribution should be such as to maximize the aggregate global welfare of individuals. In which case, coupling this utilitarian default with the luck neutralization principle does not yield the sought-for result that there should be global equality in prospects, but only the conclusion that what counts as maximal aggregate welfare ought not to be skewed by arbitrary factors like nationality. The only way the neutralization of the effects of nationality can result in global egalitarianism is if it already presumed that the global distributive default is egalitarian. And this is question-begging, says Sangiovanni, for the case for global egalitarianism is exactly what is at issue.[5] To take another example, a luck neutralization principle within a conception of democratic equality need not result in global egalitarianism, even if nationality is presumed to be arbitrary, if that conception of democratic equality denies that distributive equality is a global concern. Neutralizing the effects of nationality would result at best in whatever non-egalitarian global baseline this account of democratic equality endorses.

Sangiovanni's argument makes the convincing point that luck neutralization alone does not guarantee distributive equality unless we are already committed to some egalitarian default. But his argument only shows that luck neutralization does not entail global egalitarianism, and not that luck egalitarianism does not. The reason for this is that luck neutralization is not exhaustive of luck egalitarianism, nor does luck neutralization imply a luck egalitarianism commitment. The invocation of the luck neutralization principle within an account of democratic equality in my above example is deliberate: it is meant to show that accepting the luck neutralization principle does not sufficiently nor necessarily make a position a luck egalitarian one. As I have proposed in Part II of this work, luck egalitarianism is not just about luck neutralization understood as a principle of redress. Luck egalitarianism is an account of the basis of equality, why an egalitarian default is warranted and what qualifies as an acceptable departure from this default and what does not. The luck neutralization principle offers a specification of the ideal of egalitarian distribution. It specifies the

---

[5] As Sangiovanni himself notes, his argument parallels Hurley's criticism that luck neutralization does not entail an *egalitarian* pattern of distribution (Hurley 2003: Ch. 6). Because Sangiovanni thinks that the comparative argument does not succeed, he countenances another argument, which takes luck neutralization to restore non-comparatively persons' counterfactual condition (what the person would otherwise have if it weren't for the interference of luck). Since my claim will be that luck egalitarianism can respond to his comparative challenge, I will leave aside his counter-factual alternative.

ground of equality, that is, why equality matters, and the conditions under which departures from equal distribution are acceptable. Luck neutralization does not by itself justify an egalitarian default. It can help specify the basis of this default only if it is understood as a principle within luck egalitarianism.

Within luck egalitarianism, the luck neutralization principle is part of the specification of an egalitarian commitment, and is not merely a principle of redress aiming to restore some *independently defined* default comparative baseline. Consider the different roles that luck neutralization plays in democratic equality and luck egalitarianism. The difference between luck egalitarianism and democratic equality is not whether luck neutralization has a function in either of these accounts, but in how each understands the egalitarian default and the conditions under which departures from this default are acceptable. For democratic equality, the default is justified by reference to the ideal of democratic reciprocity, and departures from this default are identified by reference to the constraints of democratic reciprocity. Now luck neutralization can come into play within this account of equality as a way of explicating what equality, already accepted as a commitment, requires. For example, as noted in Chapter 4, it might be held that it runs against democratic reciprocity if fellow citizens can suffer comparatively poorer life prospects simply because of bad luck. Luck neutralization in this case will lead to some restoration of the egalitarian default as given by democratic equality. But if we take democratic equality to be the paradigm of equality and apply it to the global context, presumed to be one in which the criterion of democratic reciprocity does not apply (or at least in the same way), then there will be no global egalitarian default, and any subsequent application of the luck neutralization principle against the arbitrariness of nationality will not generate global distributive equality. Thus, it is not surprising that, if one does not already adopt a luck egalitarian understanding of the baseline of equal distribution in the first place, utilizing the luck neutralization principle to mitigate the arbitrary effects of nationality need not result in global egalitarianism.

On the other hand, luck neutralization within luck egalitarianism is already presumptive of an egalitarian default. As an account of distributive equality, what luck egalitarianism seeks to do is to explicate why equal distribution is the baseline from which deviations have to be justified. It takes the equal moral agency to be the basic starting point and interprets this ideal to mean that, as equal moral agents, all are entitled to equal life prospects unless choice (but not circumstance) determines otherwise. The luck neutralization principle is derived from an understanding of what moral agency entails, and is part of the specification of the egalitarian default. If this is the understanding of why equality matters, and when exceptions to it are acceptable, then luck egalitarianism comes to the global debate already armed with an egalitarian default, and therefore luck neutralization in the global domain will tend towards equality in distribution.

In other words, relative to the argument from national arbitrariness, the case for a global egalitarian default is situated further upstream, as it were. That is, the global luck egalitarian argument that holds that national arbitrariness ought to be mitigated comes to the debate already committed to a global egalitarian default. It is already granted that mitigation of arbitrariness should tend towards equal distribution. This is not any more question-begging than is an alternative view of equality, like Sangiovanni's, that denies that there is such a default. Sangiovanni's argument that the neutralization of national arbitrariness does not entail global egalitarianism follows if we accept that there is no necessary global egalitarian default (that neutralization of arbitrariness will lean towards). But this is as much a substantive claim as the claim that there is a global egalitarian default, and has to be defended. Thus the presumption in Sangiovanni's objection is as much in need of defense as the presumption of the global luck egalitarians. But this is a debate about the grounds of equality and is prior to and distinct from the argument from neutralizing national arbitrariness.[6]

To be sure, some justification of the luck egalitarian ground of equality has to be made. My attempted defense of luck egalitarianism in Part II of this work is precisely to offer an alternative account of the egalitarian default to that offered by democratic egalitarianism (of which Sangio-vanni's relational idea of equality is a version). If the arguments there are acceptable, then the case for a global egalitarian default is already given under luck egalitarianism, and the neutralization of national arbitrariness does tend toward a global egalitarian distributive pattern. Although more

---

[6] Sangiovanni (2007) has elsewhere provided a powerful case for relational justice based on reciprocity in the context of social cooperation. See Caney (2008) and Abizadeh (2007) for a response to Sangiovanni on this point.

positive arguments have to be provided for interpreting the ideal of equal moral agency in the way proposed by luck egalitarianism, I have attempted to show in the earlier chapters that the common charge that so interpreting this ideal is implausible can be responded to. Sangiovanni's objection is a forceful one, and addressing it helps clarify what luck egalitarianism is about (or should be seen to be about, so I claim). First, it allows us to reiterate that luck egalitarianism is not coextensive with luck neutralization. As I have suggested, non-luck egalitarian views can adopt or incorporate the luck neutralization principle in their theories of equality. What makes an account distinctively luck egalitarian is not just that it relies on luck neutralization, but its understanding of the egalitarian default and the acceptable limits of departures from this default. To make the general point again, the luck neutralization principle as a principle *within* luck egalitarianism is not simply a principle of redress, that is, a principle that aims to restore distribution to some independently defined baseline, but is part of the specification of that baseline. Second, the luck neutralization principle is not intended, in itself, as a full justification of an egalitarian default. Rather, when conceived as a principle within luck egalitarianism, it is part of the set of ideas that provides an interpretation of what equal moral agency entails with respect to distributive justice.[7]

---

[7] As Vallentyne points out, few luck egalitarians intend the luck neutralization principle to do the work of justifying the egalitarian default. Its purpose is to offer a formulation of equality (Vallentyne 2006: 435–6). Vallentyne is responding to Hurley's parallel objection that luck neutralization fails to justify an *egalitarian* pattern of distribution.

# 8

# Clarifications and Conclusions

As the structure of this book aims to reflect, the questions of the site, ground, and reach of distributive equality are distinct, each being concerned with different aspects of equality. Greater clarity about the nature of equality can be obtained, so I hope to have shown, if these questions are examined in their own right. To make the same point from the "answer" side of the matter, institutional egalitarianism, luck egalitarianism, and global egalitarianism are responses to different questions of equality, and we can recognize the merits of each of these views of equality better if the specific questions they are addressing are not confused with one another.

For example, as I have argued, luck egalitarianism is best appreciated when it is understood distinctly as an account of the ground of distributive equality. That it is a response to the question of the ground of *distributive equality* shows that luck egalitarianism does not absurdly entail that the imprudent decision-maker now in severe straits is not entitled to social assistance. Humanitarian considerations distinct from distributive considerations can kick in here, in spite of the person's bad choice. That it addresses *the ground* of distributive equality means that it should not be evaluated as a substantive distributive principle and expected to meet conditions that it is not designed to meet (such as directly furnishing the currency and pattern of egalitarian distribution). Similarly, treating the site of egalitarian justice and its scope to be distinct issues avoids the mistake of thinking that a response to the site question also immediately limits the scope question. That the principles of egalitarian justice are trained at institutions is a separate matter from that of the reach of the relevant institutions to which they are directed. That egalitarian justice is institutional, for example, does not foreclose the possibility that it is also global in reach.

To be sure, that these are distinct questions does not mean that they are isolated from each other. How we respond to one question can shape our responses to the other two. Indeed, one of the goals in this work is to propose an account of equality that relates these different aspects of equality. But these are distinct questions and ought to be discussed as such.

Let me recap the main ideas covered in the previous chapters. I suggest the plausibility of an institutional approach to egalitarian justice that is grounded in luck egalitarian considerations and that is global in scope. The main rationale for the institutional approach, I argue, is that it is able to present a feasible means of demarcating the bounds of justice from those of other moral demands, specifically that of personal life (taken here to include personal relationships). The institutional approach is not a means of lightening the load of justice for individuals, but is a reflection of the proper demands of justice in light of value pluralism.

The luck egalitarian ideal defended in Part II takes luck egalitarianism, understood as a grounding ideal of equality, to be of limited application in terms of its moral domain. It is concerned specifically with the question of distributive equality, distinct from that of other matters of distribution, such as those pertaining to humanitarian assistance and rescue. I also propose that luck egalitarianism can be interpreted in a way that is consistent with the Rawlsian idea (to twist it into a slogan pace Hamlet) that "There is nothing either just or unjust, but institutions make it so." This involves reading luck egalitarianism institutionally, namely, that distributive egalitarian commitments arise only in the context of systemic social practices that turn arbitrary matters into differential advantages for persons. I argue that luck egalitarianism can be constructively given this institutional interpretation without losing its significance and distinctiveness as an account of why equality matters.

Part III extends the luck egalitarian account proposed to the global context, and proposes that since the global order is constituted by certain institutionalized practices that convert arbitrary matters into differential advantages for persons, global egalitarian obligations on luck egalitarian grounds are generated. Unlike some competing accounts of why equality matters, the institutional luck egalitarian account I proposed, while grounded in institutions, does not require a *specific* normative characterization of the relevant institutions, as in the case of democratic equality. That is, the relevant global institutions need not be described or idealized as institutions of social cooperative or democratic political institutions before egalitarian commitments are motivated. The fact that global institutions or systems of entrenched practices have the effect of rendering luck into social advantages or disadvantages is sufficient for activating global egalitarian commitments.

As mentioned at the start of this work, my goal is to render more plausible institutional egalitarianism, luck egalitarianism, and global egalitarianism. These are accounts of different aspects of equality whose plausibility has recently been challenged. By clarifying the basis and contours of these accounts of equality, admittedly parting ways in some respects with extant accounts, and in addressing some of the main objections to these views, I hope to be able to restore some philosophic confidence in these accounts of equality. I will not claim that I have offered conclusive arguments for institutional, luck, and global egalitarianisms; my main goal in this work is to show that these accounts of equality are plausible and worthy of further development and philosophical investigation. In closing, I will clarify some of the main claims advanced and consider some possible objections.

## 8.1 Equality and its site

Must equality have only one site of application? Why not say that equality takes different substantive forms depending on the social domain in question and can apply as an ideal at different moral realms or sites, so to speak? To clarify, I do not hold that taking the site of egalitarian justice to be located in the basic structure means that equality as *a general moral concern* is inapplicable in other sites. As a moral ideal, equality understood as equal consideration clearly is relevant in interpersonal relations (and not only when these relations are institutionally mediated). Equal moral consideration applies *within* private associations such as in the workplace, arguably within familial groups, and so on. But this will be moral equality understood in a very general and abstract way, and what equal concern amounts to in each kind of these relationships or arrangements can take different forms. One of the claims of this work is that equality understood as a concern of *distributive* justice applies to the basic institutions of the social order, and that the substantive principle of distributive equality is directed at these institutions and need not directly regulate also, for example, interpersonal relations or other associational arrangements within the social order. To put this point in a different way, the idea is that principles of justice for institutions need not be identical in substance or form to principles regulating other aspects of social life, such as personal relations within the rules of institutions. For example, it is not a compromise of egalitarian justice when personal conduct within the rules of institutions is neither egalitarianly motivated nor affecting so long as these institutions are in fact regulated by an egalitarian principle. To illustrate, while Rawls's difference principle can be the relevant distributive egalitarian principle for the basic structure of society, it is less clear that this principle or its grounding commitment is applicable in interpersonal relations or within associations like the family.

Yet, in contrast with statist conceptions of equality, I argue that restricting the site of distributive equality to institutions does not necessarily limit the reach or scope of equality to the state. Unless the institutional site of justice is taken to be coextensive with the institutions of a political society, a sovereign state, it remains a further question whether there are institutions of the relevant sort outside the boundaries of the state that can be the subject of justice. I have attempted a strong global egalitarian conclusion, namely that reasons why distributive justice matters, and matters institutionally in the domestic context, apply as well to the global order, and hence domestic distributive egalitarian commitments have their global counterpart.

Moreover, that the site of justice is institutions does not mean that the ground of justice must also be similarly understood. Justice may require the formation of certain kinds of institutions, such as cooperative institutions, but the cause of justice itself need not be dependent on the presence of these particular kinds of institutions. That is, while justice may require cooperative social institutions to *be realized*, it does not follow that cooperative institutions are necessary in order for justice to *be generated* as a concern. The question of the circumstances under which justice is of concern is distinct from that of the conditions of its implementation. I have tried to argue that the fact of entrenched social forms and sustained and systemic practices is both necessary and sufficient for generating concerns of distributive justice. Specifically, I suggest an institutional luck egalitarian ideal that holds that justice becomes a cause of concern when sustained social arrangements and practices have the tendency to turn arbitrary facts into disparate social advantages.

So while distributive justice is contingent on there being common sustained practices, and these are often institutional in form, this does not render distributive justice into an associative obligation as the idea of "associative" is typically understood in the literature. That is, there is no requirement that some political associational ties between persons be present in order for distributive commitments to kick in. The fact that there is a social order that impinges on persons is sufficient for activating distributive demands among those responsible for the order and all others who are affected. There is no requirement in this account, for example, that participants in a distributive scheme be members of a political association like the state as in typical "associative" accounts of distributive justice.

## 8.2 The presumption of value pluralism: In luck egalitarianism

My discussion invokes the idea of value pluralism at various points. By value pluralism, I mean the idea that there are different and non-reducible domains of values. One way that value pluralism plays a part in my discussion is in my distinction between humanitarian assistance and duties of distributive equality and my limitation of luck egalitarianism to just the domain of distributive justice.

Concerning this point, it might be objected that there is nothing in my account of luck egalitarianism that justifies its limited application, and that in fact my invocation of values pluralism seems ad hoc (Stark and Landesman 2010; Schemmel). To clarify, my claim is just that on the presumption of value pluralism, we can treat luck egalitarianism as an ideal that applies within a specific moral domain (that of distributive justice). The presumption of value pluralism is not unreasonable unless we ought to accept that value monism is the default view of the nature of morality. But this is, of course, hardly the case. Nor, more importantly, is my limitation of luck egalitarianism to a circumscribed moral domain at odds with luck egalitarianism as such, for there is nothing within luck egalitarianism that necessarily rules out value pluralism. It may be the case that many luck egalitarians affirm monism and hence will find my limited reading of the applicability of luck egalitarianism problematic. But this will be on account of their presumed background monism (which informs their understanding of the applicative range of luck egalitarianism), not on account of their luck egalitarianism (see A. Macleod 2010). A monistic luck egalitarian will of course expect the luck egalitarian ideal to apply across the whole of morality. But since there is nothing in luck egalitarianism as a principle that necessitates monism, independent reasons must be given for affirming this view of morality if this is to be a real objection to my limited domain view of luck egalitarianism. And this is a debate in meta-ethics and not luck egalitarianism. My purpose is to show that if we presume value pluralism, we can usefully conceive luck egalitarianism specifically as a principle about distributive equality. In doing so, I argue that we arrive at a more plausible account of luck egalitarianism that still provides a distinctively luck egalitarian understanding of why equality matters, and that can respond to the standard issues that egalitarians are in the first instance concerned about.

My understanding of luck egalitarianism as a distributive egalitarian ideal does not directly rule out the possibility that luck egalitarianism can be a more basic moral principle that applies in other domains of value, and can regulate, say, interpersonal non-institutional relations. Indeed, a luck egalitarian coming to the debate already affirming some version of value monism (with the luck/choice principle operating as the dominant principle for all of morality) might adopt an "act luck egalitarianism" that allows for indirect approaches toward realizing the goals of luck egalitarianism, including allowing for special principles for institutions as a form of division of labor. Thus the act luck egalitarian might hold that my limitation of luck egalitarianism to the domain of distributive equality is unnecessary and unwarranted.[1] But, again, this is a meta-ethical debate and there is no basis to take monism or pluralism to be the meta-ethical default. The act luck egalitarian relies on a meta-ethical presumption as much as my pluralistic account does. Moreover, the act luck egalitarian has to show why this across-the-board application of the luck egalitarian principle does not have absurd implications (a problem that my restricted account avoids). I don't claim that the act luck egalitarian is definitively unable to show this, but she at least has that challenging burden.[2] Finally, even when

---

[1] I am here interpreting a comment offered by Peter Vallentyne.
[2] Thus for brute luck egalitarians like Vallentyne, Anderson's objection that luck egalitarianism must absurdly compensate the ugly person is not at bottom a problem for principle: it is not counter-intuitive for society to compensate ugly persons as such, but society normally ought not to because of informational limitation reasons and social opportunity costs.

luck egalitarianism is restricted to the domain of distributive justice, it still offers a very distinctive account of equality and an account worth developing. I have expressed some doubts in the preceding discussion about extending luck egalitarianism as a general moral principle, but my positive claim is that luck egalitarianism can coherently be understood narrowly and still be a valuable and distinctive position. Indeed, it is worth noting that luck egalitarianism was originally conceived as a position *within distributive equality*. That is, it was given life as an ideal within the debate on distributive justice, not in debates in moral philosophy as whole.[3] My view is that we can and should retain its original but modest purpose, and in so doing we can better understand its real relevance and appeal.

In sum, my limiting luck egalitarianism to the special domain of distributive justice is not arbitrary unless (i) we assume that value monism is the default meta-ethical view or (ii) we assume that somehow luck egalitarianism must entail value monism. The crucial point is that luck egalitarianism, even understood specifically as an account of institutional egalitarian justice, is still a distinctive account of equality (in contrast with, say, democratic equality) and is worth considering in its own right.

## 8.3 The presumption of value pluralism: In the institutional approach

Thus the presumption of value pluralism does not beg the question in favor of my account of luck egalitarianism. It specifies the given moral landscape in which I have attempted to situate an account of luck egalitarianism. The same perhaps cannot be said of its invocation in my discussion of the site of justice. Here the presumption of pluralism already puts the burden of proof on those who insist that justice should have trans-institutional site of application. Recall that it is in affirmation of the plurality of moral domains that the institutional approach is justified; that is, it is defended as a means of

---

[3] This is not to deny that there has been important discussion on moral luck (Nagel, "Moral Luck" in Nagel 1979; B. Williams 1981). But the distinctive formulation of luck egalitarianism, as the idea that distributive justice should track choice and not luck, arose in discussions on distributive justice (as in Arneson, G. A. Cohen, and Dworkin). To be sure, Anderson is responsible for coining the term, but the term captures a family of positions distinctive within distributive justice.

demarking the appropriate boundary between the domain of justice and the domain of personal life.

Thus it is important to clarify the thrust of the discussion in Part I. The aim is to assuage the initial worry that an institutional focus is implausible, since it implies that individuals who are permitted to act on non-egalitarian terms within egalitarian institutional rules are expected also to endorse and support egalitarian institutions. It attempts to do this by showing how this division of principles to distinctive domains is not only plausible but required, if we see it as a response to value pluralism. That is, the institutional approach is not so obviously misconceived once we make more explicit the pluralism that compels this way of thinking of the site of justice. Because of competing personal ends whose values are not necessarily all reducible to the value of egalitarian justice, persons committed to justice and to irreducibly valuable personal ends must find a way of allowing for personal pursuits in conformity with justice. The institutional approach provides the solution. Instead of treating it as a lightening of the load of justice, one might rather see it as a reinforcement of the weighty demands of justice: it says: "you may freely pursue your personal goals but only if you in collaboration with others have set up and maintain institutions based on justice. This is the basic prerequisite of free personal pursuits."

Moreover, to the extent that some of the main critics of the institutional approach do not explicitly deny moral pluralism, their objections become all the more difficult to sustain. It does not help the critics' position for them simply to say that they accept competing values to distributive equality and that they grant the existence of "prerogatives" that can permissibly limit egalitarian demands. For this merely restates the problem that the institutional approach is meant to solve, which is how can we feasibly demarcate and operationalize this boundary between distributive justice and permissible personal pursuits? That is, the question is: how can we determine and identify the space of prerogatives to deviate from justice? The institutional approach provides an answer to this question; the trans-institutional view simply defers it.

In short, the claim is that the rationale for the institutional approach is better appreciated on the presumption of value pluralism, and that opposition to that approach must either present a case against moral pluralism or be at risk of defending an account of distributive justice that contradicts other moral values.

## 8.4  Cosmopolitan egalitarianism

I have argued that if luck egalitarianism is the basic ideal as to why equality matters, the scope of equality is also consequently global. This argument is mostly directed at statist egalitarians, that is egalitarians who deny equality's global scope. Recently, however, there are some commentators who, while rejecting the statist egalitarian position, nonetheless do not come all the way to the global egalitarian side. They hold that the statists have exaggerated the non-institutional character of the global order in their attempt to mark the difference between the domestic and global domains. Accepting the normative premise of the statist egalitarians, that is that distributive egalitarian commitments are generated only when certain institutional forms are in place, they argue that some degree of global distributive obligations obtains globally, given that there are significant global institutional practices of different kinds. Examples of these specific institutions include trade regimes, international regimes governing intellectual property rights, policies on global environmental protection, and so on. But because the totality of these specific institutions does not amount to a global *basic structure*, we don't get all the way to a full-fledged global egalitarianism. Thus, on this view, while statists over-exaggerate the non-institutional character of the global order, the cosmopolitans have ignored institutional differences between the global and domestic contexts. To identify this supposed distinctive position, let us call it the "intermediate" globalist view.

The intermediate approach holds that certain demands of distributive justice are in force in the global order because of the presence of certain institutionalized global practices. But these global distributive commitments are said to be not egalitarian ones. Yet it is not often clear in what sense these commitments are not egalitarian commitments. To take a recent view, Aaron James has argued, for example, that fairness in the distribution of the benefits trade requires equal distribution of the benefits as a default, and departures from this benchmark are acceptable only when they are to the benefit of the less-well-off (James 2011). So stated, however, it is not easy to see why James's is not a global *egalitarian* commitment. After all, it takes equal distribution to the baseline (by specifying what fairness would require), and specifies conditions for deviating from the benchmark of equality, and its scope is global to the extent that the trade practices to regulate are global in extent (ibid.: Ch. 5).

Indeed, James's principle, even if limited to the practice of trade, has the general form of the difference principle. Thus more needs to be said as to why this is not an egalitarian ideal.

Perhaps one reason for believing this to be an alternative to global egalitarianism (rather than an account thereof) might be that, in the global case, the targeted institutional practice is a very specific and limited one (say, the institution of international trade) rather than a complex system of institutions, as in the domestic case. But it is not clear why the density and complexity of the target (the practice to be regulated) has the property of rendering a principle aimed at it egalitarian or not egalitarian by definition. Even if it is claimed as a matter of definition that egalitarian distributive principles can be aimed only at the "basic structure" of a social order, it does not follow that the basic structure must by definition consist of a critical mass of specific institutional practices. Why isn't the combined set of global institutions, taking into account their complex relations with each other, such as trade regimes, intellectual property rights law, rules governing corporate conduct, international laws governing economic practices, and the like, sufficient for constituting a global basic structure?

The basic structure that is the proper target of the distributive egalitarian principle is the set of institutions that has pervasive and profound impact on persons' prospects and that is amenable to public regulation; and what comprises this relevant institutional set can vary from social domain to social domain. In the global context, the set of relevant institutions that makes up the global basic structure is possibly more limited than those of domestic society. So the global basic structure may be less massively constituted than domestic ones. Yet so long as the institutions making it up have profound and pervasive impact on persons' life prospects and are subject to regulation, it is not clear why the global basic structure is by definition not an appropriate target of egalitarian regulation.

To borrow Blake's aptly descriptive terminology, global justice can be concerned with "relative deprivation" or only with "absolute deprivation" (Blake 2001: 258).[4] That is, it can evaluate persons' prospects comparatively (by reference to how others are faring) or only absolutely (by reference to some fixed standard). The threshold of absolute deprivation can of course be defined differently, some more robustly than others. But an

---

[4] To recall, Blake argues that global justice is committed to mitigating absolute deprivation but not relative deprivation.

account of global justice is not comparative just because it has a very substantial threshold. So, if some of the intermediate views differ from typical statist views (at least take themselves to differ) simply in terms of where they fix the threshold of absolute deprivation, they are not conceptually different from the statist position.[5] They remain essentially absolutist and non-comparative with respect to the question of deprivation. A basically sufficientist account of distribution remains sufficientist no matter where the target of sufficiency is drawn. However, if an account claims to be concerned not just with absolute deprivation but also relative deprivation, then it is not always obvious how it is not an egalitarian account. To be sure, if egalitarianism is not just comparative but also takes equal distribution as the default (as defined in Chapter 1), responsiveness to relative deprivation does not entail egalitarianism. Still, proponents of an intermediate view that is comparative will have to clarify the basis and form of their distributive commitment to show how it is really "intermediate" and not egalitarian. In the case of James, for example, the intermediate global distributive principle when explicated seems to be basically egalitarian.[6]

## 8.5 Other questions

I suggest in Chapter 4 that a luck egalitarian grounding principle for equality could support something like Rawls's difference principle. But it is possible that there are other ways of realizing the luck egalitarian principle, and I have left this matter of identifying the most plausible distributive principle that is grounded on luck egalitarianism largely to one side.

Another question of equality that I have largely put to one side is that of the metric of equality. Now to contextualize parts of the preceding

[5] In this regard J. Cohen and Sabel's response to Nagel is an objection about Nagel's location of the threshold of sufficiency, rather than a rejection of a sufficientist approach to global justice.

[6] One suspects that the real reason why James himself takes his global account to be non-egalitarian is because he draws his principles from the fact and implications of global practices, rather than from some non-institutional moral consideration (James 2011: Ch. 1 and 4). But if so, this means then that what James is arguing for is a distinctive (and indeed insightful) way of understanding the ground of global egalitarianism, not a rejection of global egalitarianism per se.

discussions, I have presumed that the proper currency or metric of distributive equality is resources, although my main arguments, I maintain, are
neutral with respect to this issue. Still, a full defense of luck egalitarianism
and institutional justice must eventually specify the proper metric of
equality. Following the basic claim of this work, the question of the
currency of equality is another distinct question to be examined without
confusion with another. But, following another claim of the work, responses to each of these distinct questions, although addressing different
aspects of equality, will influence each other. I think how we specify the
ground and site of equality will play an important role in how we work
out equality's currency. Our view of the proper luck/choice cut will
inform our view of the proper metric of distributive equality; and that
we take the proper site of equality to be institutions will also be an
important consideration in that whatever metric we adopt must be one
that can feasibly be institutionally regulated. The currency of distribution
has to be also commonly affirmed as the appropriate currency by members
of the relevant social order, and this point will be important when the
discussion concerns global distributive justice. Thus, although the questions as to the pattern of egalitarian distribution and the currency of
distribution were questions I put to one side, I hope that my discussion
of the site, ground, and scope of equality can have some bearing on our
understanding of equality's pattern and currency.

# Bibliography

Abizadeh, A. (2007). "Cooperation, Pervasive Impact, and Coercion: On the Scope (not Site) of Distributive Justice." *Philosophy & Public Affairs* 35/4: 318–58.

Anderson, E. (1999). "What is the Point of Equality?" *Ethics* 109/2: 287–337.

Armstrong, C. (2010). "National Self-Determination, Global Equality and Moral Arbitrariness." *Journal of Political Philosophy* 18/3: 313–34.

Arneson, R. (1989). "Equality and Equal Opportunity for Welfare." *Philosophical Studies* 56: 77–93.

——(2000). "Luck Egalitarianism and Prioritarianism." *Ethics* 110/2: 339–49.

Barry, B. (1995). *Justice As Impartiality*. Oxford: Oxford University Press.

——(2005). *Why Social Justice Matters?* Cambridge: Polity Press.

Barry, C., Ypi, L., and Goodin, R. (2009). "Associative Duties, Global Justice, and the Colonies." *Philosophy & Public Affairs* 37/2: 103–35.

Barry, N. (2006). "Defending Luck Egalitarianism." *Journal of Applied Philosophy* 23: 89–107.

Beitz, C. (1989). *Political Equality*. Princeton: Princeton University Press.

——(1999 [1979]). *Political Theory and International Relations*, 2nd edn. Princeton: Princeton University Press.

——(2001). "Does Global Inequality Matter?" *Metaphilosophy* 32/1 and 32/2: 95–112.

Blake, M. (2001). "Distributive Justice, State Coercion, and Autonomy." *Philosophy & Public Affairs* 30/3: 257–96.

Brock, G. (2009). *Global Justice*. Oxford: Oxford University Press.

——and Brighouse, H. (eds.) (2005). *The Political Philosophy of Cosmopolitanism*. Cambridge: Cambridge University Press.

Brown, A. (2009). *Ronald Dworkin's Theory of Equality: domestic and global perspectives*. London: Palgrave Macmillan.

Caney, S. (2005). *Justice Beyond Borders*. Oxford: Oxford University Press.

——(2008). "Global Distributive Justice and the State." *Political Studies* 57: 487–518.

Casal, P. (2007). "Why Sufficiency Is Not Enough." *Ethics* 117/2: 296–326.

Cohen, G. A. (1989). "On the Currency of Egalitarian Justice." *Ethics* 99/4: 906–44.

——(1992). "Incentives, Inequality and Community," in G. B. Peterson (ed.). *The Tanner Lectures on Human Values* vol. xiii. Salt Lake City: University of Utah Press.

—— (1997). "Where the Action is: on the site of distributive justice." *Philosophy & Public Affairs* 26/1: 3–30.

—— (2000). *If You're an Egalitarian, How Come You're so Rich?* Cambridge, MA: Harvard University Press.

—— (2006). "Luck and Equality: a reply to Hurley." *Philosophy and Phenomenological Research* 72: 439–46.

—— (2008). *Rescuing Justice and Equality.* Cambridge, MA: Harvard University Press.

Cohen, J. (2002). "Taking People as They Are?" *Philosophy & Public Affairs* 30/4: 363–86.

—— and Sabel, C. (2006). "Extra Rempublicam Nulla Justitia?" *Philosophy & Public Affairs* 34/2: 147–75.

Daniels, N. (1990). "Equality of What: welfare, resources or capabilities?" *Philosophy and Phenomenological Research* 50: 273–96.

—— (2003). "Democratic Equality: Rawls's complex egalitarianism," in S. Freeman (ed.). *The Cambridge Companion to Rawls.* Cambridge: Cambridge University Press, 241–76.

Donagan, A. (1987). "Consistency in Rationalist Moral Systems," in C. Gowans (ed.). *Moral Dilemmas.* Oxford: Oxford University Press.

Dworkin, R. (1977). *Taking Rights Seriously.* Cambridge, MA: Harvard University Press.

—— (1983). "In Defense of Liberal Equality." *Social Philosophy and Policy* 1/1: 24–40.

—— (1992). "Liberal Community," in Avineri and de-Shalit (eds.). *Individuals and Community.* Oxford: Oxford University Press.

—— (2000). *Sovereign Virtue.* Cambridge, MA: Harvard University Press.

—— (2003). "Equality, Luck, and Hierarchy." *Philosophy & Public Affairs* 31/2: 190–8.

—— (2006). *Is Democracy Possible Here?* Princeton: Princeton University Press.

Estlund, D. (1998). "Liberalism, Equality, and Fraternity in Cohen's Critique of Rawls." *Journal of Political Philosophy* 6/1: 99–112.

Fabre, C. (2006). "Global Distributive Justice: an egalitarian perspective." *Canadian Journal of Philosophy* (supplementary vol.) 31: 139–64.

—— (2010). "Distributive Justice and Freedom: Cohen on Money and Labor." *Utilitas* 22/4: 393–412.

Fleischacker, S. (2004). *A Short History of Distributive Justice.* Cambridge, MA: Harvard University Press.

Fleurbaey, M. (1995). "Equal Opportunity or Equal Social Outcome." *Economics and Politics* 11: 25–55.

—— (1998). "Equality Among Responsible Individuals," in J.-F. Laslier et al. (eds.). *Freedom in Economics.* New York: Routledge.

Frankfurt, H. (1987). "Equality as a Moral Ideal." *Ethics* 98/1: 21–43.

Freeman, S. (ed.) (2003). *The Cambridge Companion to Rawls*. Cambridge: Cambridge University Press.

—— (2006a). *Justice and the Social Contract*. New York: Oxford University Press.

—— (2006b). Distributive Justice and the Law of Peoples," in R. Martin and D. Reidy (eds.). *Rawls's Law of Peoples: a realistic utopia?* Oxford: Blackwell.

—— (2007). *Rawls*. London: Routledge Press.

—— (2008). "Review of Otsuka, *Libertarianism without Inequality*." *Mind* 117: 465–71.

—— (2009). "Distributive Justice." Unpublished paper.

Goodin, R. (2007). "Enfranchising all Affected Interests, and Its Alternatives." *Philosophy & Public Affairs* 35/1: 40–68.

Gould, C. (2004). *Globalizing Democracy and Human Rights*. Cambridge: Cambridge University Press.

Hayward, T. (2006). "Global Justice and the Distribution of Natural Resources." *Political Studies* 54/2: 349–69.

Heath, J. (2005). "Rawls on Global Distributive Justice: a defense." *Canadian Journal of Philosophy* (supplementary vol.) 31: 193–226.

Held, D. (1992). "Democracy: from city states to a cosmopolitan order?" *Political Studies*, Special Issue, 40: 10–39.

Hurley, S. (2003). *Justice, Luck, and Knowledge*. Cambridge, MA: Harvard University Press.

James, A. (2011, forthcoming). *Fairness in Practice: a social contract for a global economy*. Oxford: Oxford University Press.

Jones, C. (1999). *Global Justice*. Oxford: Oxford University Press.

Julius, A. J. (2003). "Basic Structure and the Value of Equality." *Philosophy & Public Affairs*. 31/4: 321–55.

—— (2006). "Nagel's Atlas." *Philosophy & Public Affairs* 34/4: 176–93.

Kant, I. (1953 [1785]). *Groundwork of the Metaphysics of Morals*, trans. H. J. Paton. New York: Harper and Row.

—— (1991 [1795]). "Perpetual Peace," in Hans Reiss (trans. and ed.). *Kant's Political Writings*, 2nd edn. Cambridge: Cambridge University Press.

—— (1991 [1795]). *The Metaphysics of Morals*, in Hans Reiss (trans. and ed.). *Kant's Political Writings*, 2nd edn. Cambridge: Cambridge University Press.

Kelly, E. (2000). "Personal Concern." *Canadian Journal of Philosophy* 30/1: 115–36.

Knight, C. (2009). *Luck Egalitarianism: equality, responsibility, and justice*. Edinburgh: Edinburgh University Press.

Kymlicka, W. (1990). *Contemporary Political Philosophy*. Oxford: Oxford University Press.

Lippert-Rasmussen, K. (2001). "Equality, Option Luck, and Responsibility." *Ethics* 111/3: 548–79.

Macedo, S. (2007). "When and Why Should Liberal Democracies Restrict Immigration," in Rogers Smith (ed.). *Citizenship, Borders and Human Needs*. Philadelphia: University of Pennsylvania Press.

Macleod, A. (1985). "Economic Inequality: Justice and Incentives," in K. Kipnis and D. Meyers (eds.). *Economic Justice: Private Rights and Public Responsibilities*. Totowa, NJ: Rowman and Allanheld.

——(2010). "Luck Egalitarianism and Imprudent Choice." Amintaphil Conference, Rochester, NY, October 2010.

Macleod, C. (2011). "Parental Responsibilities in an Unjust World," in D. Archard and D. Benatar (eds.). *Procreation and Parenthood*. Oxford: Oxford University Press.

Miller, D. (1988). "The Ethical Significance of Nationality." *Ethics* 98/4: 647–62.

——(1995). *On Nationality*. Oxford: Oxford University Press.

——(1998). "The Limits of Cosmopolitan Justice," in D. Mapel and T. Nardin (eds.). *International Society*: 164–81. Princeton: Princeton University Press.

——(1999). *Principles of Social Justice*. Cambridge, MA: Harvard University Press.

——(2000). *Citizenship and National Identity*. Cambridge: Polity Press.

——(2007). *National Responsibility and Global Justice*. Oxford: Oxford University Press.

Miller, R. (2010). *Globalizing Justice: the ethics of power and poverty*. Oxford: Oxford University Press.

Moellendorf, D. (2002). *Cosmopolitan Justice*. Boulder, CO: Westview Press.

Moore, M. (2001). *The Ethics of Nationalism*. Oxford: Oxford University Press.

——(2010). "Defending Community: nationalism, patriotism and culture," in D. A. Bell (ed.). *Ethics and World Politics*. Oxford: Oxford University Press.

Murphy, L. (1999). "Institutions and the Demands of Justice." *Philosophy & Public Affairs* 27/4: 251–91.

——(2000). *Moral Demands in Nonideal Theory*. New York: Oxford University Press.

Nagel, T. (1979). *Mortal Questions*. Cambridge: Cambridge University Press.

——(1991). *Equality and Partiality*. New York: Oxford University Press.

——(2005). "The Problem of Global Justice." *Philosophy & Public Affairs* 33/2: 113–47.

Navin, M. (2011). "Luck and Oppression." *Ethical Theory and Moral Practice* Online First: 10 January 2011.

Nozick, R. (1975). *Anarchy, State and Utopia*. New York: Basic Books.

Nussbaum, M. (2000a). *Women and Human Development*. Cambridge: Cambridge University Press.

——(2000b). "The Costs of Tragedy: some moral limits of cost–benefit analysis." *Journal of Legal Studies* 29/2: 1005–36.

Nussbaum, M. (2001). *The Fragility of Goodness*, rev. edn. Cambridge: Cambridge University Press.

—— (2006). *Frontiers of Justice: disabilities, nationality, and species membership.* Cambridge, MA: Harvard University Press.

Otsuka, M. (2002). "Luck, Insurance, and Equality." *Ethics*, 113/1: 40–54.

—— (2003). *Libertarianism Without Inequality*. Oxford: Oxford University Press.

—— (2008). "Freedom of Occupational Choice." *Ratio* 21: 440–53.

Pierik, R. (2006). "Reparations for Luck Egalitarianism." *Journal of Social Philosophy* 37: 423–40.

Pogge, T. (1989). *Realizing Rawls*. Ithaca, NY: Cornell University Press.

—— (2000). "On the Site of Distributive Justice: Reflections on Cohen and Murphy." *Philosophy & Public Affairs* 29/2: 137–69.

—— (2002). *World Poverty and Human Rights*. Oxford: Polity Press.

Rakowski, E. (1991). *Equal Justice*. Oxford: Oxford University Press.

Rawls, J. (1971). *A Theory of Justice*. Cambridge, MA: Harvard University Press.

—— (1993). *Political Liberalism*. New York: Columbia University Press.

—— (1999a). *The Law of Peoples*. Cambridge, MA: Harvard University Press.

—— (1999b). *Collected Papers*, S. Freeman (ed.). Cambridge, MA: Harvard University Press.

—— (1999c). *A Theory of Justice*, rev. edn. Cambridge, MA: Harvard University Press.

—— (2001). *Justice as Fairness*, E. Kelly (ed.). Cambridge, MA: Harvard University Press.

Reiss, H. (trans. and ed.) (1991) *Kant's Political Writings*, 2nd edn. Cambridge: Cambridge University Press.

Ripstein, A. (1994). "Equality, Luck, and Responsibility." *Philosophy & Public Affairs* 23/1: 1–23.

Risse, M. (2004). "Does Left-Libertarianism Have Coherent Foundations?" *Politics, Philosophy & Economics* 3/3: 337–64.

Roemer, J. (1996). *Theories of Distributive Justice*. Cambridge, MA: Harvard University Press.

Ronzoni, M. (2009). "The Global Order: A Case of Background Justice? A Practice Dependent Account." *Philosophy & Public Affairs*: 37/3: 229–56.

Rousseau, J. J. (1987 [1762]). *The Social Contract*, Cress. D. (trans.). Indianapolis, IN: Hackett Publishing.

Sandbu, M. (2004). "On Dworkin's brute-luck–option-luck distinction and the consistency of brute-luck egalitarianism." *Politics, Philosophy & Economics* 3/3: 283–312.

Sangiovanni, A. (2007). "Global Justice, Reciprocity, and the State." *Philosophy & Public Affairs* 35/1: 3–39.

——(2011, forthcoming). "Global Justice and the Arbitrariness of Birth." *Monist* 94/4.

Sanyal, S. (2012). "A Defense of Democratic Egalitarianism." *Journal of Philosophy* 109: 413–434.

Scanlon, T. M. (1987). "The Significance of Choice." *The Tanner Lectures on Human Values*, vol. 8, McMurrin, S. (ed.). Salt Lake City: University of Utah Press.

——(1998). *What We Owe to Each Other*. Cambridge, MA: Harvard University Press.

——(2003). "The Diversity of Objections to Inequality," in T. M. Scanlon. *The Difficulty of Tolerance*. Cambridge: Cambridge University Press.

Scheffler, S. (1982). *The Rejection of Consequentialism*. New York: Oxford University Press.

——(2001). *Boundaries and Allegiances*. Oxford: Oxford University Press.

——(2003a). "What is Egalitarianism?" *Philosophy & Public Affairs* 31/1: 5–39. Reprinted in Scheffler (2010).

——(2003b). "Equality as the Virtue of Sovereigns: a reply to Ronald Dworkin." *Philosophy & Public Affairs* 31/2: 199–206. Reprinted in Scheffler (2010).

——(2005). "Choice, Circumstance, and the Value of Equality." *Politics, Philosophy & Economics* 4/1: 5–28. Reprinted in Scheffler (2010).

——(2006). "Is the Basic Structure Basic?" in C. Sypnowich (ed.). *The Egalitarian Conscience: essays in honor of G. A. Cohen*. Oxford: Oxford University Press. Reprinted in Scheffler (2010).

——(2010). *Equality and Tradition*. New York: Oxford University Press.

Schemmel, C. (2012). "Luck Egalitarianism As Democratic Reciprocity: A Response to Tan." *Journal of Philosophy* 109: 435–448.

Segall, S. (2007). "In Solidarity with the Imprudent: A Defense of Luck Egalitarianism." *Social Theory and Practice* 33/2: 177–98.

——(2010). *Health, Luck and Justice*. Princeton: Princeton University Press.

Sen, A. (1980). "Equality of What?" in S. McMurrin (ed.). *The Tanner Lectures on Human Values*, vol. 1, 353–69. Salt Lake City: University of Utah Press.

——(1992). *Inequality Reexamined*. Cambridge, MA: Harvard University Press.

Shiffrin, S. (2010). "Incentives, Motives, and Talents." *Philosophy & Public Affairs* 38/2: 111–42.

Shue, H. (1980). *Basic Rights*. Princeton: Princeton University Press.

Smith, A. (1993 [1776]). *The Wealth of Nations*. Oxford: Oxford University Press.

Stark, C. and Landesman, B. (2010). "Three Problems with Luck Egalitarianism." Paper presented at the Amintaphil Conference, Rochester, NY, October 2010.

——(2011). "Luck, Equality, and the Cosmic Order." Unpublished paper.

Sypnowich, C. (ed.) (2006). *The Egalitarian Conscience: essays in honor of G. A. Cohen*. Oxford: Oxford University Press.

Tan, K. C. (2004a). "Justice and Personal Pursuits." *Journal of Philosophy* 101: 331–62.

Tan, K. C. (2004b). *Justice Without Borders*. Cambridge: Cambridge University Press.

—— (2005). "Cosmopolitan Impartiality and Patriotic Partiality." *Canadian Journal of Philosophy* (supplementary vol.) 31: 165–192.

—— (2006). "The Boundary of Justice and the Justice of Boundaries." *Canadian Journal of Law and Jurisprudence* 19/2: 319–44.

—— (2008). "A Defense of Luck Egalitarianism." *Journal of Philosophy* 105: 665–90.

—— (2010a). "Rights, Institutions, and Global Justice," in *Pogge and his Critics*, A. Jagger (ed.). Cambridge: Polity Press.

—— (2010b). "Poverty and Global Distributive Justice," in D. Bell (ed.). *Ethics and World Politics*. Oxford: Oxford University Press.

Vallentyne, P. (2002). "Brute Luck, Option Luck, and Equality of Initial Opportunities." *Ethics* 112/3: 529–57.

—— (2006). "Hurley on Justice and Responsibility." *Philosophy and Phenomenological Research* 72/2: 433–8.

—— Otsuka, M., and Steiner, M., (2005). "Why Left-Libertarianism Isn't Incoherent, Indeterminate, or Irrelevant: A Reply to Fried." *Philosophy & Public Affairs* 33/2: 201–15.

Van Parijs, P. (2003). *Real Freedom for All*. Oxford: Oxford University Press.

Walzer, M. (2007). "Deliberation, and What Else?" in M. Walzer. *Thinking Politically: Essays in Political Theory*. New Haven: Yale University Press.

Wenar, L. (2008). "Property Rights and the Resource Curse." *Philosophy & Public Affairs* 36/1: 2–32.

Williams, A. (1998). "Incentives, Inequality, and Publicity." *Philosophy & Public Affairs* 27/3: 225–47.

Williams, B. (1981). *Moral Luck*. Cambridge. Cambridge University Press.

Wolff, J. (1998). "Fairness, Respect and the Egalitarian Ethos." *Philosophy & Public Affairs* 27/2: 97–122.

# Index

institutional luck egalitarianism 88,
 141–5, 153, 165
institutions, *see* basic structure; global
 institutions; institutional approach

James, A. viii, 194–6
Julius, A.J. 161–2
justice
 ancient and modern views of 82–3
 defined as equality 2, 6, 7–12
 and distributive justice 8–13
 and humanitarianism 9–10, 101–2,
  150–1
 primacy of 29, 30, 39–44
 principles mutually dependent 45–6
 and social justice 6–7
 *see also* equality; global justice;
  institutional approach; personal
  pursuits

Kant, I. 35 n. 20, 83 n.
Kelly, E. 48 n. 22, 74
Knight, C. 141 n.
Kymlicka, W. 7, 89, 92 n. 4

Landesman, B. viii, 132 n., 142 n.
left libertarianism 8 n.
libertarianism 8, 11 n. 9
Lippert-Rasmussen, K. 95 n., 117 n.
luck
 option vs. brute 76–7, 95
 relevant sense of 91–2
luck/choice principle 89, 91–7,
  98–9, 141
 a presumption in egalitarian
  theories 96–7, 98–9, 108–9, 182–4
luck egalitarianism
 as an account of why equality
  matters 14, 105 n., 105–8, 192
 not asocial 130–6
 basic ideas of 88–90
 defined as 2, 3, 75–8, 98–9, 187
 and difference principle 109–14
 domain limitation 14, 119–21
 as grounding principle 106–8, 133–4,
  109–10, 113–14
 institutional basis of 14, 126–9
 vs. luck neutralization 91, 182–4
 luck that matters 91–2, 93–4, 96–7
 not metaphysically implausible 136–41
 modest account summarized 108

not morally implausible 119–30
 objections against, summarized 4, 116
 not principle of redress 129–30,
  131–4, 183
 and Rawls 99 n., 108–9
 as relational 134–6, 190
 as a response to inequality 90–1,
  190, 191–2
 *see also* choice; global luck
  egalitarianism; luck; luck/choice
  principle

Macedo, S. 161
Macleod, A. viii, 52, 67, 190–1
Macleod, C. 27 n. 6
Melenovsky, C. viii
Miller, D. 9, 9 n. 4, 130, 172, 173–81
Miller, R. 155 n. 7
Moellendorf, D. viii, 3, 152, 155 n. 7
monism, *see* value monism
Moore, M. viii,175, 179
Murphy, L. 51, 65,

Nagel, T. 4, 21, 27, 29, 39 n., 41 n., 92 n.
  2, 95, 101, 109 n. 19, 121, 145 n.,
  150–9, 161–3, 192 n. 3, 196 n. 5
nationality
 arbitrariness of 15, 174–85
 constrained by global justice 177,
  178, 180
 morally relevant 176–7
 special obligations due to 175–6
Navin, M. viii, 132
Nozick, R. 8, 11 n. 9
Nussbaum, M. 47, 48, 174

occupational choice, *see* freedom of
 occupation

Paletta, D. viii
partial concern, *see* special obligations
personal pursuits
 not asocial 26
 and conceptions of the good 26, 27,
  28–9, 30
 constrained by justice 39–43, 48–9,
  177–9
 and injustice 48–9, 73–4, 79–81
 and point of justice 26–31
 vs. selfish pursuits 59–62
 value-independence of 27, 28

Lightning Source UK Ltd.
Milton Keynes UK
UKOW04f0304290114

225446UK00004B/7/P